FOLLOW
THE YELLOW
BRICK
ROAD

Other books authored or co-authored by
Richard Saul Wurman

Information Anxiety
Cities: Comparison of Form and Scale
Urban Atlas: 20 American Cities
Making the City Observable
Yellow Pages of Learning Resources
YellowPage Career Library (12 vols.)
What-If, Could-Be
Guidebook to Guidebooks
What Will Be Has Always Been: The Words of Louis I. Kahn
Various Dwellings Described in a Comparative Manner
Our Man Made Environment Book 7
Man Made Philadelphia
The Nature of Recreation
Hats
The Notebooks and Drawings of Louis I. Kahn
Access Travel Guides (16 vols.)
USAtlas
On Time Flight Guides
Twin Peaks Access
Wall Street Journal Guide to Money and Markets
Olympic Games Access (Summer and Winter)
Football Access
Baseball Access
Medical Access
Dog Access
Polaroid Access
Office Access (Steelcase)

"Richard Sau...   ...ven if he
is fifty year...   ...at many
earlier diffic...   ...ructions.
I still wrestl...   ...let twice
daily.' The...   ...to give
clear ins...   ...dels I
learned fro...   ...limited
value for...   ...sed it

"Richard Sa...   ...a route
map, i...   ...e."
JOHN ...   ...lopment,

"Richard Sa...   ...greatest
innovator in...   ...enres in
publishing....   ...maps to
places, but ...   ...require
the greate...   ...more
valuable t...   ...in our

STEPHEN ...   ...University,

DEMCO 38-296

DATE DUE

FOLLOW THE YELLOW BRICK ROAD

LEARNING TO GIVE, TAKE, AND USE INSTRUCTIONS

RICHARD SAUL WURMAN
with
LORING LEIFER

Introduction by
John Sculley

Drawings by
Ed Koren
and
Larry Gonick

BANTAM BOOKS
NEW YORK • TORONTO • LONDON • SYDNEY • AUCKLAND

P95 .W87 1992
Wurman, Richard Saul, 1935—
Follow the yellow brick roa
: learning to give, take,
and use instructions

antam Books are published by Bantam Books,
division of Bantam Doubleday Dell Publishing
roup, Inc. Its trademark, consisting of the words
3antam Books" and the portrayal of a rooster, is
egistered in U. S. Patent and Trademark Office
nd in other countries. Marca Registrada. Bantam
ooks, 666 Fifth Avenue, New York, New York
0103.

Wurman, Richard Saul, 1935 -
    Follow the yellow brick road: learning to give,
        take, and use instructions /
        Richard Saul Wurman with Loring Leifer.
    p. cm.
    Includes bibliographical reference and index.
    ISBN 0-553-07425-3
    1. Oral communication. I. Title.
P95.W87 1992
302.2`242 —dc20   916956   CIP

Published simultaneously in the
United States and Canada

PRINTED IN THE UNITED STATES OF AMERICA

0 9 8 7 6 5 4 3 2 1

Thanks to the authors and publishers listed below who
graciously granted permission to reprint copyrighted
material, I was able to reprint excerpts from the following
sources:

"A Man and His Vegetable" by Hodding Carter IV in
Esquire (2/90). Reprinted by permission of author.

"Asking Workers What They Think" by Claudia H.
Deutsch. Copyright (c) 1990, *The New York Times*
Company. Reprinted by permission.

"Cabinet Decision" by Jack Smith. Copyright 1991, *Los
Angeles Times*. Reprinted by permission.

Ideas and Information: Managing in a High-Tech World
by Arno Penzias. Reprinted by permission of W. W.
Norton & Company, Inc. Copyright (c) 1989 by Arno
Penzias.

"Instructions" by Marshall Brickman. Reprinted by
permission; (c) 1976 *The New Yorker Magazine,* Inc.

"Jones at Monterey, 1842" by James High, published in
JOURNAL of the WEST (April 1966), pp 173-186. Used
with permission.

"Keith Waterhouse Decodes the Poetry of the Brochure"
in *Condé Nast Traveler*. Reprinted by permission of
Harold Ober Associates. Copyright 1989 by Keith
Waterhouse.

"Left Brain, Right Brain: Who's on First?" by Terence
Hines, Ph.D. Copyright 1985, the American Society for
Training and Development. Reprinted with permission.
All rights reserved.

"Management Secrets They'll Never Teach You at
Business School" by Julie Solomon. Reprinted with
permission from *Working Woman*. Copyright (c) 1990 by
WWT Partnership.

"Nurturing the Next Work Force" by Sandra Salmans.
Copyright (c) 1990, *The New York Times* Company.
Reprinted by permission.

Sex, Drugs, Rock & Roll by Eric Bogosian. Copyright ©
1991 by Ararat Productions, Inc. Reprinted by permission
of HarperCollins Publishers.

"Stimulating Creative Problem Solving: Innovative Set"
by Melba A. Colgrove in *Psychological Reports* 1968, 22,
pp. 1205-1211. Reproduced with permission of author and
publisher.

"Struggling to Understand Manual-Ese" by Michael
Schrage. Copyright 1989, *Los Angeles Times*. Reprinted
by permission.

"Two Practical Strategies Young Children Use to
Interpret Vague Instructions" by James Ramsey Speer in
Child Development. Copyright (c) 1984, The Society for
Research in Child Development, Inc. Reprinted by
permission.

Very Good Management by David Burkett. (c) 1983.
Reprinted by permission of the publisher, Prentice-Hall,
Inc., New Jersey, a division of Simon & Schuster, New
York.

"What Else Is New?" by Mynard Good Stoddard.
Reprinted from *The Saturday Evening Post*, (c) 1989.

"What Type of Supervisor Are You" by Eugene
Raudsepp. Reprinted by permission of *Supervision* (c)
The National Research Bureau, Inc., 424 North Third St.,
Burlington, Iowa 52601-5224.

*You Just Don't Understand: Women and Men in
Conversation* by Deborah Tannen. Copyright 1990.
Reprinted by permission of William Morrow and
Company, Inc.

Zen and the Art of Motorcycle Maintenance by Robert M.
Pirsig. Copyright 1974. Reprinted by permission of
William Morrow and Company, Inc.

to the memory of my beloved father
Morris Louis Wurman

Isadore Clyre is frantically rifling through papers on his desk. He is looking for the figures on long-staple cotton. The stockholders' meeting is this afternoon and he will have to explain why the third-quarter earnings are down 10 percent.

Isadore Clyre has problems with his employees, his bosses, his son, and even his girlfriend.

The biggest problem is that he's not clear about why he has so many problems.

In fact, Izzy's not clear about a lot of things.

Izzy Clyre has a problem with instructions. He isn't aware that almost all communications contain a good measure of instruction, either explicit or implicit.

Instructions are a fundamental part of life. They motivate communications.

Instructions are the key to knowledge and information.

If people recognized the importance of instructions, we could get a lot more out of personal and professional relationships.

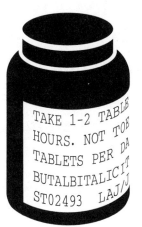

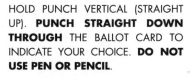

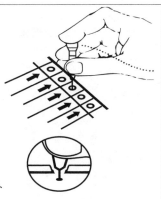

STEP ③ HOLD PUNCH VERTICAL (STRAIGHT UP). **PUNCH STRAIGHT DOWN THROUGH** THE BALLOT CARD TO INDICATE YOUR CHOICE. **DO NOT USE PEN OR PENCIL**.

Para votar, sostengo el instrumento de votar y perfore con él lo tarjeta de votar en el lugar de los candidatos de su preferencia. **No use pluma ni lapiz.**

D 第二步

請把帶鏈之選舉針，由小孔內垂佰插入 打孔校票．

TALKING ON THE JOB: SEEING INSTRUCTIONS IN THE CONTEXT OF WORK

3

What makes work so bad? It's easy for executives to imagine their employees complaining they don't get paid enough, their office partitions aren't high enough, their bosses aren't nice enough, and too much is expected of them. But at the top of most employees' gripe lists are problems in communication – not understanding what is expected of them, feeling excluded from important information, working under people who give vague and confusing instructions.

A MILLION WORDS!

MESCOLATE PIANO, con un cucchiaino, il caffè, in modo che il caffè sgorgato per primo, più denso, si mescoli con quello meno denso, sgorgato successivamente.

MÉ LANGUEZ LE CA-FE LENTEMENT à l'aide d'une cuiller, de façon à ce que la café débité d'abord, qui est plus dense, se mélange avec le café moins dense débitépar la suite.

RUHREN SIE DEN KAFFEE LANGSAM mit einem Loffel um, damit der anfangs ausgetretenen Kaffee, welcher starker ist, sich mit dem nachher ausgetretenen gut vermischt.

STIR THE COFFEE SLOWLY with a spoon, so that the first part of the coffee to ooze out, which is more concentrated, is mixed with the weaker, last part.

IF I'VE TOLD YOU ONCE…: TYPECASTING INSTRUCTION-GIVERS AND -TAKERS   *53*

In reality, no one is solely an instruction-giver or -taker. No one is ever high enough to rise above the need to follow instructions. You may be the CEO, but you still need to follow the instructions if you want to drive a car or put together a bicycle for your kid or make your stockholders happy. You have to listen for the implicit instructions in conversations with your advisers, with your friends, with your family.

All right. You protest that you bear no resemblance to the instruction-givers and -takers described in the previous chapter. In fact, should the Nobel committee establish a category for instruction-givers and -takers, you would be the first nominated. But your work environment is still far from paradise. Mistakes abound; work has to be redone; people operate with different understandings of the same project.

Personal idiosyncrasies aren't the only obstacle to giving and taking instructions.

6

A sign appears high over the road about 75 feet before many of the stoplights in British Columbia. It reads: "Prepare to Stop When Amber Flashing."

Most of us are conditioned to follow instructions.

Most of us want to follow instructions.

We're stymied by a variety of reasons, most having to do with the generally poor quality of instructions.

There are exceptions to the rule.

Generally, we are not well-trained in communicating.

Very young children communicate with a nonverbal language.

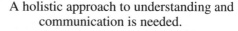

7

Literature inspires, communication instructs. Communication—especially in the workplace—has a preordained mission. Just because messages are phrased correctly doesn't mean they will get a point across. No matter how dazzling the message is, the intruction-taker still has to understand the metaphors, allusions, and comparisons.

Communication is more than vocabulary, it's word management.

FOLLOW THE YELLOW BRICK ROAD: INSTRUCTION CONSTRUCTION 101 — 163

After I first signed the contract to write this book, my editor, Tom Dyja, came to visit me at my office. He asked where the restroom was. I explained that "you walk out of the office, turn left, then make the first right turn." He walked right past the niche where the door to the restroom was located. So I had to call him back.

1 MISSION
2 DESTINATION
3 PROCEDURE
4 TIME
5 ANTICIPATION
6 FAILURE

*I know a man who taught his son
to tie his shoe in five minutes. He
tied the shoelace into a bow, then
untied it one step at a time. He
taught his son by doing it
backwards. His son instantly
grasped the relationship of each
step to the tied bow. He showed
his son the goal (the bow), then
showed him the steps leading up
to the goal.*

Cost of acquiring a lease. In amortizing the cost of acquiring your lease, the amount of time your lease is for includes all renewal options if less than 75% of the cost of the lease is for the time remaining on the lease on the purchase date. See Chapter 11.

Improvements by lessee. You may depreciate the cost of adding buildings and other permanent improvements to leased property. To do so, use the recovery period under the new modified accelerated cost recovery program (MACRS) that applies to ~~~~ful life of these ~

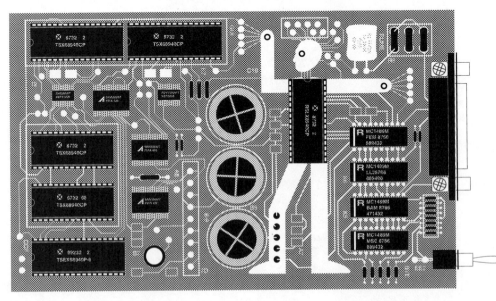

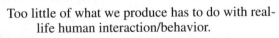

FIE-TECH OR MAN VERSUS THE MACHINE 237

In New York, no one has time to sit down and drink a cup of coffee, so many New Yorkers resort to buying a cup of coffee from a deli to drink on the run. Well, these cups all have plastic lids that are supposed to make the coffee easy and spill-free to drink on the run. (There will be time-share vacations on Neptune before this is accomplished.) The lids used to be simple plastic cylinders with a molded edge to fit snugly around the rim of the cup.

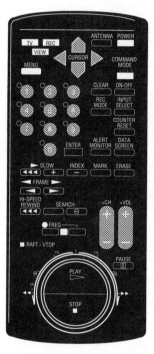

What else is new?

We all have problems with instructions.

Sex, drugs, and microwaves.

Computers never get bummed, man.

When the average American home had only a few appliances, no one thought too much about operating manuals. But now that the consumer electronic age has made button-pressing the dominant indoor activity, the jumbled jargon of instruction manuals rankles on a new plane, and the nontechnical consumer is further put off by the world of machines, finding the technical world all the more arcane.

Great Moments in the HISTORY of INSTRUCTIONS

AN INSTRUCTION WITHOUT AN ADEQUATE TERMINATOR: "GO WEST, YOUNG MAN!"

I'VE BEEN ALL THE WAY AROUND ONCE. CAN I STOP NOW?

EMPOWERMENT AND THE SPHERE OF VISION 313

The archetypal corporate interpretation of original sin is that all employees are lazy, sloppy, error-ridden potential felons who need to have the fear of God bred into them before they will perform at even the most cursory of levels. Without constant supervision and threats from above, they will lapse into slothful/sinful behavior.

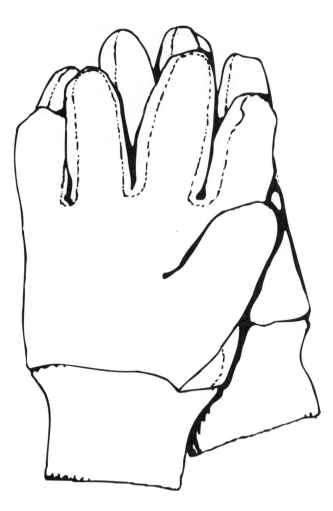

THE NEW LEADERSHIP: CONDUCTORS VERSUS CONTROLLERS   331

The loss of corporate supremacy in the United States has caused the business world to reflect on its historic leadership model based on the image of the autocratic CEO. All power is centralized and all decisions and subsequent instructions must come from one absolute source. No one else can be trusted to make decisions or understand the scope in which they must be made.

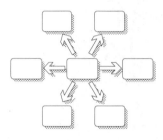

....

A new breed of leader is being forged during this time of corporate upheaval.

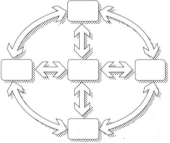

AN INSTRUCTION CRIB SHEET *353*

16

In school, students often resort to crib sheets, writing phrases or words onto a small piece of paper (or the palm of a hand), to summarize information for a test. These sheets help bring up other knowledge. This chapter is the crib sheet. Go ahead, tear it out.

Tear this chapter out.

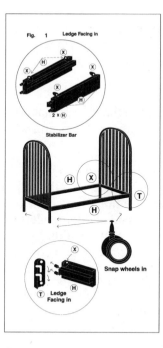

From a set of instructions for
assembling a crib.

INTRODUCTION

*I*n the same way that Richard Saul Wurman gave us an eye-opener in the macro sense about the information age in *Information Anxiety,* here he dissects the world of communication and looks at the one half of it that he claims is made up of instructions.

Delivering facts is a mass production approach to information. You assure that everybody will look at those facts in the same way or you reduce the facts to a common denominator where it's not important whether it's interesting to anybody. I think that most information doesn't get read, that which gets read doesn't get understood, that which gets even understood doesn't get remembered. I think that you have so many filters that there's probably incredibly little productivity from instructions today.

In our early years, the word *instruction* relates to school, which conjures up grim memories on the part of most students.

In our middle years, when we are mostly trying to follow the orders or instructions of others, we are fooled into thinking that we can't understand them because we aren't as intelligent as the order-givers, and thus we endow them with a false power.

Then, in later years, as some of us rise to positions of instruction-givers, we find ourselves handicapped by an inability to understand those who work around us, to operate the machines that move our lives.

What a sorry state.

It's hard to find an aspect of life these days that doesn't come with instructions. At work, at play, interacting with machines and with people involves being able to give and take instructions.

Follow the Yellow Brick Road: Learning to Give, Take, and Use Instructions recognizes the proliferation of instructions that run our lives. After reading it, I found myself paying closer attention to my colleagues, my associates, my friends, listening to what they said and more alert to their implicit instructions. Instead of the frustration I felt when I couldn't get a machine to work, I felt like I was part of a phenomenon, instead of an incompetent clod.

Wurman gives us a road map, so aptly called *Follow the Yellow Brick Road,* which guides us through this sometimes prairie, sometimes jungle, of instructions and instruction anxiety.

John Sculley

PROLOGUE

Why have the most fundamental things about our communications been left out of our learning process? We get instructions on manifold subjects, but we don't get instructions on how to follow or give instructions, which is the driving force of communications. And, without communication information is pretty useless.

We also aren't taught enough about organizing information, yet, we are a society in which so many things are based on finding things, and the corollary of organizing things is finding. How you organize data is how you find it. You can only find things based on some organizing principle.

How would you find a word in the dictionary if you didn't know the words were organized alphabetically?

There are only 5 ways of organizing information: by alphabet, category, time, magnitude, and location. Not 500, not 5000, but only 5. And it's the beginning place in communication. And in information display.

The organization and structure of instructions are as important as those of information, as instructions are a means of communicating information.

Half of all our communication is the giving and receiving of instructions. We give instructions to the waiter. The waiter recodes what we've said in his own or her own way, and takes this group of instructions in a different format, written instead of verbal, into the kitchen, and then gives instructions to a serioes of people in the kitchen to produce something. If they're given to a main chef, that chef translates the instructions often into another language to a sous-chef or other assistants. And, in order to know how to do what they're doing, they often consult a series of recipe cards or a cookbook, which is a book of instructions in itself.

We get instructions to find where a restaurant is located. Often the quality of these directional instructions isn't very good, because we've never learned how to give good instructions.

When we were growing up, many of our instructions were negative. We were told what not to do. Moses came down from the mount and proclaimed ten things we weren't supposed to do. He never told us what to do. A lot of religion is about what not to do, rather than what to do, as is child-rearing.

We have instructions in the workplace, instructions for transferring knowledge. We have instructions for how to do a particular task or make something. We have instructions for how to use something. If I want to get a smile or a laugh from an audience, I ask how many people can program their VCR? Some people have said that the whole population of the world can be divided into two groups: those who can program a VCR and those who can't. Probably at this moment there are 10 million, perhaps 100 million, electronic appliances that are flashing "12:00," because their owners couldn't follow instruction on how to set their clocks. So we have microwave ovens, VCRs, and other devices that flash "12:00" across the United States and around the world.

This book is about the structure of instructions—how we can learn how to construct, how to design, how to understand, the structure of instructions that work—and what to do about those that don't. It's about how to recognize good and bad instructions and how to recognize what type of instruction-giver and what type of instruction-taker you are.

"Hah. 'Some Assembly
Required.' I need NASA.
A Nobel physicist couldn't
put this thing together."

Isadore Clyre

*I*sadore Clyre is frantically rifling through papers on his desk. He is looking for the figures on long-staple cotton. The stockholders' meeting is this afternoon and he will have to explain why the third-quarter earnings are down 10 percent.

He suspects that he is running late and wants to know what time it is. He looks down for his digital watch, but remembers that he stopped wearing it after he lost the instruction booklet and couldn't figure out how to reset the date.

Izzy Clyre, the president of Redress Clothing Company, has a state-of-the-art stereo system/tuner/tape deck/compact-disc player in his office, but the clock has been blinking 12:00 since he took it out of the box. The blinking reminds him of his morning and he shakes his head in disgust. He woke up late this morning, after inadvertently specifying PM instead of AM on his new dream machine AM/FM digital alarm clock radio. "What in the hell is the time?" he wonders.

Izzy thinks that he has a problem with machines.

He calls for his secretary. "Get me the time, please, and see if you can get that supplier from Egypt on the phone again. I think I disconnected him when I tried to transfer the call to you to set up an appointment." She walks in with the layout for a company advertisement that is going to run in *Time* magazine.

"I just wanted to know what in the hell the time is," he says, exasperated.

A feisty woman, she replies, "Well you should have said that then. It happens to be a quarter of four." Her eyes roll upward.

Izzy wonders whether this means 3:45 or 4:15, but decides not to inquire further.

He thinks that he has a problem with his employees.

On the way to the stockholders' meeting, Izzy catches a glimpse of himself in a window. Despite his salt-and-pepper hair, he looks younger than 42. This makes him feel better until he notices that his suit jacket is drooping in back. He fears this may be symbolic of his life. Even his tailor doesn't seem to understand him.

He is still trying to straighten his suit as he walks into the stockholders' meeting. He explains that it's been a bad year for the clothing business and a 10 percent drop in sales isn't so bad relative to the state of the industry at present.

The graphics department has provided him with pie charts and bar graphs to show that the company's market share has increased, but there are so many colors that he gets dizzy looking at them and isn't quite sure what is what. He suspects that the ability of the computer to produce such colorful pictures has gone beyond the ability of people to understand them. He hopes that the board can make more sense of the material than he can. He isn't sure how the information was received. As they file out of the room, one of the directors, Alexander Abernathy, takes his hand and shakes it for a few seconds longer than seems necessary, smiling in a sad fashion. Clyre doesn't understand that the handshake is a reminder that company presidents are replaceable and this may be his last board meeting.

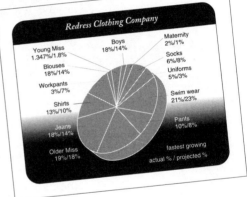

Redress Clothing Company

Young Miss 1.347%/1.8%
Blouses 18%/14%
Workpants 3%/7%
Shirts 13%/10%
Jeans 18%/14%
Older Miss 19%/18%
Boys 18%/14%
Maternity 2%/1%
Socks 6%/8%
Uniforms 5%/3%
Swim wear 21%/23%
Pants 10%/8%
fastest growing
actual % / projected %

Izzy Clyre suspects he has a problem with his board of directors.

He tries to put it out of his mind as he drives over to visit his 8-year-old son, Charlie, at what used to be his home too—a sprawling Mission-style home on 5 acres of property. For years, his wife kept telling him that she wasn't happy and he felt sorry for her. It wasn't until Bea served him with divorce papers that he realized she was trying to tell him she was unhappy with him.

Izzy realized that he had a problem communicating with his wife—but not until it was too late.

Tonight, he would stay at the house until she returned from her Chinese art class. At least she had been very cooperative about allowing him to visit Charlie, or "C" as everyone calls him. Izzy smiles as he thinks that at least someone looks up to him as perfect, or at least all-knowing and all-competent. He can't wait to see C's face when he sees the new ten-speed bicycle that he bought for him.

Izzy is still disturbed about his son's visit to his office two weeks ago. His experiences with C seemed somehow outside of his regular life, so he was always trying to bring the boy into his routines. He showed C his office and proudly introduced him to the six vice-presidents of the company, as well as the others in the executive offices. He took C to the boardroom, the new fitness studio on the premises, and to a small conference room with video equipment. The boy seemed bewildered by the place and showed little interest in anything other than the video screen that disappeared into the ceiling at the touch of a button. C didn't seem to understand what went on in the office and kept asking about where the clothes were. Izzy explained that the factory was on the other side of the world in Hong Kong and promised to take him there one day.

As Izzy tried to explain his job to C, he was struck by the idea that his work was so abstract that sometimes he didn't understand it himself. He remembered working in a clothing store as a young man and the tangible satisfaction of hearing a customer say, "I'll take it." Izzy recognized that his son couldn't grasp the abstraction of his work, but he didn't know how to explain it. C could comprehend fabric, sewing machines, and clothes, but not the stockholders, the paper-pushing, and the phone conversations about fall lines, target markets, and droughts in Egypt. Finally, Izzy told his son, "Someday this will make sense to you. Take my word for it."

His inability to make his son understand what he did at the office made him feel lonely and distant in a vague, indefinable way. He vowed to pay more attention to his son in the future.

With a look of unflappable confidence, Izzy takes the parts out of the box and finds the instructions for assembly. He thumbs through the sections on owner's responsibility and riding rules and the safety check list before reaching the assembly sections. He gives C a benevolent smile.

C runs around picking up the parts ready to go for a ride.

What could be so complicated, thinks Izzy, smiling at C with assurance. What could go wrong? It's only a bicycle. Then he notices that the print is in 6-point type. He reaches for his glasses.

He starts with the front wheel. "(1) From one side of the caliper brake, remove nut (A), washer (B), and the brake block. This will permit you to install the wheel. (2) Put the wheel between the fork tubes. Install the axle into the fork ends. (3) Install wheel retainers and the flange nuts to each side of the axle as shown. (4) Tighten the flange nuts by hand. If the flange nuts will not tighten by hand, make sure the flange nuts are the correct size. Make sure the wheel is an equal distance from each fork tube. Use a wrench and tighten the flange nuts to a torque of 20 foot pounds."

Is this English? wonders Izzy. He doesn't know what most of these parts look like and they aren't labeled.

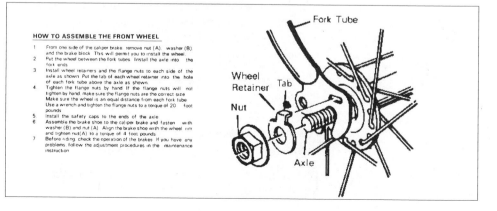

HOW TO ASSEMBLE THE FRONT WHEEL

1   From one side of the caliper brake, remove nut (A), washer (B), and the brake block. This will permit you to install the wheel.
2   Put the wheel between the fork tubes. Install the axle into the fork ends.
3   Install wheel retainers and the flange nuts to each side of the axle as shown. Put the tab of each wheel retainer into the hole of each fork tube above the axle as shown.
4   Tighten the flange nuts by hand. If the flange nuts will not tighten by hand, make sure the flange nuts are the correct size. Make sure the wheel is an equal distance from each fork tube. Use a wrench and tighten the flange nuts to a torque of 20 foot pounds.
5   Install the safety caps to the ends of the axle.
6   Assemble the brake shoe to the caliper brake and fasten with washer (B) and nut (A). Align the brake shoe with the wheel rim and tighten nut(A) to a torque of 4 foot pounds.
7   Before riding, check the operation of the brakes. If you have any problems, follow the adjustment procedures in the maintenance instruction.

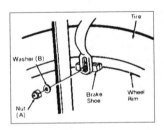

Several toy companies have toll-free hot lines for parents who think that the words "easy-to-assemble" are a cruel joke. Among them are Mattel, Lewis Galloob Toys, Fisher-Price, Little Tikes, Tyco, LEGO Systems, and Lionel Trains.

The diagram doesn't seem to bear any resemblance to the parts. He tries to page casually through the booklet and finally finds a parts list on the last two pages, 22 and 23, but the illustration is so bad that he can't tell the parts apart. He scans the list: "G/crank set steel cottered, crank cotter pin, fork assembly, derailleurs, wheel retainers, handle stems, head cups."

Izzy grows increasingly frustrated. The instructions seem contradictory; there seem to be more parts in the box than in the picture. He tries to look calm. Meanwhile, he mutters to himself, "Hah. 'Some Assembly Required.' I need NASA. A Nobel physicist couldn't put this thing together." Out of the corner of his eye, he feels the steady, despairing gaze of C, who has just come to the stunning conclusion that his father is certainly no Nobel physicist. C— who can record "Star Trek" in advance on the VCR, play Nintendo on a computer, and set the clock on the microwave—realizes that he is smarter than his father when it comes to technology.

Izzy suspects the joys of parenthood are over and wishes he wasn't such a techno-dolt. He promises his son they will figure out how to put the bicycle together next weekend and slinks away.

After this miserable day, Izzy Clyre can't wait to meet his girlfriend, Dolores Broad. It is her birthday and he has arranged a romantic dinner at La Grenadine.

Clyre has been divorced for 4 years and is terrified of making the mistakes of his first marriage again. Dolores is the first woman he has dated seriously who has inspired him to think about trying again. He suspects she also thinks about marriage. He anticipates her understanding and compassion as he recounts his day over a Scotch and soda.

"Is that grease on your shirt?" she asks.

"Don't ask," he says, rolling his eyes.

After they are seated, Izzy looks proprietarily over the menu. "Why don't I order for us."

Izzy tells the waiter, "We'll both start with the lobster bisque."

"Izzy, don't you remember, I'm allergic to dairy products," Dolores whispers.

"Oh, yes. Make that minestrone instead. Is there a cream sauce on the sole?"

"I can request that it be left off."

"Fine. One with and one without. And we'll have a bottle of Pouilly Fuissé."

When their entrees arrive, Izzy takes several bites before noticing that Dolores hasn't touched the fish. "Is something wrong?"

"This fish is swimming in butter," said Dolores.

"Gee, I guess I should have said no dairy products instead of just asking them to leave off the cream sauce."

Trying to recover from his faux pas, he suggests that they get tickets for the next season to the Metropolitan Opera.

"Izzy, please don't waste your money. You know I'm utterly tone deaf. Honestly, I wonder if you pay any attention at all to what I tell you."

In his flustered state, Clyre, desperately trying to salvage the situation, takes an envelope out of his jacket and hands it to her.

"For you dear, with all my love," Izzy says.

Dolores opens the envelope to find 2 round-trip tickets to Barbados and a brochure from the Royal Pavilion Hotel. "Honestly, Izzy, how many times have you tried to drag me to the beach. You know I'd rather watch paint dry than lie in the sun. Really, I've had it with you, Izzy. You're the most thoughtless person I've ever met."

Izzy stares at her blankly, trying to remember when she told him about the beach.

Izzy is sure that he has a problem with women.

Izzy has no idea what his real problem is.

INSTRUCTIONS: THE CORE OF COMMUNICATIONS

**There are no misunder-
standings; there are only
failures to communicate.**
Senegalese proverb

*I*zzy Clyre has a problem with instructions. He isn't aware that almost all communications contain a good measure of instruction, either explicit or implicit.

In *computerese,* instructions are measured as MIPS (millions of instructions per second).

"Instruction increases inborn worth, and right discipline strengthens the heart."—Horace, *Odes Book IV*

In every walk of life, in every human endeavor, our success, even our very survival, is determined by our ability to give and to follow instructions. We are bombarded by a litany of them from the moment our alarm clocks rudely instruct us that it's time to get up: *Step lively; watch the closing doors; walk, don't walk; curb your dog; merge right; hold onto the handrail; do not enter; detour for road construction; do this; don't do that.* All advertising is subliminal instruction: *Buy this, do that, look like me.*

When we take an airplane, we get safety instructions. When we attend a business meeting, when we talk to our co-workers, when we buy a new appliance, when we order dinner in a restaurant, when we tell a friend how to get to our house, when we follow a recipe, when we visit the doctor, we enter into the world of instructions. Even when we talk about our feelings, we are instructing others in our emotions.

Izzy is unaware of this. He doesn't recognize that he spends his days giving and receiving instructions. When he talks to his employees, to his stockholders, to his son, to his friends, he is giving them instructions. He directs people to write reports, to study markets, to get him files. He tells his friends what he likes, what he wants; he gives them instructions into what kind of person he is.

Because he is unaware that instructions are involved intrinsically in all his communications, he makes a lot of mistakes in his dealings with other people and is often disappointed by them. He missed the message that one of the stockholders was trying to warn him, and sent his secretary away mad.

He didn't realize that when he ordered dinner at the restaurant he was initiating a relay race of instructions. The waiter conveyed Izzy's instructions to the kitchen, where people were preparing food based on the instructions of the chef, who in turn was following the instructions of recipes.

During his relationship with Dolores, they had conversations that were really the exchange of implicit instructions: "If you want to know about me, if you want to get close to me, this is information you should remember." And Izzy forgot.

When your paramour tells you that the color purple makes her happy and the color green makes her see red, this information contains a subtle direction that the way to her heart is paved in purple. If you give her a green scarf, you are showing either a lack of attention to her desires or an unwillingness to follow her implicit instructions.

Because Izzy doesn't recognize the dominant role that instructions play in his life, he often confuses and frustrates people, often doesn't get what he wants from his professional and personal relationships, and often is overwhelmed with the technology that moves his world.

If you ask people to define instruction, they might claim it's that incomprehensible dribble that falls out of packing crates or it's what teachers try to do to you in school. The more serious might describe it as the act of sending messages or transferring information. They might list synonyms like *education, learning, direction, assignment, schooling,* or *study.*

In the *Webster's New Universal Unabridged Dictionary* (Deluxe 2nd edition), *instruction* is defined as "an education; knowledge, information, etc. given or taught; any teaching; lesson; directions; orders." The root of the word comes from the Latin word *struere,* which means "to pile up," "to arrange," "to build."

All of these definitions are correct, but none of them recognize how pervasive instructions are in our communications.

Instructions are one of the most *fundamental* aspects of human life. Instructions are the driving force of communications; either explicitly or implicitly, they motivate us to communicate. Yet how many schools offer a course called *Instruction 101*? It should be as common as spelling or American history. Perhaps we tend to ignore instructions because they are so fundamental.

Other neglected subjects are *How to Organize Information, How to Ask Good Questions,* and *How to Understand Failure* – all essential to giving and taking instructions.

For the most part, we don't really look at our office everyday because we expect it to look the same. We don't notice what's in our closets because we figure it's probably the same junk that was in there last year. Habit numbs awareness. I call this the *habituality effect.* We usually look past our immediate environment to the events we expect will make some difference or change in the routines. People look forward to taking a trip, buying a new car, changing jobs, or redecorating the living room because it gives them something new to notice in their environment. But often the habits and routines that people look past or ignore are the essential aspects of their lives.

"The most important fact about Spaceship Earth: an instruction book did not come with it."—Buckminster Fuller

Instructions and their relationship to communications are two such aspects. They are essential to how we relate to those around us, how well we perform our jobs, how much we come to understand of the world around us. How to find information, how to organize and understand it, and how to transfer and exchange it through communications are the most important work of our lives.

Without instructions, most information is useless. Information sitting in a file cabinet is not very valuable if no one knows where to find it or how to understand it or how to use it. Instructions give it value by making it understandable to the parties who can put it to use.

HOW DID INSTRUCTIONS GET SUCH A BAD RAP?

Instructions probably aren't our happiest memories. Most of us grew up with a litany of them.

Don't shout.

Don't play with your food.

Stop fidgeting.

Don't slam the door.

Look at me when I'm talking to you.

Stop hitting your sister.

Pick up your toys.

We all recognize the role instructions play at home, having had our share of them from zealous parents: "Don't touch the stove; stand up straight; do your homework; eat your broccoli; don't make that expression, your face might freeze; you'll go blind if you do that." We recognize them in the classroom as well.

But how many people recognize that instructions continue to run our lives—personally and professionally? They pervade our lives to such a degree that giving them and following them have become almost involuntary responses, like blinking or breathing. Yet instructions are what enable us to please those around us by giving us the means to successfully complete assigned tasks. They are also the means for others to please us by realizing our wishes. Instructions are the key to knowledge and information.

Almost all endeavors involve some form of instruction: being told what to do, telling others what to do, finding out how to use something, how to find something, fix something, or do something.

If people recognized the monumental importance that instructions assume in their lives and acknowledged the role that instructions play in communications, we could get a lot more out of these experiences and enrich our personal and professional relationships. If people began to understand the structure of instruction, they could build their own more effectively.

Q: *Name something that involves an understanding of geometry, spatial relations, algebra, manual dexterity, strategic planning, and allotment of resources.*

A: Making a dress.

Q: *Name something that involves many chemical processes, arithmetic, timing, aeration, biology, and behavior of materials.*

A: Following a recipe.

Q: *Name something that involves politics, economics, kinesiology, game strategy, psychology, and sociology.*

A: Baseball.

When I was in architecture school, someone told me that architects don't build buildings. The public thinks they do, but they don't. (Publishers don't print books either. Printers print books.) Architects are really in the instruction business; they develop the instructions for building buildings.

Composers don't give us music, they give us the instructions for making music, carefully written out in a universally accepted language. Bach didn't leave us preludes and fugues, he left us the instructions for playing them. The pianists who

"Pleasure is a shadow, wealth is vanity, and power a pageant; but knowledge is ecstatic in enjoyment, perennial in frame, unlimited in space and indefinite in duration."
—De Witt Clinton, "Thoughts on the Business of Life," *Forbes* (5/15/89)

"Some research (e.g. Kassin & Wrightsman, 1979) indicates that subjects receiving instructions before the testimony are significantly less likely to convict the defendant than are those who receive the instructions either after the testimony or not at all. Such pretrial instructions give jurors a cohesive structure within which to organize testimony and thus direct attention to relevant issues."—Donna Cruse and Beverly A. Browne, "Reasoning in a Jury Trial: The Influence of Instructions," *The Journal of General Psychology* (Vol. 114, No. 2)

follow the instructions are free to contribute their own expression as they interpret the music.

Choreographers don't create dances; they create the *instructions* for dances, using specifications of time, space, and the human body so that dancers can bring them to life.

In this late 20th-century world of rules and regulations, sophisticated systems of machinery, and global communication networks, our facility in the art of instruction will play an increasingly pivotal role in our lives. The old maxim, "If you want something done right, do it yourself," is now an inadequate response to the times. We can apply it to changing a tire or making a mousse, but at some point we are going to have to rely on instructing others to perform functions necessary to our lives.

Nowhere is this more apparent than in the workplace, and nowhere are faulty directions more costly—in terms of both dollars lost and employee morale diminished.

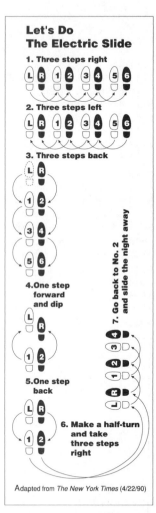

Choreographers don't create dances— they create instructions for dances.

"Last year a Gallup survey of personnel and medical directors at 201 big and small corporations showed that, on average, 25% of their companies' employees suffered from anxiety or stress-related disorders. Typically, the emotionally exhausted or depressed employee lost 16 days of work a year. According to the Research Triangle Institute, a North Carolina research firm, these disorders (and their frequent companion, substance abuse) cost the U.S. $183 billion annually in lost productivity, job errors, and doctors' bills."—Thomas A. Stewart, "Do You Push Your People Too Hard," *Fortune* (10/22/90)

LESS PAY, MORE SAY?

I've found that the singular complaint of the work force in this country isn't working conditions, salaries, or bonus packages. It's the irrational, inarticulate superior—the person whose instructions are frustrating or downright impossible to follow. Although I've seen this problem mainly in middle and upper management (the areas in which I usually work), numerous studies have documented that the problem of poor instructions permeates all rungs of the business ladder.

"When office workers were given a list of office characteristics to select from: ten items were rated as very important more often than salary....After honesty and ethics (87%), the following rate as most important: the opportunity to develop skills (84%), management recognition of individual contributions (81%), job security (79%), challenging jobs (79%), the chance to contribute (77%), good benefits (77%), management who cares for the individual as a person (76%), goals and direction provided by management (76%), and freedom from health hazards (73%)."
—Steelcase Office Environment Index: 1989 Summary Report (conducted by Louis Harris and Associates)

"If you command wisely, you'll be obeyed cheerfully."—Thomas Fuller, MD, *Gnomologia*

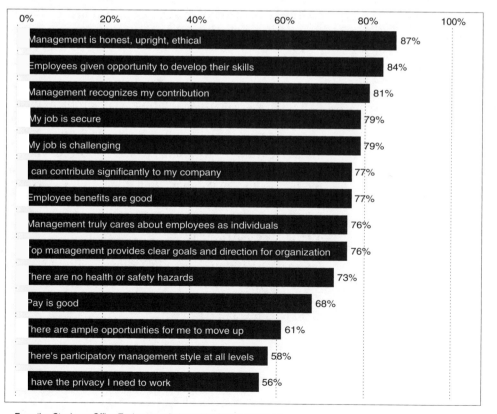

Management is honest, upright, ethical					87%
Employees given opportunity to develop their skills					84%
Management recognizes my contribution					81%
My job is secure					79%
My job is challenging					79%
I can contribute significantly to my company					77%
Employee benefits are good					77%
Management truly cares about employees as individuals					76%
Top management provides clear goals and direction for organization					76%
There are no health or safety hazards					73%
Pay is good					68%
There are ample opportunities for me to move up					61%
There's participatory management style at all levels					58%
I have the privacy I need to work					56%

From the *Steelcase Office Environment Index: 1989 Summary Report*

The fact that you can't run your VCR might mean you have problems running your company as well.

"In the last decade, the United States sold Saudi Arabia and Kuwait billions of dollars of state-of-the-art weapons—but when the crunch came, Kuwait crumbled and the Saudis cried out for help.

"Both countries turned out to have nothing but 'phantom armies'— peopled by troops who can't fight and armed to the teeth with complex gadgets only American hired guns know how to use, military experts say."
— Lucette Lagnado, "Phantom Armies Are Helpless," New York Post (8/8/90)

In service businesses, like law, medicine, advertising, architecture, instruction plays a direct and obvious role—understanding the needs or "instructions" of the client and communicating those needs via instructions to others. But even product-based companies depend on instructions—training workers how to operate manufacturing equipment, instructing a sales force, and following the instructions of consumers as to what kinds of products they want.

In the novel *Babel-17*, by Samuel R. Delany (Bantam Books, 1982), one character shows another a weapons lab. When the latter comments that the weapons are all very powerful and valuable, her guide disagrees and shows her a roomful of plans and instructions for building the weapons. "These are the true weapons," the guide says.

Instructions are supposed to help us, but without an understanding of their complexity, we are often confused, befuddled, misled, and frustrated by them. When people aren't aware of the importance of high-performance instructions, how can they be expected to give them?

Faulty or inadequate instructions are not a problem that requires expensive solutions. The problem will not be solved by more sophisticated communications technology, higher salaries and more benefits, or elaborate training programs. It will be solved when people understand the importance of instructions and the factors that make them so hard to give and to follow.

FIVE EASY PIECES

Instructions are more than just a message to do something. They are a system that can be broken down into 5 components—giver, taker, content, channel, and context.

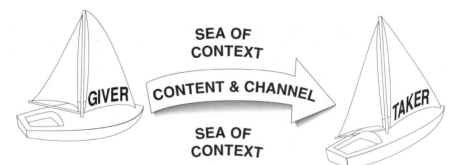

GIVERS originate instructions. They want something done, either consciously or subconsciously. They must then choose who to ask (the taker), formulate a message (content), decide how the instruction should be formed (channel), and take into account the environment in which the instruction is to be delivered (context). Each choice that they make in the process should influence the next step.

TAKERS. In a successful system, those who act on instructions are more than just passive followers. Instruction-takers should be active; they must interpret a message and perform on it, making decisions along the way. They have a responsibility to communicate their understanding of an instruction to the giver, to let the giver know if they don't understand an instruction. If people thought of themselves as instruction-takers instead of as followers, they might feel more in control and find instructions easier to follow.

CONTENT. This is the message itself— independent from the way it is presented. There are essentially 3 kinds of instructions: those that are past-oriented, concerned with transferring knowledge; those that are oriented to present action, such as building something (be it an idea or a tool shed) or operating something; and those that will require some action in the future, such as directions from bosses or even the casual, implied instructions received in social interactions. The content of all these instructions is based on the same 5 building blocks: purpose, objective, core, time, anticipation, and failure. (*See Chapter 8.*)

CHANNEL. This is the form and dressing of the message. Instructions can be expressed by different means—words or pictures—and in different media, or in a combination of these. They can be oral, told as a story or sung in a song, or written in the form of a note or a formal document. They can be illustrated graphically, imaged on videotape, expressed directly or indirectly. The channel is the medium by which the content is communicated.

CONTEXT. The context is the setting in which the instruction is delivered. It is the largest and most complex component in the instruction system. Context has 3 different levels of meaning from the immediate to the global. *Level 1* encompasses the *immediate environment* in which the instruction is given. Is it delivered in a boardroom or a back room? To fire up a sales force, a convention might be in order, but it would hardly be the setting to ask your accountant to keep an eye on a comptroller you suspect is stealing from the company. *Level 2* involves the *broader applications* of a particular instruction. What will be affected by performance of the task? If you tell someone to drill a hole in a piece of metal, is he or she making a trailer or a toaster part? *Level 3*—the broadest aspect of the context component—is the *economic or social state* of affairs surrounding all parties concerned. In the workplace, this can mean the state of the company or the economy in general. In social settings, this can mean the state of the relationship between the giver and the taker. A husband who instructs his wife to iron his socks when they are in a warring phase just short of divorce court will find that context has a bearing on his request.

All of these aspects will affect the outcome. Errors and omissions within any of these components can cause even the simplest instruction to go awry. Sometimes, accurately worded instructions don't get carried out because they are delivered to the wrong person in the wrong form. The instruction-giver's responsibility is to choose the content, the channel, and the context; the margin for error is high. The instruction-taker bears responsibility as well—to let the giver know whether he or she has chosen well by responding to the instruction. Takers must be able to recognize problems or omissions and to ask for clarification if an instruction doesn't make sense.

This puts tremendous demands on both the giver and the taker. Not only must they be able to recognize the instructive aspects of communication, they must both possess an understanding of the instruction system and be able to interpret messages not as discrete bits of information, but as components in a larger system.

WHAT ARE THE SIGNS?

Developing these abilities will help people to improve the quality of instructions that they give and to improve their response to instructions they must follow. The first step toward improvement is learning to identify weak points in the system and in one's own capacity as an instruction-giver and -taker.

You might have a problem with giving or taking instructions if:

> Your employees' eyes often glaze over when you are talking to them.
>
> You ask if there are any questions about what you've just said and there aren't.
>
> More than once a week, someone says to you, "Well, why didn't you say so in the first place?"
>
> More than once a week, you say to someone else, "Can't you understand plain English?" or "If I've told you once, I've told you a thousand times."
>
> Your favorite complaint is "No one understands me."
>
> When your instructions aren't followed to your satisfaction, you respond with "I ask you to do the simplest thing and what happens? You screw it up."
>
> The mere word *delegate* doubles your blood pressure, because you are sure no one can do the job as well as you.

- You have trouble translating your vision into goals that can be understood by your subordinates.

- You'd rather subtract an hour than figure out how to reset all of your clocks for daylight savings time.

- Every time you try to transfer a call on your office phone, you disconnect someone.

- You don't buy equipment because you don't think you can operate it.

- You don't buy toys for your kids because you know you won't be able to assemble them.

- You deny ever having a problem with instructions.

"We now know how people learn. We now know that learning and teaching are not two sides of the same coin. They are different. What can be taught has to taught and will not be learned otherwise. But what can be learned must be learned."—Peter Drucker, *The New Realities*

HOW TO HOW TO

Think of how much more productive your employees could be if you improved your instruction technique—as a giver and a taker. Think of how much more satisfying work might be if we all understood what was expected of us and could make it clear when we did not. But where do we go for help, even if we decide we have a problem?

There is virtually nowhere to turn for help in the matter. Whereas you can find instructions on how to assemble almost everything, on how to perform almost any feat, even on how to feel, think, talk, or act, there is nowhere to go for instructions on how to follow or create instructions.

Literature on education abounds; so does material on the specific area of instructional design. But these are oriented toward specific groups—such as children or technical writers. What has been neglected is an examination of the role informal instructions play in everyone's daily life.

These everyday instructions that lead us to action have little to do with the field of instruction as it occurs in the classroom setting. The roles are defined clearly in the classroom. There is a teacher and a student. There is some implicit agreement that the student is there to learn and the teacher is there to teach. The vicissitudes of work roles erase these distinctions. The person giving rules one minute may be following them the next.

Another difference between formal education and everyday instructions is that the former emphasizes subject matter and the latter the learner or performer. Rightly or wrongly, the educational system focuses on the content—the emphasis is on the curriculum and the most effective method of teaching it. What is the best way to present math? How can we measure the effectiveness of our teaching methods? Schools teach you about isosceles triangles and the Peloponnesian War, but not about how to give or receive instructions.

Schools are about *how to,* not about *how to how to.* Most of our formal education takes place in a classroom setting. But most of what we learn takes place somewhere else.

In our personal and professional lives, the emphasis is on the performer. If a superior tells you to design a software program for keeping an inventory of goods, how you execute the task is the critical matter. Unfortunately, no one pays much attention to how the request was formulated. If you screw up, the eyes will be on you and not on the person who delivered the instruction.

> "Whereas most of the reading tasks in school involve 'reading to learn,' most of the reading done at work is 'reading to do.' Here people not only have to understand what they read but have to be able to apply the knowledge gained from reading."—P. Wright and A. J. Hull, "Reading to Do: Creating Contingent Action Plans," *British Journal of Psychology* (Vol. 79, 1988)

For the most part, what we are taught in school doesn't demand a reaction. Informal instructions invariably do. They demand more than passive memorization. Whether you are following explicit or implicit directions, they require your response. The skills required to deliver and to respond to informal instructions are neglected sorely in our educational system. Yet you will be judged all of your life on how well you follow them, whether by your spouse, your friends, or colleagues in the workplace both above and below you.

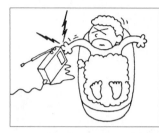

Skill at taking instructions can be very important. Above: redrawn from instructions for Aiwa radio. Below: from the Toyota Tercel 1984 Owner's Manual

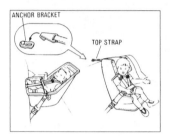

"**Precise communication becomes vitally important. To reduce the risk of misunderstanding between tower and cockpit, a controller is forbidden to tell a pilot to 'hold for takeoff.' The mere mention of 'takeoff' could trigger a response in the mind of the pilot and cause him to throw the throttles open prematurely. The correct command: 'Taxi into position and hold.'**

"**....As the jet proceeds across the U.S., a constant danger is that controller and pilot will somehow misunderstand each other.**"

—"What's He Doing? He'll Kill Us All!" *Time* (4/11/77)

THE PENALTIES

The penalties for being a poor instruction-giver and -taker are far-reaching. Both can frustrate their co-workers, alienate those around them, and create inefficiencies and errors. Sometimes, the penalty for faulty instructions is petty. If you enter through an exit door, you are likely to get by with a dirty look from those who are following the rules. If you don't pay attention to equipment manuals, you may disconnect a few callers, lose a few files, and deprive yourself of available technology; the consequences are relatively minor. But poor instructions—from the standpoint of both the giver and the taker—can result also in devastating errors, accidents, and catastrophes. The number of accidents that have occurred because someone was given inadequate or confusing instructions is staggering—Three Mile Island, the Union Carbide explosion in Bhopal, the Exxon oil spill, the plane crash in Tenerife.

On January 25, 1990, Avianca Airlines Flight 52 en route to New York from Bogotá, Colombia, crashed on Long Island after running out of fuel because of communication problems between the crew and the air traffic controllers. The plane, which had been delayed because of bad weather, was running low on fuel, but the pilots neglected to use the prescribed words—"fuel emergency"—and the plane wasn't granted emergency landing status. Seventy-three people were killed.

On a personal level, the consequences can be just as tragic. A mother in England who was bottle-feeding her newborn baby could not understand the instructions to increase the amount of formula as the weeks passed. So the baby, who was otherwise well cared for, starved to death.

The number of patients who can't or don't follow their doctors' instructions is staggering. And I'm not talking about patients who laugh when told to take off a few pounds or stop smoking. I'm talking about patients who think they *are* following advice.

"Only about 11 percent of women who take birth control pills use them correctly all the time, a new study shows. The results help explain why 6 percent of pill users get pregnant within a year, although perfect use results in a failure rate below 2 percent....Most pill users are advised, for example, to take pills at the same time each day, to take a missed pill as soon as possible and to use a back-up birth control method during their first month on the pill or after they miss two pills or more."

In the article, "Most Users of the Pill Don't Follow Directions," in *USA Today* (2/21/90), Kim Painter cited a study of 612 women at three clinics in the Detroit area. Among the mistakes made at least once were:

- 83 percent took pills at different times of day.

- 58 percent didn't take a pill every day: 16 percent didn't make up missed pills or stopped taking pills before the end of the month.

- 40 percent didn't use back-up methods, like diaphragms or condoms, when needed.

Ninety-seven percent of all materials on drugs written for patients cannot be understood by the average consumer, according tom Dorothy L. Smith, president of the consumer health Information Corporation, a company in MacLean, VA, that specializes in patient education

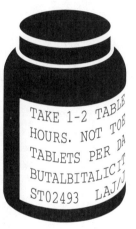

WHERE TO START

This book provides an overview of the role instructions play in our lives, as well as scrutinizes the very structure of instructions. By understanding how each component in the system plays a part in the effectiveness of an instruction, you can begin to understand the morphology of instructions. What makes them work? What makes them fail? With examples of good and bad instructions, you will learn ways to be a better instruction-giver and instruction-taker. The book will address the following topics:

- What are the different parts of an instruction and how can they be put together to make a comprehensible whole?

- What are the different categories of instructions?

- What do anticipation, time, and failure have to do with instructions? (*See Chapter 8.*)

- Why can't your employees seem to follow your instructions?

- How can employers learn to spot people who are compatible with their communication style so that they will understand instructions more easily? (*See Chapters 3 and 4.*)

- How can you give instructions that will incite the creativity of your employees and inspire them to do a better job than you could do? (*See Chapter 14.*)

- Why do you have to call your children when you want to use your VCR?

- Where do instructions come from and who writes them?

- Why can't technology companies come up with better operating manuals? (*See Chapters 11 and 12.*)

- Where do instructions usually go awry?

- How can instructions be improved?

- How can you learn to follow them for better results?

HIGH-PERFORMANCE INSTRUCTIONS

Instructions are not the enemy. They are an itinerary for action. They are guides to thinking and doing. Good instructions or directions are the

building blocks of accomplishment. Instructions fuel movement, whether they are directions to someone's house or a request to prepare a report.

A well-crafted instruction is a gift—both to the giver and to the taker. It can connect us to information, technology, and knowledge itself. A successful instruction permits high performance by inspiring attention and sparking understanding. Giving instructions that perform is a craft and needs to be recognized as such. The ability to give and follow them offers boundless rewards. With it, you can master machines, increase productivity, and inspire others to action.

Learn how to use your chopsticks!

Tuck under thumb and hold firmly

Add second chopstick and hold it as you hold a pencil

Hold first chopstick in original position move the second one up and down. Now you can pick up anything!

Sometimes very simple instructions, using both pictures and words, can be very effective. Above: from the wrapping for a set of chopsticks.

TALKING ON THE JOB: SEEING INSTRUCTIONS IN THE CONTEXT OF WORK

"Only 41 percent of office workers claim that they are very satisfied with their job—a five percentage point decrease since last year." *Steelcase Office Environment Index: 1989 Summary Report* (conducted by Louis Harris and Associates)

"*W*hen God foreclosed on Eden, he condemned Adam and Eve to go to work. Work has never recovered from that humiliation.

"From the beginning, the Lord's word said that work was something bad: a punishment, the great stone of mortality and toil laid upon a human spirit that might otherwise soar in the infinite, weightless playfulness of grace," said Lance Morrow in "What Is the Point of Working?" in *Time* (5/11/81).

What makes work so bad? It's easy for executives to imagine their employees complaining they don't get paid enough, their office partitions aren't high enough, their bosses aren't nice enough, and too much is expected of them. But at the top of most employees' gripe lists are problems in communication—not understanding what is expected of them, feeling excluded from important information, working under people who give vague and confusing instructions. When employees see their superiors as their main roadblock to getting their jobs done, the culprits are likely to be irrational or incompetent instruction-givers.

A table in *Corporate Communications: A Comparison of Japanese and American Practices* by William V. Ruch reveals that the most important job elements to an employee were rated as the least important to their foremen who were asked to predict what their people viewed as important. The top three were "Appreciation of work done, Feeling 'in' on things (full information), and Help on personal problems." The foremen assumed that "Good wages, Job security, and Promotion" would be the issues dearest to their employees' hearts.

Importance of Job Elements, As Seen by Employees and Foremen

Job Element	Employee's Rating	Foreman's Rating
Appreciation of work done	*1*	*1*
Feeling "in" on things (full information)	*2*	*2*
Help on personal problems	*3*	*3*
Job security (steady work)	*4*	*4*
Good wages	*5*	*5*
Interesting work (belief in importance of job)	*6*	*6*
Promotion	*7*	*7*
Management loyal to workers	*8*	*8*
Good working conditions	*9*	*9*
Tactful disciplining (respectful treatment)	*10*	*10*

Source: Merrihue, Managing by Communication, *p. 42, as reported in* Corporate Communications: A Comparison of Japanese and American Practices, *by William Ruch*

PERCEPTION GAP

The difference between what management and employees think is important represents a staggering gap in most American businesses. When management has a distorted picture of how their employees view their jobs and what is important to them, miscommunications, inefficiencies, mistakes, and ill-will are bound to result.

According to T. Harrell Allen in *The Bottom Line: Communicating in the Organization,* "research indicates that 50 percent understanding between supervisor and subordinate on job descriptions is about the best level of understanding that is generally reached."

The situation in most offices never reaches 50 percent. Ask most subordinates to define their job duties, major obstacles to getting their work done, priorities, and future requirements of the job; then ask their supervisors the same questions and you might wonder if both of these people are working for the same company. Yet these are the aspects of most jobs that should rate the highest levels of understanding between subordinates and their bosses, for job duties and requirements are

often written out in detailed employee handbooks. How much agreement is there in your office between employees and their bosses as to job descriptions?

In-depth interviews conducted by the American Management Association found a high level of discrepancy between middle-managers and their upper-management bosses in basic job descriptions and requirements even when the superiors were allowed to hand select the subordinates with whom they worked most closely.

Comparative Agreement Between Superior-Subordinate Pairs on Four Basic Areas of the Subordinate's Job (Percentages Based on Study of 58 Pairs in Patterned Interviews)

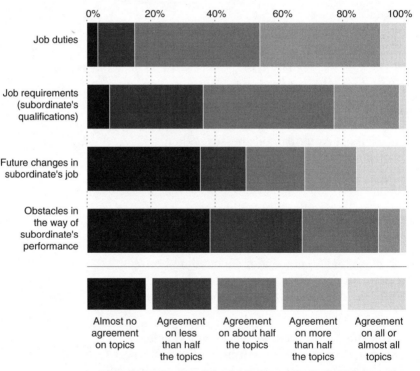

Adapted from *Superior-Subordinate Communication in Management*

More than 75 percent of the 222 pairs studied received a rating of 2 or lower on a scale of 1 to 4 (the highest degree of agreement). The only category in which superiors and subordinates agreed slightly more than they disagreed was in job duties.

When management and employees don't see eye-to-eye on such basic issues as job duties, which are often spelled out in employee handbooks, the communication gap is likely to manifest itself in other areas as well. If your boss doesn't have the same view of your job as you do, all of his or her instructions will come filtered through this disparity. When you think you are the company bookkeeper and your boss thinks you are his or her private secretary, neither of you will perform at full capacity.

What most companies fail to realize is that even if all employees are adequately trained to perform tasks and operate machinery, the problems are only half-solved. The day-to-day operations will require constant communication between staff members, between staff and management. The main component of these communications is instructions. The communication of instructions is how management tells employees what to do, how it translates its vision into products and services. It is the means by which work gets done.

Poor communications mean more than just Joe in quality control not informing Sam in pattern cutting that fly fronts are showing up in the trouser backs. It means that essential instructions are not getting through, or they are misunderstood and misinterpreted.

According to Keith D. Denton in an article, "Giving Instructions: It's Not As Easy As It Seems," in *Supervisory Management* (9/83), instructions don't get followed for reasons beyond their inherent understandability. Other factors can result in non-compliance, such as:

❶ The tone of voice used by the instruction-giver.

❷ The instruction-taker resents the giver.

❸ Distractions during the giving of the instruction.

The workplace runs on instructions, but they are of little value if they can not be accurately

"Thus the findings in general provide empirical evidence that substantial communication problems exist at high management levels in organizations—problems which one can expect to be reflected in poorer organizational efficiency and distortion of organizational goals at lower levels in the hierarchy."—Norman R.F. Maier, L. Richard Hoffman, John J. Hooven, and William H. Read, "Superior-Subordinate Communication in Management," *American Management Association Research Study #52*

As companies look for ways to cut costs in the budget-minded 1990s, full-time staff will be pared down with more reliance on freelancers. This means that more people will be out in the market having to sell their services, perhaps explaining them to people in different fields altogether. Just polishing your job description for your boss and your friends at cocktail parties won't be enough. An ability to "instruct" others as to what you can do for them becomes imperative.

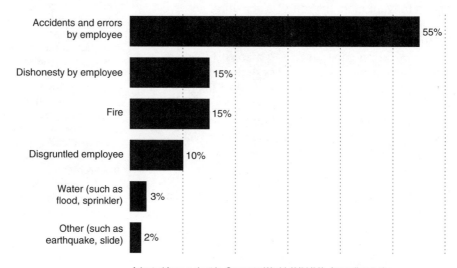

Adapted from a chart in *ComputerWorld* (2/20/89). According to the
Executive Information Network, the causes listed above are the chief causes
of systems failures.

communicated. Poor communications can affect
every area of operations. Often employees must
labor under the ill-formed instructions of their
superiors, who perhaps have erroneous ideas about
their underlings. These workers don't lack in
abilities; they lack in instructions because too many
bosses are incapable of making their employees
understand just what is expected of them.

SEEING LABOR AS PEOPLE

The importance of communication and instructions
in the workplace has little historical precedent. In an
industrial economy, employees were looked upon as
physical equipment, like drill presses or forklifts,
and prevailing management philosophy called for
them to be treated as such, oiled and tightened up as
little as was necessary to insure their continued
operation. This policy worked adequately in an
industrial society, where products were
manufactured on an assembly line by people who
performed single tasks. Employees did not require
sophisticated information or instruction. Job training
was sitting down at your new job and having the guy
next to you say, "You're supposed to drill a quarter

**According to an article in
the *International Journal of
Technology Management*
(1987) by Harlan Cleveland,
"The Twilight of Hierarchy:
Speculations on the Global
Information Society," the
inherent characteristics of
physical resources allowed
the development of hier-
archies of power, class,
influence, and privilege.
The characteristics of information do not allow such
hierarchies because information is "expandable,
substitutable, diffusive,
shareable, and not
resource-intensive."**

inch hole in this piece of metal and send it down the line." The margin for misinterpretation of the instructions was minimal.

In 1927, researchers from Harvard University conducted a study at the Hawthorne Works of the Western Electric Company in Illinois. They found that productivity increased when workers were moved to a room with more lighting, when additional breaks were permitted, and when the lunch hour was lengthened. The researchers weren't so surprised until they conducted further tests. They reduced the lighting, the number of breaks, and the length of lunch hour, and they found that productivity increased in this case as well.

They determined that this resulted because, for the first time, the employees were being treated like human beings and they responded to the attention by increasing their efforts. Thus was born the human factor in management philosophy.

The human relations school didn't really catch hold until after World War II, when the business community discovered the idea that attention to communications might serve some practical, economical purpose. As jobs grew more complex, groups and committees were formed where once work was done by an individual. Groups, by their nature, had to deliver messages, to share information, and to reach a consensus to fulfill their commissions.

In a workplace that was becoming increasingly complicated, communications began to rise in importance.

> "In the 1950s, attention turned to choice of effective media, written or oral, and the respective advantages and disadvantages of each. Particular methods began to be recommended for communicating information from management to employees; employee handbooks, company newspapers and magazines, and bulletin boards.

> "....Also in the 1950s, methods of upward communication received great attention:

attitude surveys, suggestion systems, and interviews among them. Management began to realize that employees have ideas for improvement of their own work methods, the basis for the quality circle, which is growing in use and popularity today."—William V. Ruch, *Corporate Communications: A Comparison of Japanese and American Practices*

Look at the appellation *human resources* for example. Perhaps it was created to augment the stature of personnel departments, but instead it dehumanizes, turning people into one more resource like minerals or money.

Organizational communications became a buzzword in the 1960s, when material was generated on the subject from almost every discipline—sociology, business management, psychology, anthropology, linguistics, and even the hard sciences. Communication was examined not as a linear process, "but in the context of a changing environment in which communication is an interactive series of behaviors fraught with error," stated Ruch. "Special attention began to be paid to informal communication, communication barriers, non-verbal communication, and international and intercultural communication."

Unfortunately, many companies are still towing a grossly inadequate, Neanderthal attitude toward management communications—a philosophy forged on the assembly line. Looking toward employees as a valuable source of information on business operations still remains a radical idea in many American businesses—and they are paying a high price for their reluctance to change.

"When I see a sign that reads, Department of Human Resources, I cringe. It smacks of a meat market, where you can buy a leg, an arm, a brain, a strong stomach, or even a whole person, if you can afford it."—Roy T. Cottier, "Communications: A Management Strategy, Not A Professional Technique," *Vital Speeches of the Day* (7/1/87)

WHY INSTRUCTIONS WILL BECOME EVEN MORE IMPORTANT

Improving the quality of office instructions involves an understanding of the context component in the system—in its broadest application. (*See Chapter 2* for the three levels of meaning of context.) The particular work environment in which instructions are given, the state of a particular industry, and the current economic situation in general will affect the creation and interpretation of instructions. Numerous economic and cultural forces are at work which will expand the role of instructions in the workplace and require a higher caliber of communications. These forces are also going to make instructions harder to communicate.

- The more sophisticated communication needs of an information-based economy.

- Corporate instability and the concomitant rise of anxiety in the work force.

- Increased job-hopping.

- Greater consequences of poor instructions in a high-tech society.

- New demands on companies to communicate in different languages and tailor their products to different cultures, as a result of the globalization of markets.

- Changing demographics of the work force.

- Illiteracy in the workplace.

In the last twenty years, the transformation from a product- or industrial-based economy to a service- or information-based one has become complete. More than 50 percent of all businesses deal not in tangible products but in information. Information is now the dominant base of our economy, and with it comes a concomitant need for communication. Dealing with people, i.e., customers, clients, salesmen, and co-workers, requires more sophisticated skills than working on an assembly line.

Emphasizing communication is no longer an avant-garde option for forward-thinking companies; it is a necessity.

When the product is information, humanity becomes a factor. In a world run by ideas, people are the resources. Work is affected by the ability of bosses to communicate tasks, by the employee's interpretation of the instruction he or she gets, by the moods and personalities of the people in the office.

American executives now devote 94 percent of their time in communication-related activities, according to George Plotzke, market manager of AT&T's technology group. Oral communication accounts for 69 percent of that time, with 53 percent spent in face-to-face meetings and 16 percent on the

"Traditional information sources and management techniques have become less effective or obsolete linear information, linear thinking, and incremental strategies are no match for the turbulence of today's business climate. Extrapolating fails to recognize new unknowns. And temporizing solves nothing."
—Warren Bennis and Burt Nanus, *Leaders*

"Less than half of chief executive officers believe that the millions they spend on technology actually support their companies' business plans, according to a survey by an international consulting firm.

"The CEOs and CIOs [chief information officers] cited five cultural barriers to improving the efficacy of information technology resources: a failure to change some of the basic ways of doing business, people's failure to take the time to learn and use the existing systems, a failure to train people properly, an organizational culture that resists change, and turf battles that impede change."—Richard Layne, "Technology Falls Short for Most CEOs, Study Says," *American Banker* (11/8/89)

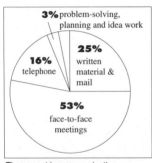

Time spent in communication-related activities

"Business is cracking the whip. A looming labor shortage, global and domestic competition, and the emphasis on speeding up work and getting costs down have made many corporations lean and mean—make that really mean. Says William McGowan, CEO of MCI, a company known for both hard work and high morale: 'Getting across the message that we've got to be competitive, that times have changed is putting a lot of stress into the business environment.' "
—Thomas A. Stewart, "Do You Push Your People Too Hard," *Fortune* (10/22/90)

I can't tell you how many companies I've called and had someone say, "Well, we're in the midst of an internal re-organization and we'll be able to give you what you want once we get organized." I think eternal re-organization might be more accurate.—RSW

telephone. Dealing with written material and mail accounts for 25 percent of their time, and problem-solving, planning, and idea work account for 3 percent. Middle managers spend somewhat less time communicating—80 percent for middle managers and 70 percent for first-line managers.

FEAR AND LOATHING IN THE OFFICE

The very vocabulary of corporate America is dispiriting to employee imagination and establishes a poor atmosphere for creatively carrying out instructions. The word *executive* has such violent connotations, sharing a root that means "to put to death." Executives fire orders, command respect, and marshal the troops. It is a word of intimidation, designed to instill fear, not inspiration, conjuring up pictures of wrathful despots who delight in throwing their weight around. Phrases like "dominate the market," "crush the competition," "butt heads with rivals," and "run it up the flagpole" are common parlance in boardroom bandying. Sometimes it seems that the language of enterprise was lifted directly from the army or the football field—neither an arena noted for its imagination or creativity.

Today's business climate fosters anxiety and defensive responses. With takeovers, mergers, unstable economies, and widespread job migrations, people are robbed of the freedom of being able to admit they don't understand, to ask questions, to disagree with a superior. This promotes an atmosphere of insecurity and mistrust. Our lives are more complicated, run by more machinery, demand more knowledge; anxiety proliferates during an age that demands a more assured response.

In a stable office environment, co-workers are more likely to cooperate, to share information, and to help each other. In a more volatile one, the likelihood is higher that the person next to you may be after your job. This dog-eat-dog attitude in the office reduces the incentive to share information or to instruct your office neighbor in company protocol. Yet this is the bedrock of corporate life and the economy increasingly relies on it.

Anxiety and fear inhibit constructive response to instructions. By their nature, they dominate other emotions and are the last feelings you want to evoke when giving important instructions. They are paralyzing; they pave the way for errors and misunderstandings. When your primary emotion toward your job is the fear of losing it, you are likely to be too anxious to follow orders.

Feeling that your job is always on the line also brings back test anxiety—the school-days' fear that your future will be determined by your performance. Only the most well-adjusted or the most oblivious perform at their peak when the weight of their *FUTURE* hangs in a perpetually tenuous balance.

Jan Carlzon, president and CEO of Scandinavian Airlines System Group, took over the then-troubled airline in 1981, when it suffered a $20-million loss. He turned the company around—turning a profit after his first year—by focusing on the front-line people who have contact with the customers. "In my experience, there are two great motivators in life. One is fear. The other is love. You can manage an organization by fear, but if you do you will ensure that people don't perform up to their real capabilities," said Carlzon, in an interview in *INC.* (5/89). "A person who is afraid doesn't dare perform to the limits of his or her capabilities....People are not willing to take risks when they feel afraid or threatened. But if you manage people by love—that is, if you show them respect and trust—they start to perform up to their real capabilities. Because in that kind of atmosphere, they dare to take risks. They can even make mistakes."

Jan Carlzon's restructuring of SAS Airlines involved turning the organizational chart upside down. Middle managers were redefined as support for the people who have direct customer contact instead of as supervisors who were supposed to make sure frontline people were following instructions. Frontline people were given the authority to make decisions.

"You must provide a framework in which people can act. For example, we have said that our first priority

"While much attention is paid to purely economic values, often it appears that top management seems unable to cope with the explosive people problems which result from rapid changing work environments and clashing corporate cultures."—Stephen A. Finch, "How to Manage Office Relationships," *Supervision* (5/88)

"No passion so effectually robs the mind of all its powers of acting and reasoning as fear."—Edmund Burke

"Minds, nevertheless, are not conquered by arms, but by love and generosity," —Benedict de Spinoza, *Ethics*

The president and CEO of Scandinavian Airlines will face new challenges after the restructuring of the European Economic Community in 1992. The intrepid Carlzon, proclaiming that the war in the air will be won on the ground in the 1990s, plans to diversify SAS into other travel-related business such as hotels.

is safety, second is punctuality, and third is other services. So, if you risk flight safety by leaving on time, you have acted outside the framework of your authority. The same is true if you don't leave on time because you are missing two catering boxes of meat. That's what I mean by a framework. You give people a framework, and within the framework you let people act," said Carlzon in the interview.

(*See* Information Anxiety.)

Scandinavian Airlines is now one of the most successful business-class airlines in Europe. Three years after Carlzon took over, it was named the Airline of the Year by *Air Transport World* magazine.

Anxiety is the worst response, whether you are following the directions for using a computer or the directions of the company president for drafting a memo.

Fear tends to get in the way of listening. It evokes a flight response. The instruction-bearer becomes the dreaded one. You try to second-guess the instructions, to demonstrate your task-fluency by exclaiming your understanding prematurely in an attempt to escape an uncomfortable situation. This fear is picked up by the instructor and, most likely, will make him or her uncomfortable as well.

Your chances of understanding the spirit of an instruction are slim and none if your first response to it is to fall into a morass of anxiety and self-doubt, wondering, "What happens if I make a mistake, what are the liabilities, how can I do this without causing any trouble, what could go wrong, how can I protect myself from problems, could it lose money, could someone sue me, could I wreck the equipment?"

The motive becomes stalling not solving, hedging your bets instead of making decisions. Then, if you feel a decision is imminent, you can always call in expensive consultants with the thinly veiled task of supporting the decisions rather than reacting genuinely to them. "Let's cover our asses. Maybe we'd better do a mall-intercept study in Des Moines." Research should be inspired by a need to know, not used to spread the blame in case something goes wrong.

People fear failure, because they don't see it as the road to success. By getting wound up in anxiety about failing, people often make more mistakes, because they are so busy fearing that they are going to make them.

When I teach, I'm demanding. I tell my class, "What I want is difficult and most of you are going to screw up." I told my assistant when I hired her that "whatever you do, it's not going to be good enough. But I won't hold it against you, therefore, don't hold it against yourself." I wanted to take away the fear of failure, by saying it's okay to fail. I wanted her to know that she could make mistakes, that she wasn't alone in making them. Few people are permitted this knowledge. Instead they carry the solitary and private fear that they are going to screw up, sure that everyone else knows how to do what they can't.

LET THEM MAKE MISTAKES

Instructions require putting yourself in the place of the project or the machine. Instructions require imagination, bridging the gap between the mind-set of the machine and the operator or between the perspective of one person and another. Instructions involve the freedom to take risks, to make mistakes, to push the wrong button.

A friend of mine used to work at Rizzoli Bookstore. Sometimes books that have been on the shelves for a long time lose their price tags. The book clerks usually call down to the stockroom and ask for a price. But these are invariably the books whose records have long since disappeared. So the stockroom manager will spend 15 minutes looking for something that probably doesn't exist anymore and the fearful book clerk who has been indoctrinated into blindly following the rules has to tell the customer that there is no price, which is tantamount to saying, "We cannot sell this book." My friend gave up on this fast. She reckoned that if she made up a reasonable price and the customer bought the book, she could increase store profits by freeing up space on the shelves for books that sold more quickly. Soon, she got a reputation in the store as the one to ask if you needed a price. No one ever questioned where she got her information; they were all delighted to give up on the fruitless calls to the stockroom. They were absolved of responsibility because they had "checked for the price."

If she feared not following the rules, the books would still be on the shelves gathering dust and many customers would have walked out thinking: Does this store really want to sell books?

> "Jim Burke actually encourages mistakes at Johnson & Johnson, saying, 'I decided that what we needed more than anything else was a climate that would encourage people to take risks.'…Burke went on to tell of his own experience with a mistake: 'I once developed a new product that failed badly, and General

Johnson called me in, and I was sure he was going to fire me....Johnson said to me, *I understand you lost over a million dollars.* I can't remember the exact amount. It seemed like a lot then. And I said, *Yes sir. That's correct.* So he stood up and held out his hand. He said, *I just want to congratulate you. All business is making decisions, and if you don't make decisions, you won't have any failures. The hardest job I have is getting people to make decisions. If you make that same decision wrong again, I'll fire you. But I hope you'll make a lot of others, and that you'll understand there are going to be more failures than successes.' "*—Warren Bennis, *On Becoming a Leader*

WHICH WAY TO THE EXECUTIVE SUITE?

The increasing rootlessness of people also plays a role in the importance of instruction. People used to spend their entire working careers at one company where they could learn the ropes gradually, following a natural apprenticeship program. But today, jobs have become as disposable as diapers. People jump from job to job often from one industry to the next.

According to a report by the Center for Creative Leadership in Greensboro, North Carolina, most white collar workers will have from 8 to 20 bosses during their careers—depending on their rising speed. Owing to the number of corporate takeovers, buyouts, and restructurings, these bosses will often have less experience with the company than the employees do. If you haven't been on the job long enough to figure out what you're supposed to be doing, you'll have a tough time explaining duties to an underling.

With many companies experiencing a turnover rate from 20 to 30 percent a year, more people have to be trained more quickly.

De Tocqueville, in *Democracy in America,* said people "are often obliged to do things which they have imperfectly learned, to say things which they imperfectly understand, and to devote themselves to work for which they are unprepared by long apprenticeship." The book was published in 4 volumes between 1835 and 1840, but it is even more timely today.

HIGH-TECH SKILLS REQUIRED

The glut of information that must be perused further taxes human capabilities—whether it be about developments in the field or new equipment in the office.

According to Robert Horn, president of Information Mapping in Waltham, Massachusetts, the typical manager wades through a million words a week. "Not surprisingly, several problems result from this kind of information gridlock—high error rates, low recall, inordinate demands on supervisors, expensive rewriting of documentation, and a constant need for retraining people."

And the skills that the work force has to master are harder to teach. The advent of telecommunications, robotics, and sophisticated computer systems has complicated the workplace, requiring ever more science and math skills. The ability of one person to affect many has risen exponentially. In the financial world, billions of dollars can go through the hands of one person in a day. In the medical world, the machinery that sustains life requires more expertise to operate. People have to be taught how to operate and maintain complex equipment, sometimes in an afternoon, and then make decisions that may affect millions of people.

DUTIES ONCE REMOVED

The complexity of business today makes the big picture harder to grasp—how do the efforts of one person affect the whole? Workers have become distanced from their duties—figuratively and literally. In an agrarian society, a farmer plowed furrows in a field, planted seeds, and knew that corn would grow in the summer. Even in an industrial economy, workers on an assembly line got to *see* the finished product, even if their only contribution to it was to drill a few holes.

This luxury of proximity and familiarity is denied many workers today. The finished product is often information—a commodity whose real life is abstract. A recommendation, a report, a file has little tangible value in its paper and ink. The value is the ephemeral information itself, information that may have been compiled by hundreds of people from hundreds of sources.

The scope and reach of companies has scattered company functions around the world. Corporate offices can be in one country, the factory in another. Management, which might not be doing a great job communicating with employees working in the home office, must now communicate with people of different countries, whose differing languages and cultures increase exponentially the difficulty of giving understandable instructions.

The scattering of functions around the world also makes it harder for people to stay informed about different parts of a business. People work for companies in which they never see the product. A commodities trader could spend his lifetime dealing with grain and never see a stalk of wheat. A garment executive might never feel the nap on a roll of velour.

This distancing of people from products does more than induce poetic longing or nostalgia. It complicates describing a product (tangible or not), understanding company business in perspective, comprehending the totality of an issue, and giving instructions that take into account the big picture.

MESCOLATE PIANO, con un cucchiaino, il caffe, in modo che il caffe sgorgato per primo, più denso, si mescoli con quello meno denso, sgorgato successivamente.

MÉ LANGUEZ LE CA-FE LENTEMENT à l'aide d'une cuiller, de façon à ce que la café débité d'abord, qui est plus dense, se mélange avec le café moins dense débitépar la suite.

RUHREN SIE DEN KAFFEE LANGSAM mit einem Loffel um, damit der anfangs ausgetretenen Kaffee, welcher starker ist, sich mit dem nachher ausgetretenen gut vermischt.

STIR THE COFFEE SLOWLY with a spoon, so that the first part of the coffee to ooze out, which is more concentrated, is mixed with the weaker, last part.

Adapted from an multilingual instruction pamphlet for a Braun coffee grinder.

GLOCALIZATION: TAILORING PRODUCTS TO INDIVIDUAL MARKETS

Surviving in the worldwide marketplace demands not only that companies must be able to communicate to people of different countries, but also that they must understand their cultures enough to tailor products to meet the needs of different populations.

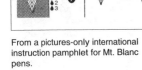

From a pictures-only international instruction pamphlet for Mt. Blanc pens.

> "Whether as citizens, as family and neighborhood members, or as workers and professionals, the vast majority of us now live in a context affected on a daily basis by international forces. This fact poses profound and far-reaching challenges....Our nation has been steeped in the history, traditions, arts, religious practices, political ideologies, and bureaucratic philosophies of Western Europe.

> "We have a long way to go to equip our citizens, our labor force, and our leadership to function in a world where the Orient, central Asia, and Latin America represent major economic and political forces."—Kerry A. Johnson and Lin J. Foa, *Instructional Design: New Alternatives for Effective Education and Training*

In the United States, Heinz uses slowness to sell its ketchup—so thick that you have to wait for it to come out of the bottle. The company tried the same approach in Japan with disastrous result. The Japanese, who are used to condiments like soy sauce that blend quickly with the food, didn't take to a product that inched out of the bottle in clumps.

A Chinese manufacturer didn't have any better results when it tried to market an automobile battery called The White Elephant in the United States.

The international marketplace has become so crowded that the ones who succeed in it will be the ones who can adapt their products and their marketing to local cultures. The ability of international companies to create products that recognize the preferences and needs of individual markets requires a competence in multicultural instructions as well.

This means that companies will have to design their products with instructions that can be customized to different languages and perspectives, as well as instruct their own suppliers who may be located around the world. A product or marketing approach that works in one country cannot be counted on to work in another.

CHANGING DEMOGRAPHICS

The challenges of integrating multiple cultures will be felt more directly in the American work force, making communications more difficult between management and employees. Traditional training programs are less likely to be effective.

The pool of labor used to be much more homogeneous. Companies hired people who had identical training, graduated from the same schools, wore the same kind of clothes, and drove the same kind of cars. You could be labeled an iconoclast by wearing suspenders in a firm where the belt was the norm or by driving a Ford in the company of Chevrolet owners. When a company's work force shared the same socioeconomic and cultural profile, it was a good bet that what worked to educate or train one would work for another.

Now the work force is multicultural. The tremendous influx of foreign-born has changed dramatically the profile of the business community. While this has succeeded in bringing new ideas into the workplace and a healthy cross-cultural polleni-zation, it has also taxed the system of employee training. Employees who come from totally different cultures have varying degrees of familiarity with English and have diverse systems for learning.

Increased immigration quotas are one cause of the more diverse work force. But another is the poor showing that Americans make in the hard sciences. Positions in these fields are being filled by foreigners.

The influx of foreigners is only one of many factors that are altering the composition of the work force and making employee training that much more complicated. The work force is aging. At the turn of the century, the ratio of elderly to young was 1 to 8; by the year 2000, it will be 1 to 2. The percentage of minorities is also increasing.

Minorities now make up nearly 30 percent of the U.S. population. They are more likely to live in

"In the 1990s the U.S. will liberalize immigration laws to attract still more work-ers. (In 1988 we admitted 643,000 immigrants, more than all other countries put together)....Japan, our prime competition, has just one race and one culture. Although that makes for a neat, well-organized society, it severely limits creativity. It is not by chance that the U.S. has 196 Nobel prizes and Japan has 5. The richness of America's human resources—including Japanese Americans—is our greatest asset in meeting the competition of the global 1990s."—Patricia Aburdene, "How to Think Like a CEO in the 90's," *Working Woman* (9/90)

poverty and suffer educational deficiencies. The high school drop out rate approaches 50 percent in some urban areas.

The high school dropout rate in the United States is 27 percent, compared to a rate of 5 percent in Japan.
—U.S. Department of Education

According to an article in *The New York Times,* "Work Force Failing to Meet Math Needs" (4/11/90), the increased demand for mathematical skills will not be met by those entering the work force in the future. "By the year 2000, the need for workers in these fields is expected to rise by 36 percent over the 1986 figure. But at the same time demographic trends indicate that the traditional pool of scientists and engineers, white males, will fall at roughly the same rate."

The article, based on a report by the National Research Council (a group that advises Congress on scientific issues), went on to say, "There will be 21 million new jobs a decade from now...with most requiring mathematical backgrounds and post-secondary education."

The NRC report said that 85 percent of the entrants to the labor force will be minorities and women, few of which enter the fields of engineering and science. Minorities account for only 6 percent of those with doctorates in mathematics; only 17 percent are women. Only 2.5 percent of the nation's engineers were black and even fewer were Hispanic. Science and math departments will have to attract these students to fill the growing number of jobs that will demand this knowledge.

Aggravating the problem is an existing shortage of qualified science and math teachers at all levels of education in the United States. The report stated that the current number of new doctoral-degreed mathematicians will not even replace the faculty lost to retirement.

Teachers—like the rest of us—cannot keep up with the developments in technology and science. The world as it was when they went to school is not the world as it is now.

> "The Educational Testing Service reported last year that Korean 13-year-olds succeeded twice as often as Americans at solving a two-step mathematical problem, such as determining an average....Other investigators have shown that average Japanese 12th graders have a better command of mathematics than the top 5 percent of their American counterparts.

> "....Unfortunately, few American students ever get to taste real science, for few of the nation's schools teach it. All parties now seem to agree that American science education serves not to nurture children's natural curiosity but to extinguish it with catalogs of dreary facts and terms.

> "....Whether out of boredom, laziness or the allure of other pursuits, American students are fleeing math and science in droves. By the third grade, half of all students don't want to take science anymore, says Edward Pizzini, associate professor of science education at the University of Iowa....Fewer than half ever take a math or science course after the 10th grade, and only 1 percent study calculus, a subject pursued by 12 percent of Japan's high-school students."—Geoffrey Cowley with Karen Springen, Todd Barrett, and Mary Hager, "Not Just for Nerds," *Newsweek* (4/9/90)

The real bankruptcy of the decade may be the bankruptcy of the educational system and its inability to educate students to work effectively in the jobs of the 1990s. Thus the business community may find itself giving instructions to a work force that is less prepared to comprehend them.

"We're graduating kids who can't even read their own diplomas," said Edward Hennessy, Jr., of Allied Signal, a New Jersey-based aerospace company, in

"How to Make Workers Better," by Andrew Erdman in *Fortune* magazine (10/22/90).

The article, based on a poll conducted by Clark, Martire & Bartolomeo, went on to say, "More than 90 percent of CEOs surveyed indicated that they spend more on educating employees today than they did in 1980. Almost all are committed to the idea that corporations must step in and help educate workers because government hasn't been up to the job. 'Management has got to pick up the challenge of education,' says E. C. Gwaltney of Russell Corp., one of the largest textile and apparel manufacturers. Referring to the students public schools are turning out, W. W. Sprague, Jr., of Savannah Foods & Industries, adds, 'Business must be involved, since the product we are getting stinks.'....Little about the way public schools are run appeals to these chief executives. They understand competition and think it would shape up the schools: Three-quarters believe parents should be able to choose the school their children will attend instead of having to patronize educational monopolies. Nearly all the CEOs polled favor basing teachers' salaries on performance and seniority, rather than on the latter alone. An object of particular disdain is the tenure system employed by many school boards."

ILLITERACY IN THE WORKPLACE

Most adult training programs assume that participants come prepared with the basics of elementary and secondary education, such as reading and writing skills. But an increasing number of students are being pushed through and out of the formal education system without being able to read and write. *Nation's Business* magazine claimed that 15 million workers are functionally illiterate—that is their skills do not go beyond the fourth-grade level.

The U.S. rate means that 1 out of 5 Americans is functionally illiterate and 1 out of 3 are only marginally literate.

According to estimates by UNESCO and the U.S. Department of Education Adult Literacy Program, a fourth of the world's adults are illiterate. Illiteracy isn't exclusively the problem of underdeveloped countries either. America's literacy rating is 49th among the 156 United Nation member countries—a drop of 18 places since 1950. The U.S. Department of Education claims that 20 percent of Americans are functionally illiterate and another 34 percent are only marginally literate.

Independent from those who cannot read is a special set of people who *choose* not to read. The abundance of entertainment available today, such as television and movies, has become a substitute for reading for millions—especially among young adults. Forty-four percent of American adults don't read even one book a year. And unused skills have a tendency to atrophy, if not disappear. The U.S. Department of Education claims that the average kindergarten student has seen more than 5,000 hours of television, more time than it takes to earn a bachelor's degree. The average adult watches about 33 hours a week, or 1,700 hours a year.

> "Experts and teachers agree that the nation's literacy problem is rooted in modern culture, where flashy distractions easily win short attention spans away from literary pursuits. Instead of reading, writing letters, or discussing politics, students spend their free time watching television, talking on the phone, zapping video monsters, and playing sports."—Joan E. Rigdon and Alecia Swasy, "Distractions of Modern Life at Key Ages Are Cited for Drop in Student Literacy," *The Wall Street Journal* (10/1/90)

The United Way estimates that the cost of illiteracy to business and taxpayers is $20 billion a year.

Employees need not be totally illiterate before they will experience problems doing their work. Three quarters of the Fortune 500 companies provide some level of remedial training for their workers at a cost of about $300 million a year, according to the American Council of Life Insurance.

> *"Do any of your employees have a workplace-literacy problem?* 'When I ask managers in my seminars that question, only a few people raise their hands,' said Miriam Shubin, the national spokesperson on workplace literacy for Olsten Corporation, a Westbury, New York-based temporary personnel company that's funding a national campaign to combat workplace illiteracy. 'But when I ask how many of them

have employees who aren't filling out forms properly, aren't taking accurate telephone messages, can't perform simple calculations or proofread—then almost everyone's hand goes up.' "—Laurel Touby, "Your Staff Can Read— But How Well?" *Working Woman* (7/90)

In 1985, Procter & Gamble, Philip Morris, and R.J. Reynolds/Nabisco each spent more on advertising than the U.S. government spent on adult basic education (about $1.1 billion).—*World Almanac, 1988*

According to Gerri Fiala, chief of the Policy Analysis Unit in the Department of Labor's Employment and Training Administration, "The problem has gotten worse in recent years. Constant changes in technology mean workers continually must update their skills, but those who already lack basic skills can't learn new ones."

In an information society, the ability to communicate successfully with your subordinates, your peers, and your superiors is of paramount importance. Information is put to use through instructions. If you want to establish a fertile field for giving and receiving them, literacy is a prerequisite. The communication of instructions demands language skills— whether reading or writing a report or carrying on a conversation. While the illiteracy problem is beyond the scope of this book, employers do need to be aware of how to recognize language problems.

INCREASED DEMANDS ON EMPLOYEE TRAINING

You have an increased number of foreigners from diverse backgrounds, more disadvantaged minorities, an explosion in the need for demanding technological skills, a more migratory work force, perpetual reorganizations, and pervasive illiteracy. Training and development will no longer be an office perk, but an essential part of the day-to-day operation of many companies.

"Training is everything. The peach was once a bitter almond; cauliflower is nothing but cabbage with a college education."—Mark Twain

"Companies are aware of the need to provide training to strengthen the relationship between management and employee. In 1988, U.S. businesses spent more than $200 billion overall on training, and employers on average offered 18 training courses," reports the American Society for Training and Development.

In the 1987-1988 school year, the total expenditures (educational and general) of all colleges and universities were $124 billion, according to the *Digest of Education Statistics 1988,* prepared by the U.S. Department of Education. That's $76 billion *less* than U.S. companies spent on education and training during the same year.

The field of instructional design has become a hot new industry. At least 100 companies offer programs to train employees to perform their functions more efficiently or to present instructions more effectively. These efforts fall under the rubric of *human* or *performance* engineering.

The goal of most adult training is to teach specific skills, such as how to operate a piece of equipment or work in a particular computer language. Adults usually have a well-defined purpose for acquiring new information, i.e., learning.

Until recently, most learning theories were based on the teaching of children, who are taught a broad spectrum of subjects. The purpose of educating children is to give them a foundation of knowledge for later life—a vague goal subject to infinite interpretations and arguments. The training needs and interests of adults differ from those of children and the methods of teaching one group won't necessarily work with the other.

Aside from a general lack of information available on the training of adults, the trainers often lack teaching experience of any kind. Trainers usually attain their positions through their expertise at a particular job or skill. No teaching experience is required to train other adults in the workplace. Therefore, those who train adults may come from any field and have varying degrees of ignorance and inexperience when it comes to teaching.

If American companies want to compete in the global market, they must bear more and more of the burden of training people and forge new methods for teaching job skills to a diverse population. But before that, they must recognize the importance of instructions and begin to isolate

problems in giving and taking them. The starting
point is to determine what kind of instruction-
giver or -taker you are. And what about the
people around you?

IF I'VE TOLD YOU ONCE....: TYPECASTING INSTRUCTION-GIVERS AND -TAKERS

"For high-level people, lack of skill is not usually what gets in their way. Their styles are just inappropriate for team playing."

Bernard Kessler, Beam-Pines Inc.

In reality, no one is solely an instruction-giver or -taker. No one is ever high enough to rise above the need to follow instructions. You may be the CEO, but you still need to follow the instructions if you want to drive a car or put together a bicycle for your kid or make your stockholders happy. You have to listen for the implicit instructions in conversations with your advisers, with your friends, with your family.

"Hobbes clearly proves that every creature

Lives in a state of war by nature.

So naturalists observe, a flea,

Has smaller fleas that on him prey;

And these have smaller still to bite 'em,

And so proceed *ad infinitum.*"—Jonathan Swift,
Poetry; a Rhapsody

"The man who commands efficiently must have obeyed others in the past, and the man who obeys dutifully is worthy of being someday a commander."
—Cicero, *De Legibus* (c. 52 BC)

And, no matter how low you are on the office totem pole, you will still have occasion to explain a task, give directions, order services, etc. You are giving instructions when you spell out your likes and dislikes to those around you.

All of us spend our days moving, sometimes seamlessly, between our roles as givers and takers of instruction. Often, in the same conversation, we switch back and forth between playing the instruction-giver and the -taker. Mr. Brown might direct Mr. White to embark on a study of peat moss. Mr. White wants clarification of the scope of the study, so he directs Mr. Brown to give him information regarding the aspects of peat moss to be covered. Successful communication demands this role exchanging. So there is always room for improvement, whether your work is dominated by giving or taking instructions.

Knowing your style in both capacities is imperative to improving your performance in both roles. Sadly, few people have a clear picture of themselves—as instructors or just as human beings for that matter. Self-image is like a funhouse mirror—probably one of life's most easily distorted images. Fat people see themselves as thin, foolish people see smart people, and docile lambs sometimes see lions. Distortion isn't always negative. Sometimes it makes life easier or at least bearable, but in the office, you need a clear sense of how you are perceived as an order-giver or -taker.

You can compensate for a distorted self-image by looking beyond the mirror and paying attention to the way people respond to you. What problems do they have in understanding you? What aspects of your personality do they complain about either openly or subversively in anquished expressions or slammed doors? What are the phrases they often use when talking with you? These all provide clues into your office image. So forewarned, see if you can identify yourself.

LOOK OUT FOR THESE INSTRUCTORS

If you notice that your employees often cock their heads sideways and look at you with a glassy-eyed, loose-lipped stare, either they are suffering from narcolepsy or they do not understand you. One way or the other, your directions are not getting through to them and you are wasting your money paying people to carry out incomprehensible instructions.

Unfortunately, the very characteristics that tend to make successful executives—creativity, ambition, and mercurial thinking—also make for poor instruction-givers. They often lack the time or patience to explain themselves clearly. Thus, they misinterpret clients' needs, bewilder and aggravate employees, diminish creativity, hinder employees' ability to do a job, and set themselves up for constant disappointment.

Bad instruction-givers squander talent and time as well as money. Their habits are perpetuated because they direct their staff in such a way as to confirm their preconceived notions. A boss who keeps peering over an employee's shoulder, fearing that he or she is incapable, is bound to make the person nervous and mistake-prone. This is a vicious cycle; the boss redoubles surveillance and makes the employee even more nervous.

> **"'I quite agree with you,' said the Duchess; 'and the moral of that is Be what you would seem to be—or if you'd like it put more simply—Never imagine yourself not to be otherwise than what it might appear to others that you were or might have been was not otherwise than what you had been would have appeared to them to be otherwise.'**
>
> **"'I think I should understand that better,' Alice said very politely, 'if I had it written down: but I'm afraid I can't quite follow it as you say it.' "**—Lewis Carroll, *Alice in Wonderland*

Remember the frustration the last time you tried to figure out an equipment manual. Did you curse and throw the manual at a wall, complaining that "I can't understand a damn word of this thing"? This may be just what the people who have to follow your instructions feel like. The next time you accuse someone of "doing exactly what I told you not to do," entertain the possibility that what you wanted them to do wasn't exactly what you told them to do.

If you think that you are a masterful direction-giver and that your faithful followers always understand exactly what you want, then you might be in real trouble. Owing to the inherent shortcomings of communication, this just isn't possible. Our understanding of language is colored by our own experience and perceptions—aspects of humanity that have infinite variations. No two people will express ideas in the same way. Brilliant instruction-givers—people who can direct their staff to perform their tasks with exquisite precision—do exist. But even they can improve their techniques.

Once you are willing to admit there is room for improving your instruction technique, the next step is to understand just where your shortcomings are in the instruction department.

The following describes a variety of bad bosses who haven't learned how to give directions. They don't represent different people as much as different delivery styles. You may recognize yourself in more than one.

- **Cover Your Ass.** These bosses have never gotten comfortable with their own position, so their primary motivation in giving you an assignment is to make sure that if anything goes wrong they will have someone other than themselves to blame it on. Finding excuses becomes a religious quest in itself. Their employees don't get to spend much time with assignments because they are occupied trying to find a scapegoat in case things go wrong. The favorite words of Cover-Your-Ass bosses are "focus group," "test market," and "mall-intercept study"— the Holy Trinity. With religious fervor, they fight off the evil temptations of personal judgment and intuition—their own or anyone else's. Every night, the entire market-research industry says a prayer for these people.

● **I'm an Important Person, I Don't Have Time to Explain.** These people are usually thinking about the next task before they have made the first one clear. They regard explanations as a waste of precious time and they brag that they won't stoop to "hand-holding" their employees. Their time is very precious because Important Persons spend most of it trying to correct the mistakes made by their subordinates, usually with new directions that they never take time to delivery properly. Of course, to do the job right the first time would save twice as much time, but then the Important Persons wouldn't feel so important and so needed. The Important Persons' favorite expression is "For Christ's sake, I don't have all day."

● **Crisis Managers** are a contradiction in terms, for nothing is managed as much as it is attacked. They take their working style from kamikaze pilots. Their speech is peppered with clichés like "going for broke,"

"staying on top of everything," "the whole ball of wax," and "shooting the wad." Foreplay to Crisis Managers is calling an "emergency meeting." They thrive on exorbitant rush charges, overnight delivery services, last-minute changes of plans, and hearing someone else say, "The sky is falling." Their phones never get put down as much as slammed down and they sound like they are on the commodities trading floor even when they are sitting in their offices. They appear to be in imminent danger of suffering from massive coronaries, nervous breakdowns, and/or apoplectic fits, but don't let this fool you. They can live long and happy lives in this state. The ones who collapse are the people who have to follow their directions.

● **Mr./Ms. Taskus Interruptus.** With flawless timing, these bosses assign a task and, just when their employee has become immersed in it, interrupt the person with a new request. Thus, their employees are deprived of a sense of accomplishment because they never get to finish a job. Sometimes this behavior is caused because people fear that their employees might donate the company to charity if they had a free moment. But, more likely, it results from arrested development on the part of the instruction-giver. When an infant's pacifier falls out of its mouth, getting it back becomes the most important quest in the world. An infant doesn't understand that the house might be on fire; mother might be rescuing brother from the washing machine; or she could be in the middle of an important phone conversation.

important phone conversation. As they mature, most children are forced to accept the idea of limited time and resources; they learn to adapt to this phenomenon by setting priorities. This escapes many executives. Whatever comes to their minds is what needs to be done NOW. Employees soon learn that the new request is always more important than what they were doing. Task Number 1 gets put aside for Task Number 2. While doing Task Number 2, they are fair game for further interruptions. Sometimes tasks undergo generations of interruptions. It becomes increasingly difficult to remember all the tasks that were put down temporarily. Employees are likely to get confused and make mistakes. "Let's see, where was I? Was I supposed to review the Barber case or case the barber?" You might think working under such a person would be intolerable, but, fortunately, Mr. and Ms. Taskus Interruptus tend to retain other more appealing traits of childhood as well. They are often very creative, optimistic, playful, and just plain fun to be around, but underlings can grow resentful if they are expected to act in a more mature manner than their bosses.

● **Over-the-Shoulder Supervisor.** These people fear that they are the only ones capable of doing anything and that the only way you are going to be able to carry out their orders is if they supervise you at every step of the way. Of course this kind of approach tends to make subordinates nervous and, in a state of heightened anxiety, they are likely to commit just the kind of errors the bosses were sure they would make in the first place. The bosses give elaborate step-by-step directions that are so detailed that they tell you not only who to call, but how to use the phone. Then, five minutes after giving the instruction, they poke their heads into your office and say, "You're staying on top of this now, aren't you, Miss Jones?" Their employees get so caught up in the intricacies that the goal gets lost in the shuffle.

● **Why Don't You Let Me Do That for You.** No one could possibly do the job as well as these people. These are the obssessive-compulsive versions of the Over-the-Shoulder Supervisors, who, while they may watch you like a hawk, will not take tasks away from you. The problem is that Let Me Do Thats have such a fixed idea of the solution that no one can do the job in the exact way that they could. Their employees are also prevented from going beyond their bosses' directions or from coming up with better ways to do things. These bosses have been told by everyone—and usually are aware of it themselves—that they should learn to delegate authority, but when they try to assign tasks, they invariably wind up repossessing them. These people live at the office and are surrounded by a staff of people who take very long lunch hours, keep in close touch with their friends, and do catalog-shopping at their desks to pass the time.

● **If You Love Me, You'll Do This, or Management by Guilt.** This type may be a workaholic who has no life outside the company and assumes that no one else does either. They play the role of parent with varying degrees of good nature. If an

employee has to tell her MBG boss that third
quarter sales figures will not be available
until after the fourth quarter, what does she
fear most? Getting yelled at? Getting
fired? Being embarrassed in front of
her co-workers? No. She fears that
baleful, bassett-hound look. "Oh,
Ms. Foididdle. This makes me very
sad," says Mr./Ms. Management-
by-Guilt, as he/she shakes his/her
head slowly. "I'm so disappointed. I
just don't know what to do with
you. You're like a daughter to me."
MBGs are fond of familial
references and they tend to attract
susceptible underlings who
imagine that their boss is really
their father or mother. The
employees of these people are
usually so burdened by
guilt that they barely have
the strength to work. But
eventually they realize that
their bosses will not come over
when the baby-sitter cancels, make
canapes for cocktail parties, or remind
them of their anniversary. When this
happens, employees tend to get very
bitter.

● **Free Associators.** These people throw
out vague requests that sometimes seem
contradictory or confusing. They speak
in stream of consciousness, read
New Age literature, think in
hyperbole, and vacation in exotic
places. They are always
animated, expostulating on harmony
in the office and the creative spirit. An
assignment given by a Free Associator might
sound like this: "I want you to show the
connection between art and science. Where
is that point where they merge? The question
is in the answer. The answer is in the
question. Education is all about

connections." The employee suspects that this might be an assignment to design a poster for a museum exhibit, but is never quite sure. These people can be positively evangelical; they are great at eliciting enthusiasm and make great bosses as long as they don't turn out to have some specific goal in mind despite the vagueness of their requests. As long as they are as flexible as their instructions, these kinds of instructors can be quite inspiring for they permit the takers to use their own imagination in completing assignments. One of the most dangerous types is an outward Free Associator in the body of an Over-the-Shoulder Supervisor.

● **The Cro-Magnon Manager.** The communication skills of these people never developed beyond the crib. Consequently, they hide behind an attitude that communication, as well as quiche, is for sissies. Their directions are barked out in one-syllable grunts and they have the patience of hand grenades. It is a peculiar phenomenon that such types tend to surround themselves with people who live for language and devote themselves to reforming their Cro-Magnon bosses. A typical exchange with such a person goes as follows:

"Sir, what did you think of the letter of agreement I drafted with Blank Page Printing Company?" says the loquacious lackey.

The Cro-Magnon Manager, rifling through the mountains of memos on his desk, responds without looking up. "Huh."

"The letter of agreement, sir, did you get a chance to read it?"

"Huh? Oh, yah," he says, as he glances at the document and seems to notice something disagreeable. "Argh."

"Is there a problem?"

Finally resorting to an approximation of English, he responds, "Wrong. It's wrong."

"What is the problem, sir?"

"It's just not right."

"Could you be more specific?" the lackey asks, ever optimistic.

"I said it's wrong," says the manager, as he goes back to rearranging the piles of paper on his desk.

At this point the employee gives up and shuffles back to his or her desk to try another version with no idea of what was wrong with the first one.

- **Do As I Mean, Not As I Say.** These bosses may have a clear picture of what needs to be done, but the idea gets garbled when they try to explain it. Their instructions are muddled in contradictory phraseology, unclear descriptions, and errors in meaning. Do As I Meaners say West Coast when they mean East Coast, say Fred when they mean Ethyl, and call General Motors Major Motors and expect you to know exactly what they are talking about. These bosses prevent their staff from getting clarification on any directions by accompanying them with remarks such as:

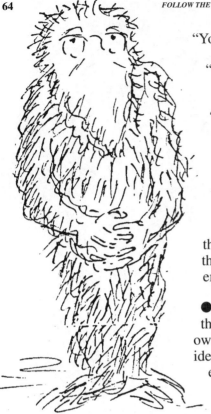

"You know what I'm talking about, don't you?"

"You can see the writing on the wall, can't you?"

"I don't have to spell it out for you, do I?"

Underlings are understandably reluctant to admit that they don't, they can't, and you do, for the implication to these questions is that you would have to be an idiot not to understand. So employees spend most of their energy trying to pretend that they do. It may be of some consolation that Do As I Meaners are as frustrated as their employees.

● **Henry/Henrietta Higgins.** This couple think their employees were created in their own image. All they have to do is think of an idea and their underlings will understand it. The employees automatically know what they know, so there is never any need to put an instruction in context. This couple believe that all of their knowledge and information gets transferred to their employees by cerebral osmosis. They mistake their employees for mind-readers. The Henry Higginses' behavior manifests itself in two diametrically opposed personalities—a supreme egotist who views underlings as merely extensions of his or her own persona and a pathologically fearful sort who is terrified of insulting anyone else's intelligence by unnecessary explanations. Either way, this couple appear to have blind faith in their employees, and blind is what the employees working for them feel like. When they tell you to call Smith, you are supposed to know that they mean Fred Smith, who is president of Smith & Smith in Smithville. Even if you can piece this together, you still need to know that Smith is vacationing in Brazil at the time, but don't expect this helpful information from a Higgins. An identifying characteristic is that they usually pound their fists on the table, wailing, "Why can't my employees think more like I do?"

● **The Carrot-on-the-Stick Wavers** are the wiliest form of instruction-givers. Their instructions appear to be complete, but they have directed their employees to a goal that is only a step along a much longer road. Just when their employees think they have realized the goal, they are discouraged to discover the road still ahead. Satisfaction is still around the corner. These bosses probably had fathers who used to tell them, "Now that you've finished cleaning the garage, you can mow the lawn." Working for a Carrot-Waver

will remind you of that detested camp counselor who kept telling you the top of the mountain was only a few yards up when, even at the age of six, you knew he was lying through his teeth.

● **Ping-Pongers.** Ping-Pongers seem to operate on a different level of consciousness than the rest of the people in the world. While many people define things in terms of their opposite, i.e., "Don't do anything cheap or small time" means "I want ritzy," these people spout out mutual exclusives. In describing his design concept to his staff, a Ping-Ponger in the architecture field might say, "I want something grandiose, but intimate; playful, but serious; large, but small." You bounce back and forth between these opposites desperately waiting for the ball to land in one court or the other, but it never does. Trying to interpret their bosses' instructions requires defying all of Western thought—a feat for which few junior designers are prepared. Ping-Pongers work well with Zen Buddhists, people from California, and anyone else who has ever seen a rock grow.

INSTRUCTION-TAKERS GUARANTEED TO GET IT WRONG

As an instruction-giver, you feel accused unjustly. The above types just don't apply to you. You always speak in a language that is understood by the taker; you clearly outline what is expected of your employees; you never give an assignment without giving the reason for it; and you are the epitome of patience. Yet, there are communication problems in your office and your employees still have trouble following your directions. Is it possible that while you are a divinely perfect instruction-giver, they are hopelessly human and flawed in the following department?

Yes. It is possible that you are surrounded by poor instruction-takers. After all, you can't be to blame for everything.

Incompetent instruction-takers are just as costly as instruction-givers in terms of dollars spent and time wasted. They can also be more dangerous. The CEO of an airline can be a lousy instruction-giver. An airline pilot who can't follow the instructions of an air-traffic controller doesn't have that luxury. Those operating the equipment can do a lot more physical damage than those who buy it.

Do you recognize yourself in any of the following instruction-takers?

- **Just Give Me the Details.** These people are always trying to second-guess you. You have just started to explain what you want them to do and they are running out of your office muttering, "Yeah, yeah, I know what you are talking about. I'll get right on it." They are in such a hurry to carry out your directions that they don't have time to listen to the request. But you don't find out that they don't know what you are talking about until they return with the evidence of the finished project. When you point out that they have done the wrong thing, they get even more flustered and harried trying to correct it. You may be tempted to yell at these people, but this will only get you more mistakes. Just-the-Details types are likely to be afraid of you, figuring that the less time they spend with you, the less chance they will incriminate themselves. One approach might be to handcuff them to a chair in your office while you fully explain what an understanding, patient person you are.

- **The Pacifist.** This inscrutable form of poor instruction-taker is the most difficult to spot. These persons will patiently listen to all of your directions, nodding at all the right moments. Pacifists have mastered a look of intelligent attention; you are just sure they are hanging onto your every word—until you see the results of their efforts. You wonder: did you explain it to them correctly? Did your message get through? You never know with Pacifists. They will never argue with you; so you have no idea whether they just don't understand you or choose not to pay attention to you. These are the types that one day start shooting at people from building tops, and their neighbors claim in the ensuing news accounts, "I don't understand it. He was such a nice man."

● **Toadying Sycophants.** In less polite circles, these instruction-takers are referred to by a term that rhymes with Pass Misser. They hover over you; they are the first to run for your coffee, to volunteer for any assignment, to fight any fire. You might ask, isn't this the best kind of instruction-taker? It is if you expect only wanton flattery, for they will look you in the eye and insist that your most preposterous ideas make perfect sense. If you are president of a company that manufactures dental prostheses and suggest that the company introduce a new line of false teeth made of balsa wood, your toady will be on the phone with the local lumber yard.

● **The Terminally Obtuse** are easy to recognize. Their mouths hang open, their shoulders droop, and they can maintain one facial expression for extended periods of time. Their favorite word is "Huh?" They move so slowly that they could walk through a room of duck down without ruffling a feather. At first, you may be tempted to suspect that they are a few pickles short of a barrel. This is not necessarily the case. The appearance of extraordinary denseness isn't always an indicator of low intelligence. The Terminally Obtuse may be trying to get out of doing something they don't want to do. If you suspect that someone is feigning stupidity, look for signs of inconsistency, such as responding to high-potential-for-reward instructions with a keen mind and low-potentials with a dim wit. For example, if the obtuse person always remembers to bring coffee to the ringmaster but forgets to clean out the lion cage, you have a strategist on your hands.

● **I'm Just All Thumbs.** This is a more appealing variation of the Terminally Obtuse. Where the former plays the moron, the latter aims for helplessness, which, when cultivated, can be quite fetching. Strategically, it is a superior tactic, for the Terminally Obtuse person will succeed only in avoiding a task; Mr. and Ms. Thumbs will get you to do it for them. They are masters in the Art of the Ditz, whether trying to park a car or to put together a barbecue grill. "I can't seem to get it. I'm such an idiot at this kind of stuff," they say while batting their eyelashes. Make no mistake, though they appear to be engaging in self-pity, they are really bragging about their inabilities. They aren't apologizing; they are *advertising* all of the things they can't do and machines they can't operate. This is part of their technique for getting someone else to do the job they don't feel like doing.

● **Wild Goose-Chasers** are always on the run—usually in the wrong direction. They have boundless energy, but no idea how to harness it. You can find them searching for left-handed monkey wrenches or unsalted herring. They are easily distracted. You could ask them for the price of beef and they might embark on a study of hoof-and-mouth disease and go on to colleges that offer animal husbandry programs. They are so earnest and intent on making you happy, it's hard to criticize them. They work well under Over-the-Shoulder Supervisors who can keep them on track.

● **Style Meisters** are obsessed with the appearance of their work. It is always neat and organized—with footnotes and margins in perfect order and replete with graphs, tables, and charts. These persons adore flashy graphics and four-color printing. They wear unstructured clothing and read only that which is printed on chrome-coated paper. Their desks are always immaculate; their taste is exquisite; and they can be counted on to know the most chic restaurants and bars in any given town. The only thing they cannot seem to do is fulfill the substance of your assignments. Their obsession with style is at the expense of content, and their work is long on glitz and short on ideas. But Style Meisters tend to flock together, so they usually wind up working in places where their shortcomings are never noticed.

- **Don't Boss Me Around.** These belligerent types perceive every instruction as an order and will never fail to let you know that they have no intention of following it. They are experts in labor law and know the number of the local Labor Relations Board, which they regularly threaten to call should you be tempted to violate any of the rules. Strangely enough, though, these people invariably follow directions quite well and, if you can stand their attitude, make competent employees. These people are often quite intelligent and concomitantly unpopular. Just don't ask them to buy a present for your spouse. They work best in environments that don't involve much interaction with others—like in ice-fishing or border patrol, perhaps.

- **Too Smart for Instructions.** This is a variation of the DBMAs above. The DBMAs are just pushy; these people are arrogant—the kind who will empty a tank of gasoline driving around hopelessly lost rather than ask directions. They see themselves as being above the need for instructions. Their egos are always on the line. Their favorite expressions are "I know that" and "You hardly need to tell me." On the positive side, they usually make a lot of mistakes so you have a good chance of getting the last laugh.

- **The Paper Warrior.** This one believes that all problems can be solved with more information. If you ask him or her to get you the figure for gross sales this month, you will get a plastic binder stuffed with charts and graphs. You will get gross sales for every year since the company was founded. You will get gross sales of all your competitors. And the only one who spends more time than this person is the one who has to wade through all the unnecessary data to find the information that was requested.

● **The Overkiller.** This is a more expensive version of the Paper Warrior who believes that all problems can be solved with more—more technology, more money, more manpower. Instead of imagination, the overkiller uses heavy artillery. Like the Pentagon, this person is expensive. Beware of the person

who starts sentences with "If we only had..." You cannot afford him. This type originated with the Cartha- ginians, who after killing their enemies would pour salt on them. Over- killers just don't know when to stop; the equation *enough is enough* computes as *more* in their minds.

● **Guaranteed to Miss the Forest for the Trees.** This common type gets so caught up in the details of the instruction that they miss the intent altogether. They thrive on the convoluted and the complex, the abstruse and the arcane. The direct line between any two points is the last place you will find them. If you asked them to count a herd of cows, they would add up the legs and divide by four. Ask a Forest-for-the-Trees type what's for lunch and you're liable to get the chemical composition of a bologna sandwich. These employees can often be found searching for overcoats that they happen to be wearing and looking for papers that are under their noses. However, they try so hard it is painful to watch them at work and few bosses are steel-willed enough to reprimand them.

● **Sure, Oh Shit.** These poor souls try to please everyone. No matter what you want them to do, they will promise to do it and then wonder how in the world they are going to manage it. They understand the word No but they will never use it. They will work harder and longer trying to do the impossible. Unlike toadies, who will butter up their bosses to improve their own position, SOSers selflessly want to make their bosses happy. If you asked for a report "yesterday," they would try to deliver it as requested. But they are often catastrophe-prone. Their cars break down en route to important meetings; they spill mustard on presentation drawings; and their buildings collapse on the day before the real-estate closing is scheduled. Somehow the adulation they seek is denied. The SOS personality was probably made to feel inadequate by parents incapable of praise and is determined to win it from a boss or other parental figure.

MANAGEMENT STYLE VERSUS WORK STYLE

Sometimes, communication problems aren't so much the result of individual personality types as the result of poor combinations of personalties. Just as bosses have different techniques for directing, workers have different styles of carrying out directions. Each will function best in a different environment, either alone or in groups, in an orderly or chaotic room, on a fixed deadline or at one's own pace. Certain types of instruction-takers can function perfectly well with certain instruction-givers, whereas others might bring work to a standstill.

There's an apocryphal story about a 7th Avenue clothing executive that illustrates how successful pairings can occur even with difficult partners. A young accountant had taken a job at this clothing company and in his first week had seen much evidence of why this CEO was known in the industry for his temper tantrums and violent outbursts. What the accountant couldn't understand was how the CEO had kept the same secretary for over 20 years. At the start of his second week, he heard a string of curses come from the boss's office, followed by a shout, a loud crash, and silence. The accountant impulsively ran toward the closed door of the CEO's office. Outside, the secretary was typing a letter. Without missing a stroke, she said, "I wouldn't do that if I were you. If he's hurt, he will call for me. If he isn't, he will be terribly embarrassed and hold it against you. And if he is dead, what's the rush?"

Pairing someone who manages by guilt with a Sure, Oh Shit personality would benefit only the company psychologist. An Over-the-Shoulder Supervisor is liable to meet his or her demise at the hands of Mr. Don't Boss Me Around. But pair a Free Associator with someone who thinks he or she is too smart for instructions and you could have a productive team, especially if that someone really is smart. And the union of Here Let Me Do This for You and I'm Just All Thumbs is a marriage made in heaven.

"The management challenge of the misfit is not simply one of removing square pegs from round holes—if the pegs represent intelligence, knowledge, experience, and drive. Those assets are not only costly to replace, but also expensive to divest considering the price of severance packages, early retirement plans, outplacement, and ever-threatening litigation. 'Faced with the cost of ending a person's employment and the risks associated with hiring somebody new, the company should be looking for new ways to use a competent person in some other area,' says Richard Jandl, a partner in the outplacement firm of MacKenna, Jandl & Associates, Lynnfield, Massachusetts."—Deborah Rhoney, "Solving the Riddle of the Misfit Manager," *Industry Week* (9/1/86)

If you can determine what types of personalities you embody in the instruction department, you can correct some of your own shortcomings and look for compatible partners who will work with the flaws you can't correct.

In an article in the *Training and Development Journal* (6/82), "Styles of Work," John D. Bies and Joel A. Turetzky list 5 components that make up a person's work style. They are as follows:

- *Behavioral factors*—what motivates a person; how committed are they; how do they follow directions?

- *Work methodology*—how does a person carry out a task via psychomotor and physiological behavior; what degree of movement or confinement do they require?

- *Interpersonal relations*—how does a person work with others; how do they react to authority; how do they work with different kinds of people?

- *Temporal considerations*—At what time of day does a person perform most efficiently?

- *Work environment*—How do physical surroundings affect the individual; how does the degree of noise, the light level, the room temperature, the air quality, and the cleanliness level influence job performance?

THESE COMBINATIONS WORK WELL TOGETHER

Just Give Me the Details

and

I'm an Important Person, I Don't Have Time to Explain

I'm Just All Thumbs

and

Why Don't You Let Me Do That for You

Toadying Sychophant

and

Over-the-Shoulder Supervisor

THESE COMBINATIONS SPELL TROUBLE

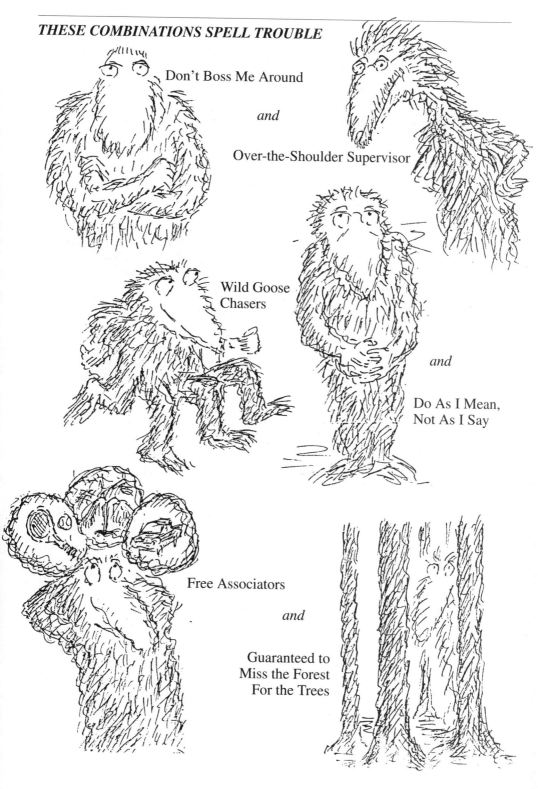

Don't Boss Me Around

and

Over-the-Shoulder Supervisor

Wild Goose
Chasers

and

Do As I Mean,
Not As I Say

Free Associators

and

Guaranteed to
Miss the Forest
For the Trees

Carl Jung devised a classification system for supervisors based on whether one is extroverted or introverted and how one perceives and makes judgements. The system can be applied to determine a work style as well. He believed that people perceive either by sensing—that is directly through our 5 senses—or by intuition—or indirectly comprehending ideas through the unconscious. People judge by thinking—by a logical system motivated by objectivity and impartiality—or by feeling—a subjective and personal system. Based on different combinations of these characteristics, he outlined 8 types:

● Extroverted Thinking Type—"But the facts are." This type is analytical, decisive, a good organizer, and a disciplinarian, but lacking in perception and concern for others.

● Introverted Thinking Type—"I'll have to give it some further thought." These people organize facts and ideas, but not people and situations; are independent, perservering, and good at problem solving. However, they tend to be stubborn, reclusive, and lacking in communication skills.

● Extroverted Intuitive Type—"I have a hunch." These enthusiatic innovators possess imagination, confidence, and an ability to stimulate others. Their biggest problem is an aversion to routine and details.

● Introverted Intuitive Type—"Silence, genius at work." These intense types are inspired by the problems no one else wants to tackle. They are creative, driven, determined, and need little companionship. They tend to be single-minded and blind to the conditions and counterforces that might affect their solutions and sometimes have the reputation of impractical geniuses.

● Extroverted Sensing Type—"The right tool for the right job." These adaptable realists are driven by facts. They notice, absorb, and remember more of the world around them than others. Their natural sense of economy, keen perceptions, and tolerance make them generators of integral solutions to

problems, instead of imposing rigid or external
ideas. On the down side, their dependence on
observations sometimes precludes vision.

● Introverted Sensing Type—"The real meaning is
not what it seems." Dependable and observative,
these types rely on facts, but see them differently.
They are adept at getting to the heart of the matter,
are perservering and patient with details and
routines. They make good administrators, but
have trouble empathizing with divergent ideas and
rather impersonal and passive socially.

● Extroverted Feeling Type—"The more the
merrier." These hail fellows are sensitive to the
emotional atmosphere, friendly, tactful, and
sympathetic. They get along well with people, but
don't do well on their own and are impatient with
slow or complex procedures.

● Introverted Feeling Type—"Still waters run deep."
These types are also sensitive, but they care more
deeply about fewer things than their extroverted
counterparts. They don't need to impress or
persuade others and are tolerant of others as long
as their own convictions aren't threatened.
Adversely, they can be overly sensitive and
frequently suffer a sense of inadequacy. —Eugene
Raudsepp,"What Type of Supervisor Are You?"
Supervision (11/80)

If you are unhappy with your type, you could always
hire a coach to readjust your personality or your
communication style. Business oaches use role-
playing, videotaping, and behavior adjustments to
correct personality problems.

"Indeed, private coaching is on the upswing, and for
good reason....'For high-level people, lack of skill is
not usually what gets in their way,' said Bernard M.
Kessler, a divisional president at Beam-Pines Inc., a
New York–based consulting firm. 'Their styles are
just inappropriate for team playing.'

"One 38-year-old management consultant recently
hired a coach to help him win the attention of his
firm's partners. In 10 meetings, complete with

videotaped role-playing sessions, he and the coach worked on making him appear more self-confident. It worked—he recently negotiated a hefty raise and bonus."—Claudia H. Deutsch, "To Get Ahead, Consider a Coach," *The New York Times* (1/14/90)

Which of the above types do you resemble? Perhaps just ask 4 people who have to follow your instructions to read this chapter and circle the personalities that most resembles you.

The next step is to recognize some of the larger forces at work that defy some of our best attempts to communicate instructions in the office.

BEYOND PERSONALITIES

"I don't want any yes-men
around me. I want people
to tell me the truth, even if
it costs them their jobs."

Samuel Goldwyn

*A*ll right. *You protest that you bear no resemblance to the instruction-givers and takers described in the previous chapter. In fact, should the Nobel committee establish a category for instruction-givers and -takers, you would be the first nominated.*

But your work environment is still far from paradise. Mistakes abound; work has to be redone; people operate with different understandings of the same project.

If our personalities were the only difficulty we had to surmount in the office, working wouldn't be such a dirty word.

There are universal, insidious, accepted corporate practices that tend to create animosity between management and employees. These practices have evolved to manage employees, but more often they confuse, undermine, and complicate the employees' attempts to do their jobs. They have little to do with individual personalties, but are inspired by business precepts that have been handed down for centuries and have become too entrenched to eradicate.

"*dybbuk*—1. An evil spirit— usually, the soul of a dead person that enters a living person on whom the dead one had some claim; 2. a demon who takes possession of someone and renders the mortal mad, irrational, vicious, sinful, corrupt."—Leo Rosten, *The Joys of Yiddish*

These fundamental forces haunt almost all work environments, from boardrooms to the warehouses. They act as *dybbuks* to create problems of communication and instruction, alienating employees and angering bosses. They are created by management policies, historical business philosophy, limitations of time and resources, and shortcomings of language and communications, and they will sabotage the best intentions of individuals. However, an awareness of their manifestations will help to temper their deleterious effects.

To alienate an employee by a conscious exercise of authority is one thing, but to do it unintentionally is another.

CONDEMNED TO MAHOGANY ROW

Executives are responsible for setting the policy regarding the exchange of information, thus the instruction policy of their companies. The burden of setting the instruction tone and of pairing the right givers with the right takers rests on the shoulders of those who run companies—those with the authority to hire and place employees. To do this, they need a clear picture of the company and of the personalties who work for it. Effective instructions must be based on accurate information. "As I see it, a healthy flow of information separates winning organizations from losers. *Deciding* means acting on information. Barring blind luck, the quality of a decision can't be better than the quality of the information behind it," said Arno Penzias in *Ideas and Information: Managing in a High-Tech World.*

But a host of factors often conspire to deny executives access to such information.

Top executives are often physically, philosophically, and politically isolated from their employees. They are isolated from their companies by their very position.

The complex chain of command, the distance between the executive suites and company operations, and the amount of time an executive spends outside of the company all serve to distance the CEO. Even CEOs of the gregarious, egalitarian variety, who promenade on the production floor, may not hear what they need to know, for the employer/employee relationship is not conducive to telling all.

"Communication difficulties are a universal problem in business organizations. All too often, we forget that communicating is a two-way process that involves listening and responding to messages as well as giving them. Too often, real ongoing communication upward to management is obscured, largely because managers won't or can't hear what is going on.

Dr. L.W. Fernald, Jr., identifies 4 types of barriers that inhibit communication between management and employees in an article, "Breaking the Barriers: Overcoming Four Communication Obstacles," in *Management World* (9-10/86). They are

❶ Intrapersonal: individual differences in perception.

❷ Interpersonal: relationships between employers and employees.

❸ Organizational: hierarchy and group size.

❹ Technological: the clarity and effectiveness of information.

"Workplace conflicts are often attributed to personality differences, but the root of the problem is usually structural. The organization's power hierarchy can distort mutual expectations....Managers who believe they are on the receiving end of unreasonable or unfair actions from their bosses, for example, may act similarly toward those below them in the organization pyramid. And the pattern may repeat itself down the chain of command."—Fernando Bartolomé and André Laurent, "The Manager: Master or Servant of Power," *Harvard Business Review* (11–12/86)

"Even executives who take precautions against becoming isolated occasionally get mousetrapped....The multiple layers of management tend to insulate the CEO from the reality of what is really happening—and what people are really thinking— at lower levels in the corporation.

"Often the god-like status conferred on CEOs can contribute to confusion. The aura can be intimidating, causing others to refrain from asking questions that might reveal their ignorance. 'People will leave my office and stop and ask my secretary, What does he want us to do?' observes Warren K. Kearns, president and chief operating officer at L. B. Foster Co., a Pittsburgh steel fabricating firm."

—Donald B. Thompson, "Isolated Executives," *Industry Week* (8/10/81)

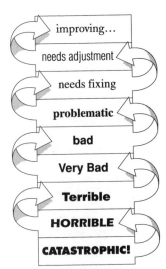

"Three conditions must be met before communications can take place successfully. Subordinates must:

❶ Know what their seniors need to hear.

❷ Be given the chance to provide this information.

❸ Work for people who can accept it in a way that will not discourage disclosure."

—Sherman K. Okun, "How to Be a Better Listener," *Nation's Business* (8/75)

Life on mahogany row is complicated further by the reluctance of most employees to bear bad news to bosses. No one wants to be responsible for delivering disagreeable tidings to a superior. So lower-level employees will tend to gloss over negative information. As the information moves upwards in the company hierarchy, it tends to be cast in a more positive light. Information may get so filtered or distorted by fear or even by just retelling that if it ever makes it to the top, it is likely to be out of date, exaggerated, or patently wrong.

While the situation rarely reaches such catastrophic proportions in U.S. companies, parallels exist and executives do make decisions based on information that may be glossed over or tempered for the bosses' consumption.

Howie, who works on an assembly line at Redress Clothing, sees that a pattern cutter isn't working properly. He suspects that it needs to be replaced, but doesn't want to report the full extent of the problem for fear his supervisor will think he hasn't maintained the machine. Howie tells his supervisor that there are serious problems with the Fineline Pattern-Cutter. With the same reservations, the supervisor reports to the factory manager that "there are problems with the pattern-cutter." As the factory manager was one of the people who recommended that the company buy Fineline, he is even more reluctant to report the problem, so he tells the general manager that the machine needs overhauling. The general manager, who knows that the three-year-old machine will cost about $250,000 to replace, doesn't want the company president to think he hasn't been on top of things, so he orders routine servicing and doesn't tell the company president. In only four rungs up the corporate ladder, a piece of equipment goes from being defunct to needing a routine tune-up.

To counteract this positive-rising effect, superiors should encourage those beneath them on the corporate ladder to bring them all relevant information and should be equally appreciative of negative information. Some people have a tendency to blame the bearer for bad news. Kings used to shoot the messengers who brought them accounts of battle defeats or peasant revolts.

No Surprises. Although CEOs rarely resort to such extreme tactics, shouting and raving after hearing about sagging sales is not uncommon—and it is not going to encourage a manager to rush to the CEO with this kind of information in the future. I think CEOs ought to have a placard behind their desks that reads *No Surprises*. No surprises means getting the bad news as well as the good. Negative news is often what the top brass most needs to know. It is what usually requires immediate action. When business is booming, who needs executive interference?

The lack of computer knowledge also fosters isolation. Computers used to be for engineers. Ten years ago, people could still afford the luxury of being technologically illiterate. They could brag about not being able to turn on a computer, work their answering machines, or program their VCRs.

Now they find themselves isolated from their most up-to-date and effective source of information. And while the capabilities of their employees were enhanced by computer literacy, their own are diminished. Also, without an awareness of the limitations of computers, executives run a greater risk of asking employees for work that can't be done or is inappropriate, time-consuming, and costly to be done by computer.

Information should flow both ways

CEAUSESCU SYNDROME

Look at the former president of Romania, Nicolae Ceausescu. Thinking that life in Romania was business as usual, he embarked on a good-will tour—9 days before his countrymen hunted him down, tried, and executed him. This was not a man who stayed in touch with his constituents.

"Sometimes managers open their doors and no one enters. That result occurs when traditional management methods chill the communication climate, creating a defensive rather than a supportive atmosphere.

"Organizational theory abounds with descriptions of the filtering phenomenon, whereby a subordinate will send up the chain only information that makes him or her look good."—Charles E. Beck and Elizabeth A. Beck, "The Manager's Open Door and the Communication Climate," *Business Horizons* (1–2/86)

Consequently, computer proficiency is becoming mandatory at higher levels of management. Techno-competence has become a prerequisite to functioning in society, and computers are commonplace in the CEO's office. Executives with access to the computers can stay informed of sales, production, and inventory figures. Stacks of unread accordion-folded printouts gathering dust on desktops don't count.

Executives who are the last to know have only themselves to blame. They hold the power to encourage information upward from their employees.

NEARER TO GOD ARE WE

Instead of taking pains to combat executive isolation, management often compounds it by resorting to unnecessary, sometimes even subconscious, displays of corporate muscle. Exercising your power is a heady temptation, especially if you've got it. However, exercised wrongly, it can work against managing your employees. While some distance may be necessary between management and labor, at some point it becomes the fodder for unrest, hostility, and recalcitrance, none of which are likely to produce quality labor.

Often, these ill-advised displays of authority are small and insidiously subtle, such as using the word *we* when *I* is more appropriate. Perhaps management fears that the opinion of one is not enough to impress the wayward employee with the gravity of the situation, but more often than not, the use of the big-brother *we* does little but raise employee dander. When a superior tells an employee, "We are not happy with your work," that employee is liable to start looking around to see if there is someone else in the room. If there isn't, the employee will either suspect the superior of hallucinating or be set on edge for no purpose. Use of the word *we* when communicating with employees is authoritarian and threatening. Such a show of communal muscle is bound to annoy an employee and unlikely to predispose him or her to following an instruction. The use of the corporate *we* should be reserved for attempts to raise esprit de corps, not used to impress employees that the eyes of the company/community/society are peering unfavorably upon them. Other offensive tactics include:

I'm the Boss, That's Why. Using your authority to explain why a subordinate should do something is a counterproductive use of power. Your employees may forget to give you phone messages, send letters, and remind you of meetings; they will never forget that you are the boss. Therefore, reminding them of this fact is unnecessary. And if you use it as a explanation of an order or instruction, you will make them suspicious that you have no other reason for the request. Humoring the boss may be a valid reason for performing a task, but it is not a satisfying motivation for a subordinate. Subordinates need to know the real whys before they can comprehend a task fully.

If at First You Don't Succeed, Scream Louder. Many employers foolishly think that if their instructions don't succeed the first time, they can try, try, try them again in a louder voice. Unless employees have hearing problems, this is not a constructive approach. If someone didn't understand an instruction communicated at a civil decibel level, it is unlikely that hearing it shouted will add to its clarity. Before raising the decibel level, try to figure out why your directions weren't followed correctly before resorting to delivering them again in a louder voice.

Always Test Their Loyalty by asking them to do frivolous favors for you outside of their work duties. Try coffee first, then move on to more time-consuming favors. It's four o'clock and you have a craving for Ben & Jerry's hazelnut ice cream. Send your secretary for a cone. If he or she is willing to do that, then try asking him or her to babysit your children. Let your employees know that you consider these tasks beneath you and that is the reason you hired them.

Everyone who has risen up the corporate ladder, especially those who have outlived the tyrannical despots who once clung to the rungs above them, feels that they deserve to be relieved of all those annoying errands that they once grudgingly performed for someone else. Resist the temptation. The animosity you breed won't be worth the antebellum thrill of feeling like you are surrounded by indentured servants. Go get that ice-cream cone yourself. It's good to get out of the office. You may have a brilliant business idea on the way.

If you can't resist asking for these favors, try turning the situation around once in while. Get coffee for your secretary. Answer the phone yourself. You staff will be less likely to accuse you of abusing your power if they see that you don't consider these tasks beneath you.

MAYBE THEY WON'T NOTICE

Some executives, so sensitive to abuses of power, bend over backwards to remind their employees of their freedom of choices. This is exemplary when the employees have the freedom of choice. In situations where they do not, such hollow promises will annoy them. A boss who tells an employee, "You don't have to work late around here," and then says to the same employee, "It would be so nice if we could get that 800-page planning commission report done by tomorrow," isn't fooling anyone. We all know that a "Thank you for not smoking" sign means *Do not smoke.*

The New York Metropolitan Transit Authority gives an outstanding example of this approach. Although it is applied to the service-and-customer relationship instead of management-and-employees, it works well to illustrate the point. I don't know whether it is an explicit policy or just something that all subway employees instinctively practice, but the MTA can bring you face-to-face with your own powerlessness faster than anything, while mocking you by pretending that you have a choice in the matter. When you are stuck underground on a train, an almost understandable voice (if you are lucky) will come blaring over the public address system and explain, "There is congestion ahead. We will be moving shortly." You know damn well there is no congestion ahead because you waited for this train for 45 minutes; you know that you will not be moving shortly; and the last thing you want is to be thanked for your patience and cooperation because you would use neither given half the opportunity.

During one of the many plumbing crises in Manhattan last year, I was riding on the IND line when a voice came blasting over the perennially out-of-whack intercom system instructing passengers as follows: "Attention passengers. Due to a water main break at 125th Street, A train service has been limited. Please refrain from transferring to the A train at 168th Street." I ignored the misuse of *due to* and wondered, what does *refrain* mean? This seems to imply that the choice is up to me. If only I can supress my impulse to take the A train, I will have a pleasant journey. What if I succumb to the impulse? This leads to more questions. What is the MTA's idea of *limited?* I know that there has been absolutely no A train service north of 59th Street for the past 3 days. Does *limited* mean 1 train every 3 days? Paralyzed with doubts and questions, I stayed on the train. I did not want the MTA to give me options. I did not want to hear that the choice is mine. I did not want them to appreciate my patience and cooperation. I wanted clear instructions—"The A train is out of service. Take the Number 1 train instead."

INCONSISTENCY IS THE HOBGOBLIN OF PRODUCTIVITY

Sometimes the problem isn't poor management; it's the inconsistent application of management policy. Having to work under a variety of management styles is confusing to employees, who are often forced to work under contradictory directions. Several studies of managerial effectiveness have shown a high degree of inconsistency in the application of company policy. According to a study cited in the article, "Measuring Managers," by David Altany in *Industry Week* (2/6/89), "some managers would discharge employees for unexcused absences before others would even issue initial warnings."

"Training employees is taken seriously in Japan. New employees spend up to 6 months in intensive training programs, which are usually held outside of the job in special training centers. Most companies observe April 1 for an annual nationally observed, nyusha-shiki, which is a ceremony for receiving newly hired employees into a company," according to Masaru Chio in "Training of Employees Is a Long-Term Investment" in *Japan Marketing/Advertising* (Spring 1985).

Few managers recognize the complexity of the process of issuing directives—the formulation of an idea, the transmission of it to someone else, the reception of the message, the decoding of it, and the signaling of understanding. Every request may be the result of countless choices and decisions on the part of the giver and, on the part of the taker, may be weighed against a history of events in the past. A host of hurdles separate the point when the manager perceives a need to give a directive from the point when it will be carried out by someone else. The subordinate could follow the directive to the letter, ignore it completely, misunderstand it and act accordingly, or follow only part of it. Three out of four outcomes could result in loss of money, resources, and time.

"Combine the number of undesirable outcomes that can occur in such routine situations with the enormous number of directives that managers issue daily and we may legitimately suspect that the aggregate dollar loss is staggering," said Eric Matthiesen and John Hollwitz in "Giving Instructions That Get Followed," *Supervisory Management* (5/83).

Employees who get conflicting or perplexing directions will be stymied by the frustration of trying to carry out impossible instructions. Workers under contradictory bosses become numb; they learn to nod yes to all instructions, then proceed to do what they think needs to be done. This promotes anger and frustration among both the instruction-givers and the -followers.

Canadian construction magnate Max Tanenbaum was a master at inconsistent instructions.

"Someone would come into his office with an idea for a deal and begin to explain it. "After a minute or two, Max would shout: 'What the fuck are you saying? I don't understand. You're standing there like an asshole, when you could go away, write a memo, I could read it and make a decision.' When the deal was brought

back 20 minutes later, typed up on one page
with two or three schedules neatly attached,
Max would begin to rant: 'What the fuck have
you given me? How am I supposed to
understand this bullshit? If you stood there and
explained it to me in three or four minutes, then
I could make a decision.' "—Rod McQueen,
"The Sorry Legacy of Max Tanenbaum,"
Canadian Business (8/83)

His inconsistencies (and impatience) made him such
a poor instruction-giver that following a series of
incapacitating strokes, his companies started into a
decline, for he had never taken the time to train
anyone to replace him.

GROUP VERSUS INDIVIDUAL GOALS OR THEM AGAINST ME

People toil in the work place for different reasons.
Some can be motivated by the promise of money or
power. Others need intellectual stimulation or
adventure. Everyone is driven by different forces.
Yet the workplace is united by corporate goals. All
of these diverse individuals must somehow be
encouraged to labor toward these group goals.

In ideal situations, group and individual goals will
be compatible. Let's say the president of a computer
company finds out that he has to have his gall-
bladder removed during the time of an important
industry convention. So he asks an ambitious vice
president to attend the convention in his place. I bet
the VP will oblige happily, for the VP will rise in
status and thus meet his or her individual goals. And
the corporate goal of maintaining a presence in the
industry will also be met by having someone in
attendance.

Let's say that the executive assistant to the same
president calls in sick. So the president asks the VP
to make some phone calls for him. The VP is going
to resent being asked to perform tasks that might be
perceived as status-diminishing, even though the
tasks might be necessary to meet the corporate goals
of conducted business.

Invariably, there will be times when individual goals will be inconsistent with those of the group. Individuals may be asked to do a job that runs contrary to their own goals.

While management cannot avoid these situations altogether, much can be done to minimize their occurrence.

- Wherever possible, management should try to assign tasks to those employees who might find them consistent with their own individual goals.

- When this isn't possible, management should explain the reason that an employee is being asked to perform a task.

- Management should make sure that employees understand just what the corporate goals are.

INSTRUCTIONS VERSUS ORDERS

What is the difference between an instruction and an order? Often conflicts arise because management has inadequately defined group goals, which are understood through instructions.

"Orders and instructions are the tool by which leaders motivate a desired action of group members towards the group objective. The terms *order* and *instruction,* therefore, are synonymous with such terms as suggestions, requests, motivation, direction and influencing, which are much less threatening terms than *order.*

"....As leaders, if we can build a strong association between orders and instructions and group goals, followers would be more willing to forgo personal objectives for the good of the group....Understanding how specific orders and instructions relate to group goals can be a powerful motivator—to the point of individuals sacrificing personal goals," said Ray Collins and Brian H. Kleiner in "Orders and Instructions" in *IMDS* (No.3, 1989).

When group goals conflict with individual expectations, employees will be more likely to perceive instructions as orders.

Most orders are good instructions in a bad overcoat. Instructions become orders when there is no flexibility, empowerment, possession, or responsibility. Orders have too many negative connotations. They provoke the rebellious child in us all. Orders are what our parents gave us when they didn't like our haircuts or friends. And we didn't follow them then either. All instructions contain some implicit measure of command, but the most successful instructions stay on the side of a request that empowers and not a command.

> "The dynamics of parent and child also can be a terrific model of management," observes Jolie Solomon in "Management Secrets They'll Never Teach You at Business School" in *Working Woman* (6/90). She turns to Nancy Samalin's book, *Loving Your Child Is Not Enough,* to illustrate this point. "One of Samalin's favorite themes is that parents should acknowledge the feelings of children. Whatever message you want to get across, the first response has to be 'I hear you,' even if you then want to argue the point. The manager who first says, 'I know you're disappointed that we lost the account,' is way ahead of the one who leaps in with 'How could you have lost this job!' "

Executives who view themselves as giving *instructions* rather than *orders* will find their subordinates trying harder to comply with them. Look at what a big mistake the medical profession made when it coined the term *doctor's orders.* They are the first things everyone wants to disobey. We might eat and smoke less if they had called them *doctor's instructions.*

DOCTOR NO-NO

"Based on the symptoms, the physician will tell the patient what to do. Because most people are trained to be obedient, especially to someone as powerful as a physician, patients say little and accept the physician's decision.

" 'You are overweight,' he announces and presents the patient with a diet and perhaps a prescription to remove the pounds. Will the patient do what he has been told to do? Not always. In fact, less often than might be imagined.

"After leaving the doctor's office, or perhaps a few days later, the patient may begin to react to the counterfeiting he experienced. Even though his diet eliminates desserts, he decides the price is much too high. He eats desserts, a few at first, more later. Cut out salt, the diet commands. The patient does, for awhile. Then gradually, the struggle to rise above subordination adds a little salt. Not much at first, maybe more later. The patient is a child again, finding ways around the authority of the physician through manipulation and rebellion.

"....The enlightened family physician attempts to know his patient much better. He is aware that some illnesses, real or imagined, are actually evidence of helplessness, suffering, or anger. He believes a person does not always need medication. He certainly believes a patient must be brought into the healing process and become a participant in moving from illness to wellness."
—David Burkett, *Very Good Management: A Guide to Managing by Communicating*

A review of several studies regarding the ability of patients to retain instructions given by their physicians shows that approximately one half of the items given to the patients are forgotten shortly after.

Many of the same dynamics operate in the business world as well. The executive who assumes a parental role and orders his employees may find that they soon cast themselves in the role of rebellious child.

MISSING THE OBVIOUS

While some instructions fail because they are perceived as orders, others fail because they weren't perceived at all. Even if you recognize the instruction content of your communications, you have to make it clear to the taker. People can't follow your directions if they don't know that is what you are giving them. Nigel Holmes, the graphics director of *Time* magazine had a suggestion for starting instructions that was brilliant in its simplicity. "Good instructions involve letting someone know that the conversation you are having with them *IS* instruction and not just idle chatter."

Perhaps, because instructions run the workplace, people don't see the need to announce them. Consequently, their subordinates must guess or interpret messages, a condition of uncertainty that could get in the way of understanding.

You might think this sounds a bit silly or at least unnecessary, but you would be surprised at how much work doesn't get done because an instruction-giver didn't make this clear. You may have asked Johnson to get you the debt-to-capital ratio for that chemical company you are trying to buy, but Johnson might think you were musing on what *you* were going to do after lunch. He didn't read the message as an instruction.

Everyone needs to know what is expected from them.

> "When interviews with both the presidents and their subordinates were compared over time, one characteristic of an effective relationship became apparent—that expectations became more concrete and specific as the relationship developed....Often they were communicated formally and explicitly....More often, however, expectations were communicated, clarified, and modified in the process of day-to-day interactions of a routine nature, such as ad hoc meetings on specific problems. Ad hoc situations emerged as the most frequent and important settings in which expectations were communicated. On-the-spot feedback was

viewed as the most effective way of clarifying expectations."—John Gabarro, "Socialization at the Top: How CEOs and Subordinates Evolve Interpersonal Contracts," *Organizational Dynamics* (Winter 1979)

PROMOTION: A DEADLY REWARD

The foundation of most business is to reward good workers by promoting them. In most workplaces, promotion, with its concomitant raises, is the *sole* reward for effort. In this way, so the theory goes, the cream will rise to the top. The only trouble with this idea is that business is not butter.

Departures from this phenomenon do exist. Managers of sports teams usually make less than the players, and publishers make less than their top authors.

The oracle of American business has declared that monetary compensation should be on par with one's management level, and so it is. Workers don't make as much money as foremen, foremen get less than managers, managers get less than directors, and so on. Therefore, to reward a worker with more money, accepted business practice dictates that they must be promoted. This pervasive practice is often counterproductive for it places people in positions that they may not want or may not be prepared to handle.

A man who works in a ceramic tile factory may be an expert on the behavior of materials. He may understand under what conditions the mixture of earth and water will produce a quality tile. And because of his knowledge, he may enjoy his work. To promote this man to manager might deprive him of the exercise of his knowledge. He might not understand the mix of people and personalities; he might not enjoy filling out forms and developing work schedules. To promote this man would be to take him out of an arena where he is making a valuable contribution and put him into one where he will make mistakes instead. To not increase his salary would demonstrate a lack of appreciation of his knowledge that might send him looking for work elsewhere.

People are promoted to positions of authority because they work harder than their peers; they possess outstanding technical knowledge; they are ambitious and work on their own initiative; they are good followers; or they are related to the president of the company. None of these attributes says in itself anything about an ability to lead people, which requires a high degree of interpersonal skills and an understanding of human psychology.

This kind of thinking inspired Laurence J. Peter and Raymond Hull to write a book on the subject, *The Peter Principle,* which stated that everyone rises to their level of incompetence and gets stuck there. Thus, the world is replete with people who bumble through jobs out of their league.

People should be rewarded in a way that encourages them to utilize their talents and not abandon them. Effort should be rewarded with money, with faith in the competence of employees, with the right to make decisions about their work—not necessarily with a shove up the corporate ladder. There is no reason why a subordinate should not make more money than a superior. Perhaps he or she has specific information or a special talent that cannot be replaced easily.

THE COMPETITIVE DREDGE

Instead of encouraging people to do their personal best, many managers make a sport of pitting employees against each other. Telling Schlepstein that "last month, Spielkistein sold twice as many pounds of hog rings as you did" will aggravate his ulcers and promote in-house rivalry instead of cooperation.

The foundation of the American economy is built on the principle of may-the-better-product win. This can be a healthy motivation to spur market effort. But this belief in competition as cure-all has entrenched itself within companies so that not only is product pitted against product, people are pitted against people. And competition isn't always healthy.

This is tantamount to heresy in many U.S. companies.

In a society that worships winners, intramural competition has become the key motivation to many employees who pursue victory with the zeal of Olympic athletes. Crushing your opponents, even if they are also your office mates, has become almost synonymous with success. Most managers believe that among their responsibilities is the training of their employees to be competitive. Then management wonders why these hungry-for-the-kill employees show more concern for their own advancement than for the advancement of company business.

The demise of teamwork induces office paranoia, and employees are less likely to take risks, to suggest unorthodox approaches, or to do anything that might expose them to failure. The Center for Creative Leadership in Greensboro, North Carolina, ranked internal competition as one of the ten most frequently cited obstacles to creativity.

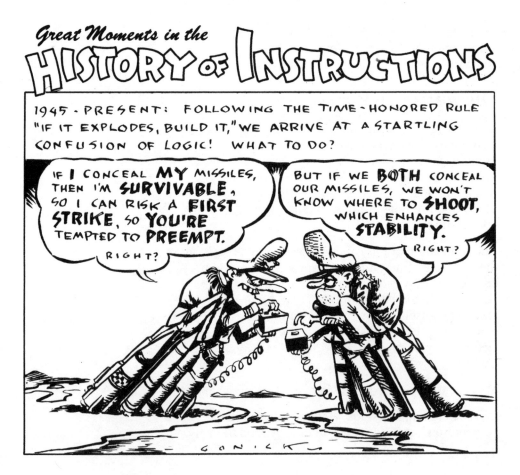

INFORMATION IS NOT THE FINAL PRODUCT

A high value is placed on information in the work place. Having the most current figures, the most comprehensive data, and the inside sources is better than a corner office when it comes to having an asset that everyone else will admire. Information, in all of its forms is eating up megabytes of computer space, filling up file cabinets, obscuring desktops, and overstuffing the bounds of briefcases throughout the world.

The managerial mania for acquiring information has become such a hobby horse that few have stopped rocking long enough to ponder what good is information if it can't be communicated. What matters is the ability—through instruction —to transfer information from the mind of one person to another.

In larger companies, if you asked managers what kind of communication program the company had, they might tell you about internal publications, staff meetings, and inter-office mail systems. These are *information* programs, not necessarily *communications* programs, and the only thing they can be guaranteed to do is add to interoffice clutter. In themselves, they carry no intrinsic properties that will add to the communication or understanding of information.

> **"Most companies have a fancy document on their shelf that they call their disaster recovery plan, but if you were to read it, it wouldn't make sense, and if you were to try to implement it, you'd start another disaster."** — Joseph F. Callahan as quoted in an article by James Daly, "No Excuse for Unpreparedness," in *Computerworld* (2/20/89)

INSTRUCTIONS ARE NOT THE GOAL

In an ideal office, there would be no need for instructions. Everyone would understand their job so well that their actions wouldn't need directions.

Because we are so far from this ideal, there is a tendency to forget that giving instructions isn't the purpose of working; instructions are a means of getting the job done in an imperfect world.

> **An old Jewish proverb says you should never leave a temple by the same door you entered.**

The limits of human communication will never make instructions obsolete, but improving their quality can reduce employees' reliance on them. The means to the end might be to communicate directions in such a way that employees understand their role so clearly they can perform their duties on their own.

This requires altering a deeply held belief that instructions are a means of control, a means of conscripting someone else to do work that you don't want or don't have time to do.

The best instructions are actually the opposite. Ideal instructions should liberate both the giver and the taker. They should empower subordinates to do their work and they should free time for superiors. Instead of spending time putting out fires, superiors might look further in the future, do long-range planning instead of short-range emergency services.

In much the same way that industrial designers— at least the good ones—try to create products that don't require so much instruction, employers should try to cultivate employees that don't need so much direction. Really good products should tell you how they want to be used—so should a good employee.

This ideal isn't so farfetched. Managers can move toward this state by changing their view of the role of instructions and by looking more closely at the role of management.

WHAT DO MANAGERS MANAGE?

The accepted answer in most companies is that managers manage people or information. These tasks require focusing on the past, in that they involve keeping track of what people have done, how well they have done it, and whether information about past business activity is accurate, and then correcting inappropriate usage of resources—human or otherwise.

These activities aren't superfluous, but they distract managers from the real essence of management: directing the future action of a company *through instructions.*

" 'Manage' is a verb meaning to achieve little effect by expenditure of great effort, as in : 'I managed to get the kids to bed.' 'I got fired, the house burned down, Shirley's mom is sick, but we're managing.' "—P. J. O'Rourke, "How to Succeed in Business? Here's the Secret," *The New York Times Book Review* (10/29/89)

In an article by Fernando Flores and Chauncey Bell in *Computer Technology Review* (Fall 1984), the question was answered as follows: "Managers are paid to discover what is missing in the work that is already going forward and to bring that into being....The effective manager's first concern is future action. However, most office systems and accompanying technology focus on the recording, manipulation, and presentation of historical data."

For example, if you manage the new products division of a toothpaste company and you decide that the market is ripe for new flavors, you might study research on acceptance of new flavors in the past, current market conditions, costs of production, etc.—all information from the past. Let's say based on your research, you decide that arugula-flavored toothpaste would be a market-buster. You present your idea with the documentation and research to your superiors. You convince them that your judgment is sound and reliable, so they encourage you to proceed.

"Ideas are for action."
—Aristotle

But nothing has really happened until you instruct the people who work for you on how to proceed to develop this product. This linguistic communication initiates action. To translate corporate policies into plans for action in the future is the heart of management, not the recording of past events. Management's mission is to bring about action through the expression of words, not to document it after it has happened.

"A recent study we conducted of 19 organizations turned up some interesting insights into barriers that block strategic action.

"The first and foremost barrier is the lack of clear, simple, and specific strategic initiatives. Many strategies are either too vague or too voluminous to be of any use. For example, one leading American company we studied defines its business as 'the creation of machines and methods to help find solutions to the increasingly complex problems of business, government, science, space exploration, education, medicine, and nearly every other area of human endeavor.' If you were a product or market manager, what action could you take to support this overall direction?"—Benjamin B. Tregoe and Peter M. Tobia, "Set a Goal and Reach It Step by Step," *The New York Times* (10/29/89)

Future actions live in language.

"How many companies have secretaries who type at 100 words per minute, sophisticated word-processors for them to use, fancy letterheads, and continuous forms, all of which regularly are rendered irrelevant by mail delivery systems that deliver the right communication late, or to the wrong person? With all the technical wonders of word-processing, letters, memos, and reports still arrive late and are misdirected, because designing to produce artifacts faster or better has no intrinsic value. What has value, potentially, is the letter delivered to the right person, and read at the right time.

"....If your attention is on the future of an enterprise, then the people who work within that enterprise must first be understood as some network of already present commitments and of possibilities for the making of other commitments in the future. The ingredients of the work are not the bodies and tools and spaces, but the questions and commitments and possibilities that bring forth things."—Fernando Flores and Chauncey Bell, "A New Understanding of Managerial Work Improves System Design," *Computer Technology Review* (Fall 1984)

ATTITUDE OVERHAUL

Bosses are not the enemy; frustration is the enemy, and it comes from instructions that are constructed badly or given carelessly without regard to the follower. Frustration also arises from being ill-prepared to receive instructions. It arises from a lack of awareness of the larger problems of communication.

In the previous chapters, I have tried to make my case for the importance of instructions and have outlined the larger issues with which we all must wrestle in the giving and taking of them. These issues can be summarized as follows:

- Instructions are a major component of communications.

- Instructions in the workplace must be understood within the larger context of current affairs and the economy.

- The transformation from an industrial- to an information-based economy broadens the role of instructions.

- Changing demographics will make the communication of instructions a more challenging task.

- The first step toward meeting the challenge is understanding what kind of instruction-giver and -taker you are. What about the people with whom you work?
  (See Chapter 4.)

- The next step is understanding the forces at work beyond individual personalities that alter the perception of instructions and obstruct the flow of information.

Most of the prior material has focused on the nature of work and the workplace, and it behooves us to keep these in mind when formulating or following instructions. But we come to work with preconceived notions and biases toward certain modes of thinking that make it harder for us to understand each other. An examination of how we learn and use language will provide more insight into the intricacies of instructions.

WHY CAN'T ANYBODY FOLLOW INSTRUCTIONS?

"Following instructions is one of the most difficult comprehension tasks encountered in daily life."

H. A. Simon and J. R. Hayes,
"Understanding Complex Task
Instructions," *Cognition and Instruction*

A sign appears high over the road about 75 feet before many of the stoplights in British Columbia. It reads: "Prepare to Stop When Amber Flashing."

Now, amber is a rather sophisticated color. First, you have to ask yourself, what does amber look like? Then you have to decide that this implies an amber

PREPARE TO STOP
WHEN AMBER FLASHING

light. You might imagine something at least the size of a stoplight. You start to look around for a big amber light. Then you notice that there are two tiny lights set in the top of the sign and wonder, is this the amber that flashes? By this time, you have probably run through the red light for which the sign was supposed to prepare you.

You didn't want to run the red light; you were trying to follow the instruction. What happened, you wonder?

According to a study conducted by Shinar and Drory in 1983, only 4.5 percent of motorists could recall the last two road signs they passed during the daytime, despite the fact that they were stopped only 200 meters away from the signs. (The nighttime recall was 16.5 percent.) Yet, another study conducted by Summula and Naatanen (1974) found that when motorists were asked to report the signs to an investigator in the back seat, only 2.95 percent failed to notice road signs.

By nature, most people want to follow instructions.

EXCEPTIONS TO THE RULE

Of course there are exceptions. Who deliberately and willfully hasn't tried to machine wash a garment clearly labeled "dry clean only."

"Most of us who take our lives at all seriously have for years been secretly tyrannized by the increasingly insistent manufacturers' washing instructions on our clothing.

"....Indeed, even though garments are theoretically more 'easy care' than ever before, it has become a powerful likelihood, that, like snowflakes, no two garments exist in the world with EXACTLY the same washing instructions.

"Scientists using supercomputers at California's Livermore Laboratory have calculated over 460 million potential combinations of washing instructions on any given garment (including, 'HAND WASH, MEDIUM' and 'LINE DRY, UNLESS YOU ARE A RISING CAPRICORN'), which means that you have the potential of having over a million sorted piles of laundry in front of you on any given day.

"....In the beginning, for about the first three million years of civilization, all of humanity's laundry came equipped with the following washing instructions: 'WASH.' Which was eventually fine-tuned to 'SMASH AGAINST ROCK.'

"But I guess we've all come too far. The only one way we can get society moving again is if we all become nudists."—Stephanie Brush, "This Suds for You," *The Washington Post* (1/15/89)

Following the rules is our entrance fee to communal society and most of us are amenable or at least resigned to following them. People have been known to behave in antisocial ways contrary to their own conventional behavior patterns—just because someone else instructed them to do so.

In a study conducted at 2 grocery stores in Blacksburg, Virginia, customers were handed a handbill with the specials of the week. Some of the flyers had different messages at the bottom related to the disposal of the flyer, such as, "Please dispose of properly" or "Please don't litter. Please dispose of in green can located at rear of store."

One had the message: "Please litter. Dispose of on floor."

> "Very few customers dropped their handbill on the floor *except when the message on the handbill requested such littering;* then several patrons at each store complied with the litter instructions and dropped their handbills on the floor.

> "Thus,...the present study merely adds to the abundance of research in social psychology demonstrating that people will obey instructions even when their compliance results in antisocial behavior."—E. Scott Geller, Jill F. Witmer, and Andra L. Orebaugh, "Instructions as a Determinant of Paper-Disposal Behaviors," *Environment and Behavior* (9/76)

"Why does any pilgrim journey to see any saint? Why does any novice seek out a guru or a master? For instruction. We wished to be instructed."—Tom Robbins, *Even Cowgirls Get the Blues*

The willingness to follow instructions is almost an involuntary response, a response not limited to pecadillos like throwing paper on the floor. When God told Abraham to sacrifice his son, Abraham was willing to follow the instruction. Human history is littered with cases in which people have gone to sometimes unfathomable lengths in the name of following orders, such as the Nazi holocaust and the My Lai massacre during the Vietnam War.

"Behavior that is unthinkable in an individual who is acting on his own may be executed without hesitation when carried out under orders."—Stanley Milgram, *Obedience to Authority*

This extraordinary willingness of people to follow the orders of perceived superiors even when it might involve compromising their own principles or ethics has been documented in numerous studies. Remember the experiments of Stanley Milgram in 1963? People were willing to administer what they were led to believe were potentially fatal electric shocks to subjects at the request of a lab-coated *experimenter.*

On a more prosaic level, most of us are conditioned to follow the rules. From infancy on, we hear, "Do as you are told. Don't ask so many questions." We drive on the right side of the road, don't stand in supermarket express lanes with more than 10 items in our basket, and faithfully fill in all the blanks on forms.

If most people are trying "to do as they are told," why do so many have problems following instructions?

Often we are not given the information that would enable us to understand the purpose of the instruction, so that we could interpret the instruction in light of the inevitable altered or unexpected circumstances.

Thus we follow instructions with such antlike industry that in our zeal to follow the letter of the order, we miss the spirit.

We get stopped along the way for a variety of reasons:

> The instruction isn't prepared in a way we can understand it.
>
> We don't pay enough attention.
>
> We fail to ask the essential questions that would reveal the intent of the instruction.
>
> The instruction is delivered in such a narrow way that it becomes an order.
>
> We get bogged down in an excess of information and don't recognize what we need to know.
>
> The instruction-giver didn't understand the importance of communicating carefully.
>
> We don't visualize the result or outcome.
>
> The instruction wasn't driven by concern for human behavior.

BACK TO THE CRIB

However, these are only explanations specific to a situation. There are more primordial causes that go back through our education to early childhood and even to the basic limitations of human understanding.

Our failure to follow instructions has to do with the way we learn language as infants, the way we are educated in school, and the low premium placed on communication in our society. We are a society of doers and watchers, not talkers. Conversation was once viewed as a pastime, a craft to which we devoted time and attention. Now it seems to be something reduced to a necessity for obtaining what we want. "Please pass the mustard" is not a conversation. Socializing once meant spending an evening in conversation with people, now it means sharing a bowl of popcorn in front of a TV.

ENGLISH: OUR SECOND LANGUAGE

Children first learn to communicate with a nonverbal, almost binary, language. They cry to indicate discomfort or need and smile to indicate pleasure. Infants will also respond to faces and tones of voices around them. Infants are mimics; when addressed in baby talk, this is how they respond. This reliance on nonverbal language is reinforced by the family unit. Most families use highly personalized codes of communication. Certain expressions, nonsense names, tones of voice, are used to deliver information. These signals have little to do with a universal word-based language.

Only when the children go out into the world, to school or to play with other children, do they realize that these family codes don't work in the community at large. Then they must learn word-based English almost as if it were a second language.

Perhaps this is why adults commonly return to baby talk in love relationships. An atmosphere of warmth and nurturing can evolve that simulates an infantile state, thus returning them to our primordial means of communication.

Childhood development literature can really be frightening when you realize how easily you could substitute the word *adult*. The shortcomings of development become the plagues of the adult.

If you tell young children to do something that they don't understand, rather than ask for clarification, they will pretend that you have made perfect sense. Even if children show fleeting signs of incomprehension, they will soon forget their uncertainties. There is a natural tendency for children to blame themselves when they can't understand something. Their inherent trust in their adult caretakers prevents them from entertaining the idea that they may be getting poor instructions. The way that children learn language may cause them to develop ineffective communication patterns. They adapt and apply behaviors learned at home to their social interactions outside the home in ways that are inappropriate in the new situations.

"Babies are sophisticated communicators long before they produce language....Infants are introduced to the process of conversational turn-taking early in development. For example, mothers of infants as young as 3 months make *space* for the baby's turn in verbal interactions, and by that same early age, infants' vocalizations are varied to fill that space.

"....Indeed the tacit trust of very young children in their communication partners may be so strong that they might be entirely unaware that those who address them could do so vaguely or ambiguously.

"....When children first communicate linguistically, they accord language no special status: they treat it as another signal system parallel with, and of no more importance than, the nonverbal one. Language understood in this way is a poor tool with which to correct a listener's misapprehensions about one's communicative intent; being accorded no special status in the complex of communicative channels, it cannot be used to modify interpretations derived from other (i.e., nonlinguistic) channels.... If young children view the utility of language in this way, it may be possible to see why they do not ask clarifying questions; to do so assumes that the linguistic channel may be used to override and modify the results of other communication channels, and these children simply do not make that assumption.

"....It has been proposed, for example, that only when children commence having extensive social relations outside the home—typically in preschool or kindergarten—do they come to accord special communicative status to language (Cook-Gumperz, 1977). This proposal supposes that the children and their caretakers develop highly idiosyncratic, multichannel communication routines and that when they enter school they learn that their routines do not work in the new setting because teachers and other children are not in on the game. So they come to highlight the one system that does prove to work, the linguistic one."—James Ramsey Speer, "Two Practical Strategies Young Children Use to Interpret Vague Instructions," *Child Development* (Vol. 55, 1984)

NONVERBAL COMMUNICATION

"When our words appear to contradict the feelings that are expressed in our faces, voices, and bodily movements, the perceived inconsistency tends to be resolved by trusting the nonverbal messages more than the verbal."—Martin Remland, "Developing Leadership Skills in Non-Verbal Communication," *The Journal of Business Communication* (Vol. 18, No. 3)

At some point, the nonverbal communication of infancy gets packed away like the pacifier and the plastic pants. Parents set to the work of honing their children's language skills, as does the education system. For after all, Western culture relies on the word as the official currency of communication. "You have my word" can be a legally binding contract.

Yet, the nonverbal signals that were preeminent in childhood continue to serve us in communication. According to some estimates, nonverbal signals—facial expressions, tone of voice, hand gestures, head-nodding, etc.—make up close to 90 percent of all communications. Deciphering the messages contained in this type of communication requires a different kind of skill *from* just understanding what a

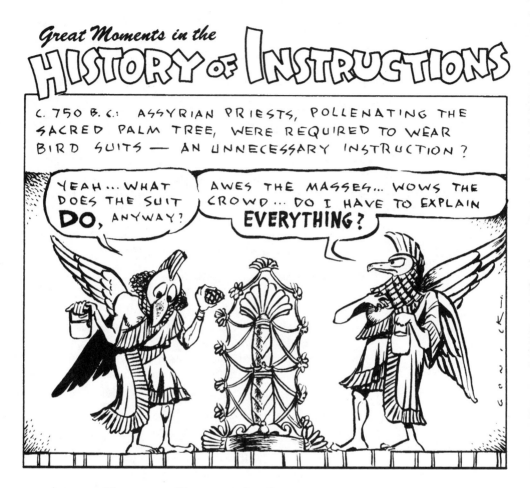

word means. The range of interpretation for nonverbal behavior is vast and often contradictory.

There's a pope joke that illustrates this point. Several hundred years ago, the pope issues an edict that all the Jews have to be out of Rome by Monday morning. It's Friday; the whole community is up in arms. What's wrong, they wonder. We've been living here for hundreds of years; we have homes and families; we have businesses. A group of rabbis and wise men meet to discuss the edict. They approach the Vatican and want a chance to argue the edict. They receive word that "the smartest among you will be allowed a silent disputation with the pope." They can't believe it. How can you argue a point silently? They are overwrought, in a quandary about what to do. Benjy, the ghetto janitor, is sweeping nearby. He says, "What's the problem? If that's your only choice, you argue silently." The rabbis decide to send Benjy to the pope.

The pope is at his desk. Benjy sits down in front of him. The pope makes a sweeping motion with his arms. Benjy pounds one finger on the desk. The pope shakes a finger at Benjy. Benjy holds three fingers up to the pope. The pope takes the communion wafer and eats it. Benjy takes out an apple and takes a bite out of it. The pope throws up his hands and says, "All right, you win. The Jews can stay in Rome."

After Benjy leaves, his bishops rush into the pope's office. "What happened?" they query.

The pope explains, "I motioned to him that we are the religion of the world. Benjy responded, 'But the Jews are the chosen people.' I told him, 'There is only one God.' He argued, 'But the Catholics have three gods.' I ate the communion wafer to show him they are as one and he ate an apple, reminding me that we all share in the original sin. So I let them stay."

Benjy returns to the ghetto. The rabbis and wise men surround him. "How did you do it?"

Benjy replies, "It was easy. He motioned that the Jews should go. I countered that they should stay. He said, 'I give you one week.' I said we need at least three weeks. He agreed and we both ate lunch."

A *grin-fuck* is the smile you get from someone who thinks your idea is absurd and has no intention of acting on it. It's used in America frequently but has been brought to the level of an art form by the Japanese.

A smile can be perceived as an expression of warmth or as baring the teeth. To some animals, bears for example, a smile is perceived as a menacing threat. In humans, for the most part, a smile is an expression of warmth and welcome, but there are also human smiles that suggest agression. I've had people smile at me with a too-big grin that made my blood curdle.

Sometimes tone of voice means more than the words themselves. I have a friend, Lanna, who insists that her son understands only her tone of voice. "I say, 'Stephan, it's time to get ready to go visit Grandma, now.' He continues with whatever he is doing. I say again, 'Stephan, it's time to get ready to go,' with more firmness. No effect. 'Stephan, it's time to get ready to go NOW,' I say with menace. He doesn't understand time or even now, but he responds to the tone of NOW."

BETWEEN HARD AND SOFT LEARNING

The maladaptive language and listening strategies of young children and the lack of formal emphasis on nonverbal communication act in concert with the biases parents and teachers place on children to inhibit their ability to communicate later as adults.

Parents, however inadvertently, begin to predispose their children toward certain biases of thought, depending on their own personality and preferences. Everytime a young child performs an act, parents can ignore it or make a fuss about it—either a positive or a negative one. When little junior smears apricot puree on a bib, parents can marvel that they have produced another Picasso or they can quietly hose him down. They can rush to provide the potential artistic genius with crayons and finger paint or they can scold him for being a slob. How do the parents respond when junior figures out how to change channels on the TV with the remote control box? By marveling at this mechanical accomplishment and rushing to provide him with more scientific stimulation, they will encourage this aptitude. By taking the remote control box away and replacing it with fingerpaints, parents will give the message that one endeavor is superior to the other.

These tiny events start the process of pushing children in the direction of art or science. And whether or not children choose to rebel or imitate their parents, they begin to get the idea that there are two kinds of people the in world—those who can program their VCRs and those who can't.

This dichotomy between art and science is further reinforced at school, where many teachers have their own biases. In elementary school, teachers, who may be teaching a variety of subjects, may have to teach subjects they would rather not and may subtly infuse their students with their own

GUILTY LOOKS

A judge's tone of voice and behavior can influence the jury, according to an investigation of 34 criminal-misdemeanor trials in California municipal courts. Even when a judge does not say anything prejudicial, his or her behavior, tone of voice, and facial expressions can signal a point of view to jurors.
—"Guilty Looks," *Scientific American* (6/86)

"The two processes, that of science and that of art, are not very different. Both science and art form in the course of the centuries a human language by which we can speak about the more remote parts of reality." —Werner Heisenberg, *Physics and Philosophy*

preferences. (This has been postulated as one factor in the poor showing of U.S. students in the sciences.) Later, at the college level, the two subjects become divided almost irrevocably—by faculty, by administration, usually by building, and by college.

The arts } The Sciences

According to a Johns Hopkins University study, 95 percent of the nation's schools have at least one computer, with 2.25 million computers in the nation's school system in 1988. That's 10 times more than there were in 1983.

Students are encouraged, if not forced, by teachers, by the curricula, and by the system itself to develop a preference for one or the other approach by the choice of a course of study. The stringent division between liberal arts, or soft learning, and the sciences, or hard learning, practically forces us to become biased in a way that prevents us from being able to translate naturally between the qualitative world of liberal arts and the quantitative world of science. Although the computer has somewhat ameliorated this situation and even English majors can be seduced by the precision of computers, a dichotomy still exists in our education between hard and soft learning.

There's an apocryphal story that takes place in a supermarket in Cambridge, Massachussetts. A man is standing in an express checkout lane designated for people "with 10 items or less." The cashier sees that he has at least 20 items in his cart. She looks up at him and says, "You must be either an MBA from Harvard who can't count or an MBA from MIT who can't read. So I'll tell you, you're in the wrong line, buddy."

Students are still encouraged to align themselves with one group or the other and to define themselves in terms of their differences with the other. The groups become adversarial factions. Engineering students regard English majors as incompetent romantics who have no sense of the world in which they live. And English majors think engineering students are microchip-obssessed nerds who lack all sense of poetry and of the finer things in life.

PRIDE AND INCOMPETENCE

By the time most students leave school, they are entrenched permanently in the notion that these two worlds are at opposite ends of some ideological spectrum. They live the rest of their lives in one camp or the other, each side staunchly defining itself in haughty differentiation from the other. Aesthetes pride themselves on being able to recognize and appreciate the finer things in life, often scoffing at those who delight in cogs and wheels, and engineers brag about being able to operate and understand all those essential devices of modern life, laughing at the ineptitude of mechanical morons.

Both postures are not only weak and ineffectual, but highly impractical given the conditions of modern life, and bragging about incompetence in either arena only worsens the gap and gets in the way of identifying problems in understanding.

"I can't even change a light bulb," the aesthetes will boast to you. "I have to call my kids to bake a potato in the microwave." They find themselves surrounded by machines that they lack the skills to operate, so they boast of their incompetence and imply that they are above the need to operate mere machinery. The insinuation of technology into everyone's life has made this kind of stance more difficult to maintain, though, and staunch aesthetes find themselves increasingly cut off from an abundance of efficiences. So they hide their insecurities and inabilities behind bravado.

Bravado colors the perspective of those with a scientific orientation as well. The less tangible world of soft learning—of interpretation and conjecture— can be just as threatening to one used to formulas and functions as a control panel can be to a comparative literature professor. Yet, the most creative technology is often conceived through application of principles of soft learning. The best programmers approach their jobs not only with a high regard for technique and specification, but with an artistic, imaginative approach to problem-solving as well.

The two modes of thought are not mutually exclusive. There is no divine dictum that forbids someone from being able to change spark plugs and appreciate a Schubert symphony. In fact, often the most distinguished artists and scientists exhibit aptitudes in both areas, which suggest that they have managed somehow to transcend the biases of

THE WORLD'S FIRST TECHNICAL WRITER?

The great literary genius Geoffrey Chaucer wrote an instruction manual for his son about how to use an astrolabe, an early version of the sextant.

Richard Saul Wurman, by Ofey. Ofey was the pseudonym of Richard Feynman.

"Certain kinds of science aspire to the condition of poetry; and on the planet of the Spiral Dancers, a long tradition of scientist-poets had elevated a branch of physics until it became a high symbolist religion. They had probed matter, dividing it into ever-smaller units, until they found at its very roots the pure, beautiful dance of life. This was a harmony of the infinitesimal, where energy and matter moved like fluids....From this discovery came the religion of Spiral Unity. If everything was energy, everything was the same. A thinking being and a table were only aspects of the same force."—Salman Rushdie, *Grimus*

conventional education and its petty divisiveness. Would anyone insist that Albert Einstein wasn't creative? Richard Feynman, who won a Nobel prize for physics, was also a painter and a musician. If Schubert were alive today, he'd be composing on the the computer.

A mission of instructions is often to move us back and forth between hard and soft learning. Machine instructions try to take hard scientific operations and explain them in abstract language; company presidents give abstract instructions in the hopes that their employees can turn them into tangible products. We have difficulty along the way because of our inevitable biases, whether we are instruction-givers or -takers. Unless the polarization is dispelled between hard and soft learning, between meaning and machines, instructions will act as barricades instead of bridges to understanding. Without an equal facility and appreciation of both hard and soft learning, the simple, understandable instruction is a mission impossible.

UNITED WE UNDERSTAND; DIVIDED WE FAIL

"I want to divide human understanding into two kinds—classical understanding and romantic understanding....A classical understanding sees the world primarily as underlying form itself. A romantic understanding sees it primarily in terms of immediate appearance. If you were to show an engine or a mechanical drawing or electronic schematic to a romantic it is unlikely he would see much of interest in it. It has no appeal because the reality he sees is its surface. Dull, complex lists of names, lines and numbers....But if you were to show the same blueprint or schematic or give the same description to a classical person he might look at it and then become fascinated by it because he sees that within the lines and shapes and symbols is a tremendous richness of underlying form.

"The romantic mode is primarily inspiration, imaginative creative intuitive. Feelings rather than acts predominate.

"....The classic mode, by contrast, proceeds by reason and by laws—which are themselves underlying forms of thought and behavior.

"....To a romantic this classic mode often appears dull, awkward and ugly, like mechanical maintenance itself. Everything is in terms of pieces and parts and components and relationships. Nothing is figured out until it's run through the computer a dozen times. Everything's got to be measured and proved. Oppressive. Heavy. Endlessly grey. The death force.

"Within the classic mode, however, the romantic has some appearances of his own. Frivolous, irrational, erratic, untrustworthy, interested primarily in pleasure-seeking. Shallow. Of no substance. Often a parasite who cannot or will not carry his own weight. A real drag on society. By now these battle lines should sound a little familiar.

"This is the source of the trouble. Persons tend to think and feel exclusively in one mode or the other and in doing so tend to misunderstand and underestimate what the other mode is all about. But no one is willing to give up the truth as he sees it, as far as I know, no one now living has any real reconciliation of these truths or modes. There is no point at which these visions of reality are unified.

"And so in recent times we have seen a huge split develop between a classic culture and a romantic counterculture—two worlds growingly alienated and hateful toward each other with everyone wondering if it will always be this way, a house divided against itself.

"What has become an urgent necessity is a way of looking at the world that does violence to neither of these two kinds of understanding and unites them into one."—Robert Pirsig, *Zen and the Art of Motorcycle Maintenance*

IF IT'S A COMPUTER, IT MUST BE COMPLICATED

A friend told me about working in an office of computer-intimidated people. They moved a computer from one room to another and when they turned it on, the mouse wasn't working. The cursor became invisible when it was moved into a highlighted area on the computer screen. They checked all the settings, restarted the computer, tried to take apart the mouse, reloaded the software program that operates the mouse, and checked to see if the mouse would work in another word-processing program. Then they concluded that the move had damaged the computer and called a repair service. The repairman turned down the brightness control, and instantly the mouse reappeared. Someone must have brushed against the knob as they moved the computer—hardly a problem worth a service call.

Because some people operate computers at only a basic word-processing level, there is a high degree of helplessness where computers are concerned. We easily assume that if something is wrong, it must be beyond our ability to fix it. Because of this response, sometimes we neglect the simplest solutions to problems. We try to start at our highest level of ability, when often that is not the level that is needed.

LEFT BRAIN/RIGHT BRAIN

In recent years, a fashionable management theory has attempted to draw a line down the middle of people's brains and then deal out various characteristics to either side like a deck of cards.

Brain lateralization, once the milieu of neuroscience, has become the *cause célèbre* of business and pop psychology to the chagrin of science. "Are you left-brained or right-brained?" is now the question of the week during morning coffee breaks.

As the theory goes—attributes and abilities can be assigned to a particular brain hemisphere, roughly based on the assumption that creative thinking happens in the right half and analytical thinking goes on in the left. The left brain is the location for logical, rational, inductive, conscious, linear thinking. Go to the right brain for intuitive, deductive, unconscious, nonlinear thinking. Science is left brain, art is right brain. The left brain is verbal, analytic. The right is natural, organic. The left processes verbal stimuli and the right processes spatial, visual stimuli.

The problem is that our quantitatively obsessed culture has caused the left half to become a bully, leaving the right cowering in a corner, weak and underdeveloped. We have been tyrannized by left-brainers and left-brain thinking, which has been kicking sand in the face of the right brain for too long.

Right-brain devotees believe some of the world's— or at least the business community's—problems could be solved with more right-brain thinking. To produce more creative business thinking, we have to beef up that poor, defenseless right brain.

This is the same kind of compartmentalized, militaristic thinking that prompts people to assume that all businessmen and scientists are stodgy and noncreative and all artists are imaginative and emotional. Have you ever sat next to someone who told you with a straight face that he was an *artist,* then proceeded to use the term *deconstruction* until you found yourself wishing he would be apply it to himself before the next course? I rest my case.

Using the patina of neuroscience, business theorists reapplied the research to a simplistic formula that contradicts many of the original findings regarding hemispheric differences in the brain.

Research done by Martha Farah, a Carnegie-Mellon University psychologist, has shown that some of the imaging abilities previously thought to be the province of the right brain appear to be controlled by the left hemisphere.

> "That there are differences between the two sides of the human brain in the way they process information has been known since 1865, when Broca first described an impairment of speech (aphasia) associated with damage to a certain part of a patient's left hemisphere. Research on these differences has shown them to be of a totally different character than those claimed by the left-brain/right-brain mythology. The actual differences in the way that information is processed in the hemispheres are much smaller and much less dichotomized than the mythology claims.
>
> "The real research findings on hemispheric differences have shown, in sharp contrast to the claims of left-brain/right-brain mythology, that differences in function between the hemispheres, while very real and extremely interesting, are, with the exception of vocal control, rather small and matters of degree. There is no evidence to support the claims that,

"I disagree with them about cycle maintenance, but not because I am out of sympathy with their feelings about technology. I just think that their flight from and hatred of technology is self-defeating. The Buddha, the Godhead, resides quite as comfortably in the circuits of a digital computer or the gears of a cycle transmission as he does at the top of a mountain or in the petals of a flower. To think otherwise is to demean the Buddha—which is to demean oneself."—Robert Pirsig, *Zen and the Art of Motorcycle Maintenance*

for example, the left hemisphere is 'logical' and the right 'intuitive' or that the left hemisphere is 'conscious' while the right is 'unconscious.'....In view of this, attempts to improve performance and training by relying on non-existent left-brain/right-brain differences are unlikely to be productive."—Terence Hines, Ph.D., "Left Brain, Right Brain: Who's on First?" *Training and Development Journal* (11/85)

"What was first thought to be a dichotomy between the abilities of the left and right hemispheres became known by the early 1970s as a gradual gradient in abilities.

"...If creativity is a function of the right hemisphere, as hemisphere mythology claims, then damage to the right hemisphere should impair creative behavior, whereas damage to the left hemisphere should not affect creative behavior....Research has not borne this out.

"... Damage to the right hemisphere is more likely to impair musical creativity than damage to the left hemisphere, whereas damage to the left hemisphere is more likely to impair literary creativity than damage to the right hemisphere. Creativity is not localized in either hemisphere. Rather creativity in a domain is impaired when those areas of the brain that underlie the basic cognitive functions required in the domain are damaged. The study of the effects that damage to the left and right hemispheres has on graphic (drawing and painting) abilities also shows clearly that neither creativity nor art are contained in either hemisphere. In artistically untrained individuals, damage to both left and right hemispheres impairs the ability to draw (Hecaen, 1981). Case studies of graphic artists who have suffered damage to either the left or right hemisphere of the brain also show the involvement of both hemispheres in graphic skill and creativity (Gardner, 1982; Gardner & Winner, 1981). The effects a lesion in either the left or the right hemisphere can have on ability and creativity in painting are similar.

"....Left brain/right brain mythology has been adopted with enthusiasm in the fields of management and training. As early as 1976, Mintzberg proposed that 'which hemisphere of one's brain is better developed may determine whether a person ought to be a planner or a manager.' After incorrectly claiming that the right brain is *holistic* and the left brain *logical,* Mintzberg assigned planning to the left hemisphere and management to the right hemisphere, as if these two were separate functions, requiring different skills."—Terence Hines, Ph.D., "LeftBrain/Right Brain Mythology and Implications for Management and Training," *Academy of Management Review* (Vol. 12, No. 4, 1987)

MISSION IMPOSSIBLE: THE TECHNO-HUMANIST

The occidental mania for seeing all things in terms of mutually exclusive opposites builds in limitations. People view themselves as either right-brained or left-brained, artistic or scientific, numbers- or word-oriented, logical or intuitive. In truth, excellence in one side of these pairs doesn't mean an inability in the other, nor are they mutually exclusive opposites. It is possible to be proficient in both numbers and words, to be artistic and scientific.

Look at logic and intuition. What appears to be an intuitive leap from problem to solution might be a series of logical steps in the evolution of thought. The chaos theory in physics asserts that seemingly random events may have a meticulous order.

Trying to label employees and assign jobs based on questionable dichotomies in brain hemispheres can squander both time and talent.

New research has shown that the brain is more holographic than hemispheric in its functioning.

Scientists are pushing against the boundaries of reason and coming up with some Star-Trek conclusions in the exploration of how people understand and learn. Dr. Rupert Sheldrake of England developed a theory of formative causation, which claims that any repeated behavior will form a worldwide energy field or a "morphic resonance" that facilitates others in learning the behavior. A competition sponsored by the Tarrytown House Executive Conference Center in Tarrytown, New York, was held to test his theories. A British psychology professor, Alan Pickering, found that when Cambridge students were shown characters from the Persian language mixed with nonsense shapes, the students were more successful in reproducing the real shapes, even though none had any knowledge of Persian. Pickering shared the first prize with a Yale psychiatrist, Gary E. Schwartz, and Arden Mahlberg, a psychologist in Wisconsin.

I used to think that my brain was the most important organ in my body, but then I thought: look who's telling me that.—Paraphrased from comedian Emo Phillips

Both halves of the brain are connected by the *corpus callosum*. This enables the halves of the brain to cooperate and complement each other. Often, injury to certain areas of the brain will cause other parts of the brain to compensate for the loss of function. The halves of the brain don't work in adversarial isolation, competing for dominance; they engage in a rich and fruitful cooperation.

The people who will triumph in the future will be those who can view the world in more holistic terms and bridge the gap between the two worlds of hard and soft learning. The techno–humanists will understand not only machines, but the implications of machines for people and society, and they will be articulate enough to communicate their perspective.

Rather than view the world as man versus the machine, they see the machine as a natural extension of man, knowing that the machine becomes the master of those who eye it fearfully. They see the connections where the rest of the world sees the gaps.

Writer Donald R. Katz sort of backed into the computer age after meeting just such a person. He was in a traumatized state after losing a computer file, so his girlfriend suggested that he call her friend, John, who might be able to retrieve the file. In an article, "Don't Be Mean to Your Machine" in *Esquire* (5/90), he wrote, "John never descends to the gee-whiz celebrations that characterize so much technological discourse, and his analysis often centers on the ways in which an innovation will change a life, on how soon it will be surpassed, on how easily a thing will break, and most of all, on how easily it can be fixed."

"....It seems the pace of technological evolution has so broadened the gulf between those two out of ten Americans who are *involved* with technology...and the eight citizens who are not, that those among the eight who want to retain control have realized they need help. The very quality of most lives has become dependent on the successful mitigation of the two sides of the curve.

"My friend John—and those thousands of others who have become like him during the last decade—represent an entirely new social species, a living bridge between the left and right sides of the collective mind....John is not a techie of tradition, because, among other things, he doesn't seek to bore further into the protective cover and introverted language of technique. He is certainly not a 'hacker,' who labors alone and blindered before a screen, often with antisocial intent....John draws information from both sides of the divide for the sake of the integration of technology by the whole. He believes technology is morally evocative, and dangerous in the extreme if it is not understood.

"He is, I believe, a prime example of techno-oracular man, a living interface between the two sides of an ever-increasing cultural chasm."—Donald R. Katz, "Don't Be Mean to Your Machine," *Esquire* (5/90)

" 'Come over this afternoon and play croquet,' said Irina Cherkassova.

" 'I don't know the game,' replied Flapping Eagle.

" 'Then it will be instructive,' she smiled. 'When you play a game you don't understand, it teaches you a great deal about yourself. And your limitations.' "
—Salman Rushdie, *Grimus*

Accepting ambiguity runs contrary to the foundations of Western thought, yet it is a concept that most of us are being forced to accept—in more and more dramatic degrees. Perhaps this explains the turn toward the East for new insights in dealing with The Great Void.

"Above, not a tile to cover the head; Below, not an inch of ground for the foot."—Zen axiom

"We learn music, for example, by restricting the whole range of tone and rhythm to a notation of fixed tonal and rhythmic intervals—a notation which is incapable of representing Oriental music. But the Oriental musician has a rough notation which he uses only as a reminder of a melody," said Alan Watts in *The Wisdom of Insecurity.* "He learns music, not by reading notes, but by listening to the performance of a teacher, getting the 'feel' of it, and copying him, and this enables him to acquire rhythmic and tonal sophistications matched only by those Western jazz-artists who use the same approach."

"The most beautiful thing we can experience is the mysterious."— Albert Einstein

Chinese life is driven by the complementary traditions of Confucianism and Taoism. Roughly, Confucianism concerns itself with everyday life, with the conventions of society. Taoism is the realm outside of the conventions, a liberation from the order. The principles of both traditions are well-respected, coexisting peacefully in Oriental thought.

THE SABOTAGE OF SELF-CONSCIOUSNESS

One of the most overwhelming obstacles that defeat giving and following instructions is self-consciousness. It destroys creativity, deprives people from feeling a sense of purpose in their work, makes them fearful and inhibited, and stops the flow of ideas. If you are always worried about how you are performing a task, about how others perceive your performance, you will never perform it well. Performance requires forgetting yourself.

My associate, Loring Leifer, should have had this in her mind when she went to vote in the last presidential election. She told me the following story.

The voting precinct in my neighborhood is staffed mainly by elderly German ladies. They believe that there is a right way to dress, a right way to speak, and a right way to live. Order above all. Heaven help you if you accidently cut in front of one of them in a grocery store checkout line or go out of your apartment with beige shoes and a black handbag. I never got used to their disapproving looks if I went to pick up the mail wearing shorts.

Come election time, I put on a sensible skirt and went to the voting precinct. I was used to hand-written ballots and was nervous about using the voting machines. All I could think about was pulling the curtain on the voting booth so I could read the directions in private out of the reach of the imperious gaze of little, old German ladies. Before I stepped into the booth, a group of them started telling me, "You pull the lever one time when you go in and one time when you go out." I imagined a slot machine or a washing machine, where you pushed the coins into the machine, then brought the tray out, pulled the lever down then brought it back up. In my mind this forward/backward motion constituted "one time." I went into the booth and tried to pull the curtain by hand. My first mistake. "Stop, stop that. The lever. Pull the lever. Don't touch the curtains," the little old ladies were screaming at me. I panicked.

I pulled the lever to the right and the curtain closed. Then I pulled the lever back and the curtain opened, exposing me in my failure to understand directions. I didn't get much sympathy. "You've lost your vote. That's it. You're finished here. You did exactly what I told you not to do. I told you once when you go in, once when you come out. Exactly what I told you not to do."

I was humiliated. I contemplated moving. I wondered how the government thought I was intelligent enough to vote, when I couldn't even operate the voting machines. If I had not felt so self-conscious, I would have been relaxed enough to take the time to learn. And maybe George Bush wouldn't have won the election.

If you can allow yourself to be innocent and honest with yourself, you can trust your own opinions and intuitions. The trouble is people have too many layerings of phony responses.

A writer who tries to edit at the same time he or she is writing makes the task doubly difficult. When you start to build a story on paper, if you put a sentence to paper and think, "Oh no, this sounds stupid. Let me try another way," the story easily gets lost in self-doubt and overactive erasures.

Employees who are motivated only by ego gratification soon find the satisfactions to be shallow. A person who works only to say, "I can do this better than you can," is missing the point. With a genuine belief in the organization's goals, people work with a sense of a purpose outside of themselves and the quality of their work improves.

We can't change the way we learned language; the way we were educated; or the way society regards conversation. We can't do much to change the economy, nor can we even do much to alter our personalities or those of the people around us. But this doesn't mean we should resign ourselves to a lifetime of misunderstandings, communication breakdowns, and solitude.

We can improve our instruction techniques as givers or receivers. Just as technology can be improved, so can people in their attitudes toward it. People can enlarge their repertoire of capabilities as well as improve their attitude toward acquiring new skills in any field of endeavor.

Improvement demands an understanding of the issues involved and the taking of positive action. The prior chapters have examined the issues surrounding the giving and following of instructions that we should all keep in mind. The following chapters address the instructions themselves and the actions or steps that we can take to improve our technique in giving and following them.

TILE MANAGEMENT OR JUMPING HURDLES TO UNDERSTANDING

"No one ever listened himself out of a job."
Calvin Coolidge

"*At the recent National SCRABBLE® Championship at the Penta Hotel, a veteran competitor pulled a frustrated amateur into a corner to offer advice: 'Son,' she whispered, looking both ways, 'the key to success in this game isn't vocabulary. It's tile management,'*" according to an article in New York magazine (8/21/89).

"A very great part of the mischiefs that vex this world arises from words."
—Edmund Burke

The rules of SCRABBLE® apply to the game of communication as well: what matters isn't vocabulary, it's word management. The goal of communication is not to find the right word, but to get your message across. Communication isn't literature. A message could meet all the requirements of exemplary prose, but still fall short as a communication. Subjects could be in perfect agreement with verbs, infinitives intact, and all participles correctly attached; the images could be imaginative and the adjectives acrobatic, but unless the taker understands the message in the way the giver meant to give it, the communication has failed. A novel can delight, impress, and overwhelm, but it does not require that it be understood as the author intended. Vladimir Nabokov's nymphet character, Lolita, was seen by some as a symbol of America and American culture, by others as Nabokov's fascination with the English language, and by still more as a satire on puritanical morality. The book is enriched by the multitude of interpretations.

Albert Einstein's mother used to say that when she tried to read her son's work, she could understand the words but not the sentences.

Literature inspires, communication instructs.
Communication—especially in the workplace—has a preordained mission. Just because messages are phrased correctly doesn't mean they will get a point across. No matter how dazzling the message is, the intruction-taker still has to understand the metaphors, allusions, and comparisons.

With an understanding of the issues involved in the instruction system from the previous chapters, you can now take positive action to become a more able instruction-giver or -taker.

Instructions are a driving force of communications, and anything you do to improve your communication skills will affect your ability to give and take instructions. In the workplace, this can produce more productive working relationships and more efficient operations by improving the exchange of messages—the primary activity of organizations.

Improvement begins simply by acknowledging all the communication situations in which you act as an instruction-giver and -taker. If you are aware that you are making a request of someone or influencing another's actions or beliefs in your conversations, you might choose words differently or more carefully than otherwise.

Then you can go on to address some of the general improvements in communication that can be made and applied to almost any instruction situation.

- At the top of the list is accounting for the condition that all communication involves translating from one person's understanding to another's by learning to apply some of the tactics of translation to our communications.

- Learning to use the context, i.e., the immediate environment and the broader applications, of your messages to surmount some of the difficulties in communication.

- Focusing on the intent and not the form of the messages.

- Replacing abstract concepts with concrete descriptions.

- Making sure your messages are getting through intact to the appropriate target.

- Honing your question-asking skills to correct misunderstandings and uncover information.

- Improving listening skills.

Tactics for improving specific instructions appear in the next 2 chapters, but if you have time to read only one chapter, this is it.

"We shall never understand one another until we reduce the language to seven words."—Kahlil Gibran, *Sand and Foam*

SO MANY MEANINGS, SO FEW WORDS

"There are about 800,000 words in the English language, some 800 of which are used in daily conversations. Because the 800 words have 14,000 meanings in total, we have trouble interpreting messages as they are intended," stated William V. Ruch in *Corporate Communications: A Comparison of Japanese and American Practices.*

This means that by simple division there would be an average of about 17 meanings per word. It's a wonder that we can communicate at all with odds like that. Every time we choose a word, we run the risk that the person to whom we are speaking will apply a different meaning than we intended. On a word-by-word basis, we have only a 1 in 17 chance of having our word understood in the intended meaning—that's if people stick to the accepted definitions.

These are the odds we start out with when we try to talk to somebody.

Among the synonyms for communicate are advise, air, brief, bring up, broach, buzz, call, coach, condition, confer, consult, contact, convey, cultivate, declare, describe, develop, discipline, disclose, discuss, display, divulge, drill, edify, educate, enlighten, exercise, exhibit, explain, expose, express, give, groom, group, huddle, imbue, impart, implant, improve, inculcate, indoctrinate, inform, infuse, inseminate, inspire, instill, instruct, introduce, narrate, notify, open, orate, parley, perfect, phone, portray, powwow, practice, prepare, put, read, ready, recite, recount, relate, report, retell, reveal, ring, school, share, state, tap, tattle, teach, telephone, tell, touch, train, transmit, tutor, uncover, unveil, vent, ventilate, verbalize.

Just look at the word *communicate* for example. There are at least 60 synonyms (among them is the word *instruct*) that can be used to define the word *communicate.* Each has its own nuances and meanings and everyone would probably explain them differently. Here's what some of them mean to me:

- *To broach*—this means to bring up a topic that you both will soon wish you hadn't, such as, "I'd like to broach the subject of our alimony settlement."

- *To air*—is to bring up a topic that will make you feel much better but is likely to cause permanent damage to the psyche of the person to whom you "aired" it. "There's something I need to air with you. That dress makes you look like a linebacker in a mermaid costume. There, I feel so good that I could be honest with you."

- *To consult*—means "I haven't done this yet and I'm going to try to pawn it off on someone else," as in, "I want to consult Johnson first; I'll get back to you."

- *To impart*—means you are going to bestow one of your pearls of wisdom on an ungrateful swine who doesn't want to hear it. "Let me impart something I learned in boot camp, dear."

- *To reveal*—is what a first party exposes about a third party to a second party, who will soon feel an irresistible urge to repeat it at many other parties.

- *To express*—is usually what someone else (who has had a lot of expensive counseling) will ask you (who have had no counseling) to do in the hopes of diminishing the clarity or intensity of your feelings. "If you could just express how you felt when I stood you up, I'm sure it would make you feel a lot better than putting your fist through the wall."

TRANSLATION: THE ULTIMATE EXERCISE

I could make myself perfectly clear; it's only the words that get in the way. Language is personal, based on an individual's own idiosyncrasies and understanding. Different people will interpret the same words or pictures differently, depending on their own perceptions and experiences. Your messages are offered in your own language, in your own terms, to someone who may understand them in his or her own language. This is why the same message never gets the same interpretation. There is bound to be some doubt or ambiguity in any communication, if nothing more than the difference between the speaker's and the listener's use and understanding of language.

This means that all messages must be translated; people must learn to think, speak, and listen in what might be viewed as a foreign language—the language of the person with whom they are

"If little else, the brain is an educational toy. While it may be a frustrating plaything—one whose finer points recede just when you think you are mastering them—it is nonetheless perpetually fascinating, frequently surprising, occasionally rewarding, and it comes already assembled; you don't have to put it together on Christmas morning.

"The problem with possessing such an engaging toy is that other people want to play with it, too. Sometimes they'd rather play with yours than theirs. Or they object if you play with yours in a different manner from the way they play with theirs. The result is, a few games out of a toy department of possibilities are universally and endlessly repeated."
—Tom Robbins, *Even Cowgirls Get the Blues*

communicating. Both sides will have to make judgments, interpret meanings, and make a leap from one person's biases to another's.

A small-town friend was directing her big-city cousins to her new house. She told them that the street she lived on was "3 blocks past a big 4-way stop." They arrived an hour late, incredulous that the *tiny* stop sign they had gone through about 25 miles back was "a *big* 4-way stop"! Their Chicago traffic experiences didn't prepare them to recognize 1 stop sign as a "big 4-way stop."

To translate a message requires finding the different words that will get your message across to someone else. If my friend had attempted to translate her message, she might have thought that her cousins have an urban mind-set and are used to multilane roads and traffic lights. She could have been more explicit and called it a stop sign. She could have alerted them to certain landmarks.

"As a communications student, I participated in a simple, yet effective, communications experiment. The professor asked each of us to take a piece of paper out of our notebooks. He then told us to close our eyes and follow these simple instructions: 1) Fold the paper in half. 2) Fold it in half again. 3) Tear off the right-hand corner. 4) Fold it in half again. 5) Tear off the bottom, left corner. 6) Tear a semi-circle off the top, left corner. 7) Open the paper to full size. He asked us to open our eyes. Not surprisingly, there were 20 different versions of torn and folded paper. Needless to say, we got the point."
—Sandi Kimmel, a program manager in member communications for Prodigy Services

Keith Waterhouse, a British playwright and novelist, offers these translations of travel brochure language that are sure to reduce vacation letdowns:

Amenities—noun used to make what is singular sound plural: e.g., shopping amenities = shop.

Brand-new complex—unfinished.

Bustling hotel in one of the liveliest areas—conga line under your window at 3 AM.

Commanding views—up a steep hill.

Extensively renovated—concrete mixer on sun deck.

Few (as in few minutes from)—many.

Friendly atmosphere—slack service.

International cuisine—melon boats.

Many (as in many other attractions)—few.

No frills—bring your own coat hangers.

Simply furnished—plywood fittings.

Spectacular scenery—halfway up a mountain.

Striking—ugly.

Sun-drenched—hot.

Thriving—overcrowded.

Two magnificent pools—two small pools, one of them drained.

Value for money—read small print.

Will be part of the amenities—not yet built.

Within walking distance—cab ride.

1 brochure mile = 3 miles.

1 brochure minute = 5 min.

1 brochure person (as in sleeps six)—1 half-person.

"Keith Waterhouse Decodes the Poetry of the Brochure," *Condé Nast Traveler* (8/89)

The abbreviation- and acronym-loving U.S. Army has its own translation guide in back of the instruction-packed IET (Initial Entry Training) Soldier's Handbook. If you think you know what jag, law, pam, salute, and sop mean, you may find differently according to the handbook's glossary:

JAG—judge advocate general

LAW—light antitank weapon

PAM—pamphlet

SALUTE—size, activity, location, unit, time, equipment

SOP—standing operating procedure

As instructions are often a part of communication that requires action and reaction, an understanding of translation is particularly critical. Neither words nor sentence construction can be exchanged directly from one language to another.

Anyone who is fluent in more than one language knows that the language itself says something about the character of the people who speak it. In certain languages, there are words for things that don't exist in other languages, words that seem to defy translation.

"Every word in every language is part of a system of thinking unlike any other. Speakers of different languages live in different worlds; or rather, they live in the same world, but can't help looking at it in different ways. Words stand for patterns of experience. As one generation hands its language down to the next, it also hands down a fixed pattern

"**Whenever we translate, we are forced to abandon the mental patterns we are used to and get the hang of others completely alien to our thinking.**"—Rudolph Flesch, *The Art of Clear Thinking*

of thinking, seeing, and feeling. When we go from one language to another, nothing stays put."
—Rudolph Flesch, *The Art of Clear Thinking*

In Yiddish, there are about 75 words for idiot. There just isn't a one-word (or even one-sentence) English equivalent for *schlemiel, schmo, schlep, putz,* or *golem*—each has its own specific derogatory connotations. Take the Yiddish adjective *farblondjet. Confused, addlepated, mixed-up, kaput, agitated,* don't even begin to describe it. The German language contains more words for death than any other. Almost one third of the Laplanders' vocabulary relates to reindeer and is applied metaphorically to describe other things.

FROM THE TYPING POOL TO PARLIAMENT

**During a flight to London on the Concorde, I sat next to Chris Jones, chief executive for J. Walter Thompson in London, who told me a story about a friend who is a permanent secretary in the British government. As one of the most prestigious positions under the Prime Minister, the permanent secretary was being introduced to a long line of Japanese government officials and businessmen, who were respectfully bowing to him. Standing at the end of the line was an Englishman who happened to speak Japanese. Overhearing the introductions, he started to laugh, explaining to the permanent secretary that he was being introduced as the *eternal typist.*

When you translate sentences, you can't just plug in one word for another and expect the meanings to translate as well. For example, after a meal, an American might say "*I am full.*" The literal French translation would be *Je suis plein,* which happens to be a rather vulgar expression for "*I am pregnant.*"

Many foreign languages have very specific terms to distinguish family relations—such as an uncle on the father's side from an uncle on the mother's or a female cousin from a male cousin. English isn't so specific. There was no one word in English to denote both brothers and sisters until recently when sociologists came up with *siblings.*

In Hindustani, the word *kal* stands for *yesterday* and *tomorrow.* In Hebrew, the word *shalom* stands for *hello, goodbye,* and *peace.* These languages demand great assumptions on the part of the listener.

ICON, BUT YOU CAN'T

The increasing globalization of men and markets has inspired a search for a more universal means of communication than words. As the theory goes, icons or pictorials can be understood by people who speak different languages. The use of icons has increased dramatically as more people move, immigrant populations increase, and Europe moves toward unification.

The trouble is that icons are subject to the same misinterpretations as words. Few, if any, symbols are universally recognized, and designers are finding that icons often transmit the opposite of the desired meaning. They must still be translated from one language or culture or mode of understanding to another.

Apple Computer has made a significant contribution to the vocabulary of icons and provides a glimpse into the challenge of making universal symbols. A common early frustration in learning to use a Macintosh computer is figuring out how to get a disk out of the computer. In the lower right-hand corner of the screen is an icon of a trash can, which is where you move files that are to be deleted. This makes sense. But it is the same place into which you must move the disk icon to eject it from the drive. While it simplifies operation, understandably, uninitiated users are reluctant to move valuable (at least to them) information into a symbol that connotes a place to throw something away.

"Easterby and Hakiel (1981) tested all known symbols pertaining to fire, poison, caustic, electrical, and general hazard. Approximately 4000 consumers participated in the survey. The comprehension of the best signs was only about 20 percent, when the criterion of correctness was stringent. When the criterion was lax, comprehension of the best signs increased to 50 percent. Markedly worse performance was observed for the poor signs (5 percent of worse with the lax criterion)."
—Mark R. Lehto and James M. Miller, "The Effectiveness of Warning Labels," *Journal of Products Liability* (Vol. 2, 1988)

The same rules apply even when you are speaking in your native tongue. If you don't think so, consider this. Have you ever had a conversation with someone of the opposite sex that left you baffled at how the simplest idea could be misunderstood so grossly? Men and women trying to communicate provide some of the most glaring evidence of what happens when language doesn't get translated. Social scientists have done much exploration of the way that men and women use and understand language and have uncovered countless gaps and misinterpretations.

Deborah Tannen, Ph.D., a linguistics professor at Georgetown University, addresses this translation problem in a book, *You Just Don't Understand: Women and Men in Conversation*. She found that men are more likely to regard conversation as "negotiations in which people try to achieve and maintain the upper hand if they can, and protect themselves from others' attempts to put them down and push them around." Women view conversations as "negotiations for closeness in which people try to seek and give confirmation and support, and to reach consensus."

Without some attempts to go beyond your own biases by translating your ideas into the language of someone else's perspective, you can get locked into conversation patterns that go downhill like a greased watermelon. Gregory Bateson has a more scientific term for these distintegrating conversations— *complementary schismogenesis,* which is defined in Tannen's book as "a mutually aggravating spiral by which each person's response to the other's behavior provokes more exaggerated forms of the divergent behavior.

"....Complementary schismogenesis commonly sets in when women and men have divergent sensitivities and hypersensitivities. For example, a man who fears losing freedom pulls away at the first sign he interprets as an attempt to control him, but pulling away is just the signal that sets off alarms for the woman who fears losing intimacy. Her attempts to get closer will aggravate his fear, and his reaction— pulling further away—will aggravate hers, and so on, in an ever-widening spiral. Understanding each other's styles, and the motives behind them, is a first move in breaking this destructive circuit," stated Deborah Tannen in *You Just Don't Understand: Women and Men in Conversation.*

Sometimes, I suspect that many arguments are caused not by two people disagreeing about a subject, but by two people who are on the same side of the fence but using two different vocabularies to fortify their positions. I know a couple who was trying to decide where to go on vacation. They had talked about going to China, a country the husband had always wanted to see. The wife, who also wanted to go, was nervous about the possible arduousness of the trip, so she said she wanted to talk to some friends of hers who had visited China before making the decision. She was ready to go, but wanted some reassurance. Her husband, fearing that she would decide against going, started questioning

"That women have been labeled *nags* may result from the interplay of men's and women's styles, whereby many women are inclined to do what is asked of them and many men are inclined to resist even the slightest hint that anyone, especially a woman, is telling them what to do. A woman will be inclined to repeat a request that doesn't get a response because she is convinced that her husband would do what she asks, if he only understood that she *really* wants him to do it. But a man who wants to avoid feeling that he is following orders may instinctively wait before doing what she asked, in order to imagine that he is doing it of his own free will. Nagging is the result, because each time she repeats the request, he again puts off fulfilling it."—Deborah Tannen, *You Just Don't Understand: Women and Men in Conversation*

her about her reservations. He translated her inde-cisiveness as an unwillingness to go and started arguing about her concerns, hoping to allay them. She interpreted this as his trying to push her into a decision before she got information that was important to her, so she entrenched herself further in her position of delay. Soon, they were having an argument as if he wanted to go and she wanted to stay home.

My wife, Gloria, is a novelist. Sometimes, she comes to me with problems that she's having with a plot. In trying to be helpful, I give her suggestions, but this seems to make her mad. She interprets my suggestions as attempts to show that I have all the answers. What she wants is my ear; she wants commiseration, not suggestions. I'm learning.

GLORIA'S PERSPECTIVE

"I think men who are used to being in charge—who have employees, give lectures, do consulting work—don't understand or have forgotten the difference between a conversation and a speech. This kind of style gives them a lot more control. Women can be control freaks too, but they will go about it differently. We learn to control by going around the circle; men control by going straight through to the center.

"Richard is the only person that I let read my manuscript before I send it to the publisher. He would never buy the kind of novels that I write—social satire. What I like about his response is he reads absolutely clear—with a fresh eye, like a smart child, without preconceptions. So his reactions are the best. I think when he focuses, he listens to ideas, he can really zap into an idea.

"But I may have been at work for 12 hours on something that is tortuously difficult and his first comment will be a punctuation error. Men give you the kind of input they would want. They don't understand the need for absolute reassurance. The easiest things for him to see first is what's wrong. He believes you don't make something better by what's right; you learn from what doesn't work;

you learn from failure. It's not very uplifting, but it works. In a way, maybe it's what we need more than what we want.

"The most common problem is he tends to feel that everything is his fault and it's his job to fix it. If you come to him with a complaint, he hears attack: 'If I was doing my job, this wouldn't have happened.' So, he tries to anticipate situations. This means that he sometimes hears things before you have said them.

"In a car together, I will say, 'We turn left at the corner,' and he says, 'No we don't, we turn left at the corner.' And I say, 'That's just what I said,' but it's not what he heard."—Gloria Nagy

The act of translation operates on many levels. Parents of young children commonly translate their own language into words they think will be more understandable to a youngster. An expert might see (although too often they don't) the need to explain an idea to a novice in nontechnical terms, such as when a doctor speaks to a patient, a lawyer to a client, a mechanic to a car owner. In these situations, the need for translation seems self-evident. But rarely do people working together recognize the need to translate their words when speaking to others, either above or below them in rank.

" 'How did you know how to do that?' he asks.

" 'You just have to figure it out.'

" 'I wouldn't know where to start,' he says.

" I think to myself, That's the problem, all right, where to start. To reach him you have to back up and back up, and the further back you go, the further back you see you have to go until what looked like a small problem of communication turns into a major philosophic inquiry."—Robert Pirsig, *Zen and the Art of Motorcycle Maintenance*

If words had universal meanings, translation would be unnecessary—and communicating would be a dull affair. The individual and idiosyncratic interpretation of words builds creative surprises and beguiling mystery into the process of communication. I wouldn't want to eliminate that, but some effort should be made to allow for it in situations where mystery and surprises are less desirable, such as in giving and taking instructions.

"Take a look at the difference in language used in men's magazines and women's magazines. Try rewriting the cover lines of *Cosmopolitan* magazine as they would appear in a men's magazine."

WHEN THE WOMEN'S MAGS SAY:	THE MEN'S MAGS SAY:
Orgasm ►	*Home Run*
Fiance ►	*Finance*
Powder my nose ►	*Shake the snake*
Breasts ►	*Too many to list*
Diet pills ►	*Steroids*
Foreplay ►	*Fore!*
Silicone ►	*Silicon*
Bath oil ►	*WD-40*
Carnations ►	*Car stereos*
Relationships ►	*Poker*

Lee Schreiber, "Counterespionage: What the Women's Magazines Are Saying About Us," *Men's Life* (Fall 1990)

> Smith, who had recently returned from a deep-sea fishing trip, was lunching with Jones at the club. Periodically, friends would pass by the table and Smith would recount in detail how he caught the giant blue marlin. Jones couldn't help but notice that Smith changed the size of the fish for each listener. Finally he asked Smith about the discrepancy and Smith replied, "But of course. You should never tell a man more than you think he will believe."

Successful translations result from the application of many skills—a sensitivity to different outlooks, a willingness to sacrifice literality for intent, and a keen ear that can detect misunderstandings. There are several tactics for improving our success as translators.

CONTEXT, CONTEXT, CONTEXT

One of the primary means of transcending the individual interpretation of words is context. Context is examined here in its first two levels of meaning— the *immediate environment* of a word or idea and the broader applications of it. Just as a doctor should look at the whole person rather than the symptom in diagnosing a disease, we must learn to look at the context of a word or idea rather than just the thing itself to decipher meaning.

Context enables people to understand things that would be incomprehensible alone. For example, proofreaders' marks wouldn't make much sense to someone who was unfamiliar with them.

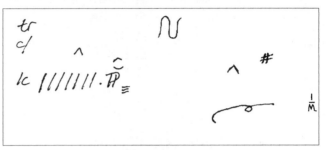

But if a novice saw them in the context of an edited page, he or she could probably figure out what they mean with little trouble.

tr One of the primmay means of
c/ transending the individual
    interpretation of wordsis *#*
lc context. context is examined here
    in its first two levels of meaning
    the immediate environement of a
    word or idea and the broader

What is the setting or environment of the word or idea? How can it be applied? Two people might define a word taken alone in different terms, but define it similarly when used in the context of a sentence. Sentences can determine meaning more than the individual words. Take the word *leak,* for example. If you had to apply one definition for it, you might say it meant fluid escaping accidentally from an object or container. The roof *leaks.* Then again, you might define it as deliberately passing information. The broker *leaked* information to his clients. You might mean *pissing,* as in, "I have to take a *leak.*" Seeing the word in the sentence sets its particular meaning.

The sentence can enable a person to understand a word that means nothing alone. Do you know what the word *estivate* means? What would your guess be if you saw it in this sentence: Bears hibernate in the winter; snails estivate in the summer.

estivate: (v.i.) To spend the summer in a dormant condition.

This can be applied to instructions. Telling someone to "turn right" doesn't mean much unless you have spelled out the direction the person should be going. Turning right can be the same as turning left, depending on whether you are coming from the north or the south. Telling a creative director to design a campaign for cereal doesn't give him or her enough information to make decisions about the job. Who is the target market? Where does the client want to advertise?

Lack of context is why tourists can't understand subway announcements. My cousins were visiting New York and decided to take the subway to the Lower East Side on a Sunday morning. At 42nd Street, they got on the F train, which according to the map was the correct train to go to Delancey Street. The train reached West Fourth Street, at which time a garbled voice came blaring over the public address system. They looked around at their fellow riders, most of whom were lying down on the seats covered with newspapers. A few of them perked up their ears, listened to the message, and got off the train. Others listened, shrugged their shoulders, and went back to sleep. Bewildered, they wondered why they seemed to be the only ones who didn't understand the message. They are both highly intelligent, articulate people, but they wound up at Atlantic Avenue in Brooklyn because they couldn't understand the conductor's message that the F train would be running on the C train track.

The other more seasoned riders didn't have to understand the whole message. All they had to hear was "C train track" before understanding that the F train was to be rerouted. But my cousins had no experience with the Metropolitan Transit Authority and its public address system. The message had no familiar context.

As an instruction-giver spells out the scope of the instruction, differences in interpretation should appear. Thus, paying attention to the context can be one way of insuring fewer mistakes in translation. You can begin to tell where the definition you use for a word diverges from another's definition of the same word when you can see it in an environment.

With our family and friends the chances are somewhat higher that we will be able to understand messages. Sharing a common background, familiarity, and the potential for repetition also increase the odds. But in the workplace, you may find yourself surrounded by people who persist in applying different meanings to your messages.

THE BIG PICTURE

You have to give the context. You have to give the connections you make in your own mind.

We all like to know toward what end we are working. When asking someone else to do something, make sure to tell them why they are being asked to do it. Whether it is a request to perform some simple task or a complex project, make sure the instruction-takers know the purpose. Make sure they know how the specific instruction will apply to the larger scope of their work. Sometimes I neglect to do this, thinking that I am saving time, but it usually winds up taking more time when work has to be redone. I asked one of my employees to bring me some of my stationery. I didn't tell her that I wanted to write a personal letter. She brought me some of the company stationery that has my name on it. All I would have had to do to avoid this was tell her that I wanted to write my brother and I wanted my personal stationery.

Most directions don't pay enough homage to the employees' need to understand where their contribution fits into the larger picture. The minimum information to complete a task isn't enough; neither is just giving the end product.

Without the big picture, the instruction-takers will be forced to imagine possible motivations that would color their work. For example, Madame X is appointed head of the customer service department of the Macro Microchip Company. She is a wizard with customer service, but before she got this job, she thought microchips were made by Nestle. She wants to learn about the product and the company as quickly as possible and she is reluctant to admit her ignorance, so she tells her staff that she would like to see all correspondence before it gets sent out. Given no other explanation, the staff sees this as the request of someone who doesn't trust them to do their jobs. They suspect she might be too controlling and tyrannical and they resent her. Had she told them that she was trying to familiarize herself with how the company works and thought that looking at correspondence would help, her staff might not only have cooperated, they might have volunteered other useful information.

Context allows us to extrapolate, to go beyond the information given. We remember things in patterns in our minds. This is why the smell of a particular perfume will bring up the image of a person. This is how we can recognize a caricaturist's sketch of a famous person from only a few lines. The shapes we see call up other shapes. This is why we have difficulty remembering completely new information.

I talked about context with John Sculley, chairman of Apple Computer, Inc. Apple has been a pioneer in the field of computers and in creating the instructions on how to operate them by placing them in the context of the computer.

JOHN SCULLEY ON THE IMPORTANCE OF CONTEXT

"I think a large part of my life was giving instructions in the context of a traditionally hierarchical experience where you didn't expect people to question your instructions, you only expected them to follow them, because they were told to, and that's no longer the way the world works. In fact, today, people will challenge any-thing they don't understand; they will fold their arms and do nothing if it doesn't excite them. That means that instructions have to have a

"The power of an odor to stimulate memory, familiar to anybody in whom a whiff of perfume or cologne has stirred thoughts of a long-lost lover, has proved itself in a research laboratory.

"College students who smelled chocolate during a word exercise and again the next day did better at remembering their answers than others denied the memory-evoking aroma....A follow-up experiment showed that the same odor must be present upon learning and testing to get a memory benefit. Chocolate and mothball odors worked equally well, suggesting that a smell's pleasantness does not affect its power to stimulate memory.

"The researcher, Frank Schab, said a memory strategy based on odor could help students study-ing for multiple exams or airline pilots training for emergencies."—"Memory: It Seems a Whiff of Chocolate Helps," *The New York Times* (7/10/90)

context that makes them interesting, understandable, and that motivates you to do something. Most instructions are still written in a very different model.

"The most important thing to me is that instructions have a context that becomes highly personalized; when I pick up a manual or get a request from someone verbally, it ought to be in a form that relates to something I care about and presented to me in a way that gets me, personally, involved with it.

"So the word *context* takes on a huge importance whereas I don't think that context was much of a priority in the past. People were more interested in delivering facts than they were in putting them into a context relevant to an individual person who was going to read it.

"If you just wanted to increase the productivity of instructions, the idea of giving them context is the highest priority and making them understandable, interesting, relevant, and inspiring becomes a lot more important than delivering facts."

Our reliance on context distinguishes man from the computer. It enables us to surmount the poor odds when it comes to word meanings, to supply the missing links in communication, and to make magic leaps from one idea to another.

Unless an instruction can be tied to an already established pattern in your mind, the chances of misinterpretation are almost 100 percent.

ABSTRACT TO CONCRETE

Translation errors can also be reduced by substituting concrete words instead of abstract ones to express ourselves.

We are constantly translating in our own minds from concrete facts to abstract principles, from specific observations to vague concepts, from hard fact to soft theory.

All language is an abstraction to some degree. Words only represent things or ideas; they are not the things themselves. A pie is only the name of a gustatory concoction that can be composed of numerous ingredients and can take numerous forms. Relatively, though, a pie is an easy abstraction to grasp. A roomful of people probably wouldn't argue too much about what constituted a pie. As words become more abstract, the margin for misinterpretation increases. At the other end of the abstraction spectrum is the word *happiness.* This word means something different to almost anyone who would define it and likely will encompass opposites. A roomful of people could spend an eternity trying to arrive at a common definition.

There is an inherent ambiguity in abstract words— an ambiguity that enables us to personalize language. However, in communicating instructions, you are trying to universalize a message or direction, so your chances of being understood will increase if you phrase your instructions with words that fall toward the concrete end of the communication continuum.

We tell kids to be more enthusiastic, work harder, be more careful. These are meaningless, vague concepts. Does *enthusiastic* mean you should smile more or jump up and down a lot? Does *working harder* mean working longer or just sweating more during the same period of time?

We also resort too often to negative abstractions, which are even more meaningless than positive abstractions. Studies have shown that very young children have trouble with negative concepts. When you tell them "Don't slam the door." They hear "Slam the door." Slam and door are familiar and well rooted in their minds; the concept of don't is not. Children understand negative messages more from intonation than meaning. (*See Chapter 6.*)

I think that these problems carry over into adulthood, and people continue to have problems interpreting negative instructions. Telling someone what they *should not* do doesn't necessarily narrow the field enough for them to know what they are *supposed* to do.

"We should have a great many fewer disputes in the world if words were taken for what they are, the signs of ideas only, and not for things themselves."—John Locke, *Essay on Human Understanding*

"Instructions can also be difficult to understand if they involve negation. File and Jew (1973) contrasted affirmative instructions describing in-flight emergency procedures with the corresponding negative information. They found that people recalled about 20 percent more information from affirmative instructions (such as *extinguish cigarettes, remove shoes*) than was remembered from the corresponding negative instructions (*do not leave cigarettes lighted, do not keep shoes on*)." —Dr. Patricia Wright, "The Instructions Clearly State...: Can't People Read?" *Applied Ergonomics* (9/81)

Sometimes, commercial buildings will have a sign on one of the doors: "Please use other door." Invariably, that's the one people try to use. The first word they see is *Please,* then they see *door,* and they go for it. If the sign said "Don't use this door," it might be more effective, at least with those sufficiently mature enough to understand the concept of *don't.*

Moses came down from the mountain and said to his people: "I have good news and I have bad news. The good news is that I got him down from 20 to 10. The bad news is the adultery one stays."—Famous agent joke

While it might be more challenging to communicate abstract ideas with concrete words, it is not impossible. In fact, you can almost always move your messages closer to the concrete.

You can almost always say the same thing with both abstract or concrete words. For example, you could tell employees not to be afraid to act on their own initiative. *Initiative* is frightfully vague. This could mean that you will allow them to work at home, to

chose their own projects, to make decisions without authorization, or to decorate their offices as they please. Any one of these instructions is bound to be interpreted more accurately than a direction to "act on your own initiative."

Without a suggestion of what you mean, most vague instructions are wasted. You can tell an employee you want him or her to do better work. But what do you mean by *better*? Better can encompass opposite behaviors. To you it might mean finishing projects in less time, turning in shorter reports, sending more memos, working more easily with other employees. To the employee, it might reasonably mean taking more time to do a task, turning in more detailed reports, sending fewer memos, and working more independently. Every instruction has to relate to the understanding of the taker.

Many people are oblivious to how dependent they are on abstract terms. Sometimes, just asking yourself if there is a more specific word to communicate your meaning will move your messages into a more universally understandable realm. Every word has either an abstract or concrete value. Happiness is abstract. A smile is concrete. Concrete words are less likely to be confused in translation. By substituting words with a higher concrete value, you will reduce some of the ambiguity of communications.

MAKING SURE YOUR MESSAGE IS GETTING THROUGH

To gauge your prowess at translating your communications, giving them in context, and expressing yourself in more concrete terms, you should begin to practice some of the following tests to confirm that you have made yourself clear.

First you must make sure your message has arrived intact to the appropriate destination and that it has been understood in the way that it was delivered. This is absolutely essential when giving instructions. The most elaborate manual isn't going to do much good if the postman loses it. A letter with instructions to your attorney has little value if the mailman delivers it to your doctor.

The easiest way to confirm that your message is understood is to ask the person to repeat your instruction. To ask, "Have I made myself clear?" is hardly enough. Most people wouldn't have the nerve to tell you that you make less sense than the Internal Revenue Service. Hearing your instructions gives you an idea what still needs to be translated.

Just because someone nods at you doesn't mean they have understood a message in the way it was intended. Not taking the time to determine this can have disasterous consequences.

DO WE ALL KNOW WHY WE ARE HERE?

"A murder trial at Manitoba in February 1978 was well advanced, when one juror revealed that he was completely deaf and did not have the remotest clue what was happening.

"The judge, Mr. Justice Solomon, asked him if he had heard any evidence at all and, when there was no reply, dismissed him.

"The excitement which this caused was only equalled when a second juror revealed that he spoke not a word of English. A fluent French speaker, he exhibited great surprise when told, after two days, that he was hearing a murder trial.

"The trial was abandoned when a third juror said that he suffered from both conditions, being simultaneously unversed in the English language and nearly as deaf as the first juror.

"The judge ordered a retrial."—Stephen Pile, *The Incomplete Book of Failures: The Official Handbook of the Not-Terribly-Good Club of Great Britain*

THE INNOCENT QUESTION

Questions are the best checks of understanding messages or instructions. They test for clarity and tell us if we are on the right track as bearers of instruction or as the receivers. Children are masters at spontaneous, incisive questions, and they use this effective tool for acquiring information. However, somewhere along the way of growing up, this inquisitiveness gets squashed—by parents, by teachers, by a growing self-consciousness that prompts us to be wary of appearing uninformed.

Physicist Isador Isaac Rabi, who won a Nobel prize for inventing a technique that permitted scientists to probe the structure of atoms and molecules in the 1930s, attributed his success to the way his mother used to greet him when he came home from school each day. "Did you ask any good questions today, Isaac?" she would say. "There are questions which illuminate, and there those that destroy. I was always taught to ask the first kind," said Rabi (Paraphrased from *Ideas and Information: Managing in a High-Tech World*).

Rabi was lucky. Most of us mere mortals were rewarded with a litany of discouragement when we embarked on question-asking missions. Do these phrases sound familiar: "Stop asking questions," "Damn it, just do it," "Shoot first, ask questions later," "Wait till I'm finished, then if you still have questions, i.e., if you're so dense you still don't understand..." These wholesale phrases designed only to make the lives of parents and teachers easier tend to repress the natural inquisitiveness associated with children—a repression that manifests itself in some peculiarly counterproductive behavior in adults.

Adults learn to use questions to show off their own acumen rather than to acquire information from others.

Almost everyone has attended a lecture, and no matter how provocative or inspiring the lecture was, invariably someone will rush the microphone to ask a question that is prompted solely by self-interest or self-importance instead of by any genuine curiosity or desire to learn more about the subject at hand.

NOT SO INNOCENT QUESTIONS

"Now when I was in the service..." Every question-and-answer period seems to bring out the audience's most narcissistic, egomaniacal tendencies at the expense of further developing the speaker's point.

Questions that are designed to elicit information or clarification of a problem are innocent questions that produce solutions. Questions that are designed to show off one's own erudition or prove someone else in error are destroyers of learning.

Preconceived ideas may inhibit the ability to follow instructions. In a study conducted in England by E. J. Robinson and M. J. Whitfield, respectively a psychologist and an epidemiologist, the researchers found that patients who asked their doctors original questions (that is questions that didn't relate to anything previously said by the doctor) had poorer recall of the doctor's advice than those who asked only clarification questions. The results showed that this phenomenon occurred no matter how the doctor responded to these spontaneous questions. The researchers theorized, "It could be that patients find it difficult to switch from presenting their views to receiving new information, and that those who choose to concentrate on the former perform relatively poorly at the latter." —"Contributions of Patients to General Practitioner Consultations in Relation to Their Understanding of Doctor's Instructions and Advice," *Social Science Medicine* (Vol. 27, No. 9, 1988)

The ability to ask questions borne out of original curiosity will serve one well in almost any circumstance—be it solving a problem, asking for directions, clarifying an assignment, or just having a conversation with a friend.

The person who asks the question usually learns more than the person who answers the question. If I ask you how old you are and you tell me 45, I have learned something. You knew you were 45 before I asked the question; you haven't learned anything.

106

34 *What if I am having a diagnostic test?*

If you need to be admitted to the hospital for a **diagnostic test**, it is probably an **invasive test** which means that the procedure **introduces tubes or probes into your body.** Because there is some risk involved, you will be required to sign a **consent form.** Again, know what you are signing and why. Be sure that the form is **only for the diagnostic procedure so that decisions concerning further surgery or treatment, if necessary, can be discussed with you.**

For example, if a woman has a breast biopsy and the doctor finds a larger tumor than expected, he or she should perform the biopsy only, not a radical mastectomy.

If you change your mind and no longer want to have a certain procedure performed, have the signed consent form returned to you.

35 *What is an arbitration agreement?*

You may be asked to sign an **arbitration agreement.** Under this system, any malpractice claim that you file against your doctor will be handled by an **arbitration panel** of 3 arbitrators, 1 chosen by you, 1 chosen by the physician and third chosen by the other 2 arbitrators, **rather than going to court.** The panel presides over a hearing which you attend with or without your lawyer, and which the physician and a representative attend. The panel then decides the verdict which is binding for you and your doctor. **You do not have to sign this form.**

Arbitration can save you court costs and a lengthy wait for a court date but may result in a lower settlement. Several states have approved arbitration for the medical field.

Make sure you fully understand the process before deciding to sign an arbitration agreement.

36 *After I fill out these forms, then what?*

A staff person in the admitting office will take information on your medical insurance, your personal and family medical history and other pertinent information about yourself.

It is best to make arrangements ahead of time, but if you have not, now is the time to ask about room types. If you smoke, or if you do not smoke and object to it, say so before you are assigned a roommate.

You will also receive an **identification bracelet** which has your name and the name of the attending physician on it. Never try to take it off. Generally, nurses are required to check your ID bracelet before giving you any medication. If you are having surgery, it is one of the ways that the nurses identify you in the recovery room.

You may receive a series of general tests, such as a **blood test, EKG** and **chest x-ray** and be asked to give a **urine sample.**

Once in your room, a nurse will record your **vital signs: blood pressure, pulse rate, respiration, temperature.** The nurse will take a more **detailed medical history.** Tell him or her about any **previous problems, allergies to food** or **drugs, reactions to drugs or doctor's restrictions,** particularly if the physician is not directly involved with the surgical procedure or hospital stay.

37 *What is my schedule during my stay?*

Hospitals start bustling early in the morning. If you do not have to be awakened early, and would like to sleep late, check with your nurse to see if this is possible. Otherwise, the hospital day goes something like this:

6:00-7:00am Nursing day shift arrives.

7:00-8:00am First surgeries of the day, and physician's rounds start. Blood samples taken, if necessary.

8:00am Breakfast.

8:00am-noon Morning baths, vital signs checked, treatments, exercises, beds changed.

Noon Lunch.

1:00-5:00pm Afternoon treatments and medications.

5:00-6:00pm Dinner.

6:00-8:00pm Evening visiting hours.

8:00-10:00pm Preparations for sleep: medications, instructions to patients if tests or surgery are to be performed the next day.

In most hospitals, you will **fill out a menu** each day for the next day's meals. You will have a choice of appetizers, main courses, side dishes such as vegetables, dessert and a beverage. Some hospitals serve better food than others, but you can usually have your advocate or companion bring in food from home or a restaurant if it does not conflict with any dietary restrictions.

38 *What are 7 things the anesthesiologist needs to know about my medical history?*

The **anesthesiologist** will interview you before your surgery in order to determine what type of anesthesia to use. He or she should ask you the following questions. If you feel any of these questions have been overlooked, offer the information.

1. Do you have any **allergies?**

2. Do you have any **medical problems** such as heart disease, diabetes or sickle cell anemia?

3. Are you **taking any medication?**

4. Have you had **anesthesia in the past?**

5. If so, **how recently?** Some anesthesia cannot be repeated until a specific amount of time has passed.

6. Have you ever had any **adverse reactions** to anesthesia in the past, such as high fever or vomiting?

7. Do you have a **history of severe bleeding?**

Page from *Medical Access,* by Richard Saul Wurman

In a good question is the answer and in the brilliant answer is the good question.

SECRET SOCIETY OF THE INSECURE

"Personally, I can think of no better head start to healthy use of technology than a well-developed habit of inquiry. For adults, this habit is hard to maintain, for while truly dumb people often live in blissful unawareness of the gaps in their understanding, most intelligent people secretly suspect that their personal gaps are large—far larger than the people around them realize. Competition in the workplace makes the expression of this ill-advised, so most of us try to hide this insecurity. In my experience, the attitudes that underlie this wasteful undercommunication between technical colleagues often carry over into interactions between technical people and the rest of society. If engineers and scientists fear a public display of their 'ignorance,' of course nontechnical people rarely question technical presentations enough to get the information they need.

"....What happens when such a secretly insecure person explains something to another with the same secret self-image (or, worse yet, to a group of them)? Since A has labeled what he understands as simple by self-definition, A can't insult B's intelligence by going into excessive detail. A's original estimate is reinforced by the obvious ease with which B appears to take in the material—nodding occasionally and never asking for additional clarification. Accordingly, A speeds things up even more, with no change whatever in B's demeanor. Off B goes at the end of the meeting, resolved to learn what A was transmitting during the exchange, wondering if A suspected his lack of understanding.

"....Many technical meetings are saved by those who feel free enough to ask questions. When a question is asked it's easy to spot at least half a dozen heads going up, others who would like to know the answer but couldn't ask for themselves."—Arno Penzias, *Ideas and Information: Managing in a High-Tech World*

This works as well in society at large. The art of asking questions can be applied to operating appliances as well. When you are trying to figure out how a new piece of equipment works, ask yourself why a function is accomplished in a certain way. Is there more than one way to do the same thing? What does "voice-hook up" mean on a fax machine? The more buttons you understand, the more comfortable you will be with the equipment.

Every project can benefit from innocent questions. Last year, I produced a road atlas to the United States. A year after moving to New York, I was convinced that you had to have a house in the Hamptons. After buying one, I realized I had to have a car to get there. We started taking more car trips, so I began buying atlases.

Most people thinking about doing an atlas might ask themselves, "What is the best way to do an atlas?" Maybe they would conduct a survey on how people like to see an atlas organized. Likely, the responses would be to list the states alphabetically, which is the way people are used to using an atlas. The "best way" question is already biased toward the production of an atlas. It's the question that was asked by all of the existing road atlases in which the states appear one to a page in alphabetical order, not necessarily in the same scale. That's definitely the most efficient way to keep track of material and produce an atlas. I wanted to ask the innocent questions. I wanted to do an atlas that was based on what people want to know about driving from one place to another.

I asked myself, How do people drive? Do people drive across the United States alphabetically? Are state or county boundaries an important issue in driving?

Of course, the answer to both is no. People drive from one point to another. Driving across state borders isn't a monumental event; people don't go through customs; borders aren't patrolled; and roads don't switch from gravel to macadam at state borders. We have a contiguous interstate road system. This suggested to me that a new organizing principle was in order. How could an atlas reflect the way people drive? What are the concerns of drivers?

Time and distance became the determinants of the *USAtlas*. At a reasonable pace, people can drive about 250 miles a day. I put a grid over the map of the United States and divided the country into 78 grids—each covering a 250-mile square and laid them out from the west coast to the east. In this way,

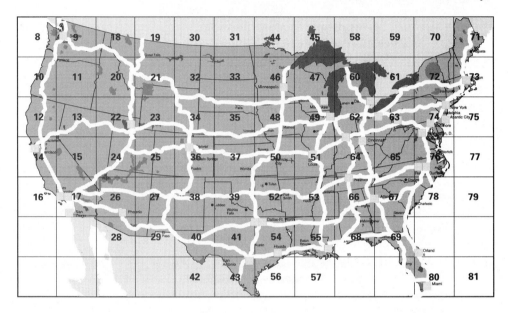

Table of Contents map from *USAtlas*, by Richard Saul Wurman

the atlas is laid out the way people drive—in geographical order, from one place to the next. You get an idea of the relative time and distance between places, of how far you can go in a day, and of what states you will be passing through. Over this square, I placed a 50-mile grid—about the distance you can drive in an hour. People also have to make decisions about whether to drive around or through major cities, so I added 42 maps of them shown in 25-mile squares. Eleven cities are shown in 5-mile squares for those who want to find specific streets in the downtown area. I made the page numbers larger because they are part of the instructions. I gave alternative ways of searching for information—the cover, the index, the table of contents, but most of all the maps themselves.

You can easily see the relationship between time and distance in the *USAtlas*. It is based on human needs and human behavior. The project all evolved from the simple question, "How do people drive?" Learning how to ask the innocent questions will enable you to understand less-than-ideal instructions.

BE CAREFUL, SOMEONE MIGHT HEAR YOU

However, asking the right questions isn't enough. You have to listen to the answers. When most people think of communications, they think of being able to convey their thoughts in a way that they will be understood by others. But, listening is actually an even bigger part of communication.

Executives spend an estimated 40 percent of their work day just listening. And the higher they rise, the more apt they are to find themselves engaged in this activity—going to meetings, counseling employees, interviewing colleagues, and gathering information.

> **"Listening is growing in stature through the ears."**
> —Anonymous

What in the world does listening have to do with giving instructions? Conscious listening is the most important tool for judging how well your instructions are being received. Even while you are giving instructions, you should be trying to assess whether your message is being understood or being received with wariness, reluctance, or irritation.

> **"To listen well is a second inheritance."**—Publilius Syrus

How many times have you cried out in conversation, *"Haven't you heard a word I've said?"* Nothing sabotages communication more successfully than someone who doesn't listen. Language aficionados often bemoan that no one knows how to talk anymore, but perhaps the real culprit is that no one knows how to listen.

> **"Most researchers suggest that the listening process consists of three sequential stages: hearing, attention, and understanding."**
> —Donald W. Caudill and Regina M. Donaldson, "Effective Listening Tips for Managers," *Administrative Management* (9/86)

We are a society that prizes the talkers, not the listeners, the positive space, not the negative. When we think about honing our communications skills, we think about expanding our vocabulary, speaking more articulately, and impressing those around us with our wit and intelligence. **But the most valuable communication, the negative, or listening component, is as essential as the positive or speaking component. You can't listen as long as you are talking.**

"Being a poor listener will stop you from advancing, from promotions, from growth. You can't really learn anything from yourself: you can only know it from other people, and in order to learn, you've got to listen," said Kenneth F. Thompson in an article by John Louis DiGaetani, "The Sperry Corporation and Listening: An Interview," in *Business Horizon* (3/82).

Most of the pauses in communication occur when the individuals involved stop to prepare their own response to a message—not solely to listen to the message. In fact, in conversation, how many times do you prepare your response to the other person while he or she is talking? This activity is hardly conducive to genuine listening.

According to Warren H. Reed in an article, "How Well Do You Listen?" in *Savvy* (1/86), the following are the most common listening barriers:

- Distractions: interruptions; cross-conversation; poor acoustics; noises and other voices within hearing distance; people moving around in a nearby room; incessant telephone-ringing; telephones answered within earshot.

- Trigger words: words, ideas, or phrases that provoke a negative response in you and sidetrack you from the main topic.

- Vocabulary: unfamiliarity with the speaker's use of language—may be specific words, phrasing, accents, etc.

- Listless or indifferent responses.

- Excessive note-taking.

"Anyone who has listened to conversations between frustrated people in ego-centric predicaments is amazed at how often each person ignores what the other is saying. For all the communication that takes place, the conversation sounds like two audio tapes made in advance of the meeting and played alternately."—Dr. Jard DeVille, "Communicating Your Recommendations," *Agency Sales Magazine* (1/87)

● Limited attention span: usually due to your lack of willingness to accept or understand new or unusual ideas and information.

A moment's pause of genuine listening in communication can provoke infinite understanding. It buys us the time to process information and to avoid jumping to conclusions or reacting emotionally to the communicator. Victor Dishy suggests that people put an imaginary drop of Elmer's Glue between their lips during conversations to improve their listening skills.

THE ELMER'S GLUE PRINCIPLE

"The drop-of-glue idea represents more than just being quiet: It reminds us to stop interfering, making assumptions, and jumping to conclusions.

"....By listening instead of talking, learning to absorb information not only with your ears but with all your senses, you will begin to perceive more of the world around you. You will expand your base of information. Being more attuned to others will make you more adept at communicating with them on their wavelength. In this way, you can start to sidestep much of the unhealthy friction cause by misunderstanding and miscommunicating with those around you.

"Remaining silent allows your perception-processing machinery time to consider whether you have all the pertinent facts. You can determine if the significance you are about to attribute to a situation is valid, if an action you are going to take is wise, and if you are on the right track in your approach.—Victor Dishy, *Inner Fitness*

Problems with language and with listening plague people throughout their lives. People can assimilate information only in manageable proportions relevant to their own capacity to understand. How many times have you stopped to ask directions to a hotel or restaurant and really paid attention to the entire response? Admit it, you stop listening the moment they point their finger, which was probably the first thing you could follow or as much as you could remember. Your inattention was due probably not to arrogance but to inability. The instructions you were getting were confusing, too complicated, or too elaborate relative to what you needed to know.

Unless you take into account how much someone can understand, your messages are meaningless. Language is a slippery, nebulous business. By translating your own language, delivering messages in context, and using concrete terms instead of abstract ones, you can shape your messages into understandable forms.

FOLLOW THE YELLOW BRICK ROAD: INSTRUCTION CONSTRUCTION 101

No matter what form the instruction takes or what kind of instruction it is, including these components will facilitate understanding by minimizing the general problems of communication and enabling the taker to visualize the instruction.

The components are:

- Mission
- Destination
- Procedure
- Time
- Anticipation
- Failure

After I first signed the contract to write this book, my editor, Tom Dyja, came to visit me at my office. He asked where the restroom was. I explained that "you walk out of the office, turn left, then make the first right turn." He walked right past the niche where the door to the restroom was located. So I had to call him back.

I didn't think this was a good sign for someone writing a book about instructions, so I tried to imagine where I had gone wrong in my directions. He was looking for a corridor, not a niche. I neglected to account for this by alerting him to the niche—giving him a point of reference from which to start.

Beyond improving communication skills, there is much you can do to improve the quality of specific instructions. With an awareness of the various parts that make up the content of an instruction, you can begin to build more structurally sound instructions.

You have to go back to the fundamentals. You can't build a tall building without understanding triangulation—that the structure stiffens and passes on stresses in a significant way. I don't think you can give or follow instructions without understanding the underlying structure. When your education starts, you learn the alphabet, then words, then sentences, then paragraphs. There is a progression. You can't miss a step and expect to get terrific results. The education system has missed out on a significant part of our communications.

We have neglected and even avoided the fundamentals. To me, our society is a lot like French cooking. The French appear to care much less about the essential ingredients and more about the sauce. We tend to focus on the dressings, the forms, the features of things, and not the essential thing.

Let's say you are sitting in a cave trying to plan a basic course in instruction construction. First you'd want to know what are the different kinds of instructions? How do they differ? What are the building blocks? Are the instructions for making a flint spear essentially the same as the instructions for operating a flour grinder?

"If you love instruction, you will be well instructed."
—Isocrates, *Ad Doemonicum*

You'd want to look at just the content of an instruction—independent of the other parts of the instruction system, independent of the channel in which it is delivered, the personality of the giver or the taker, the context in which it is set. In the cave, you'd want to know about the most essential component in the system—the content.

These are bread and water concerns. This is not about semantic translation of the Samoan language. It's not esoteric; it's not brain surgery. It's fundamental. Instructions are not an elective. (Except that I think all subjects should be electives.) It's pervasive, not esoteric. This book is trying to discover the obvious.

ALL GAUL IS DIVIDED INTO THREE PARTS

Despite the myriad different versions of instructions, there are roughly only 3 different types.

- Those that involve the *past* as in transfer of knowledge that occurs in school where students learn history, geography, biology, mathematics. Aside from memorization and regurgitation for tests, past-oriented instructions are usually passive; they don't require any immediate action. When you learn about the Battle of Waterloo, you won't have to fight it.

- Those that involve the *present,* such as operating and assembly instructions. "Push this button if you want to send a message." "Turn left at Route 66." Present-based instructions include those for all equipment instructions, as well as directions from one place to another, recipes, assembly manuals. These instructions demand immediate action.

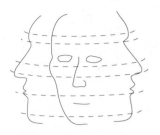

- Those that are *future-oriented.* This is the realm of interest in the workplace and in social relationships. When a boss instructs you to reduce spending in the marketing department, he or she is asking you to do something at some future point. It may be next week, next month, or next year. When a company president talks about corporate goals, he or she may be giving implicit instructions that will dictate future actions. The explicit and implicit instructions that we give to our friends and relatives also fall into this category, whether it be "Pick up a quart of ice-cream on your way home" or "I hate to dance," which carries the implicit instructions to "Stop suggesting that we go dancing."

"[Knowledge is] the small part of ignorance that we arrange and classify."
—Ambrose Bierce

"Directions for carrying our tasks often contain two qualitatively different kinds of information. The first might be termed *component step information,* the specific enumeration of the actions needed to perform the task. Another kind of information might be termed *organizational information,* information about the overall structure and organization of the task. Organizational information indicates how the component steps are related to each other and how they go together to accomplish the task at hand."—Peter Dixon, "The Processing of Organizational and Component Step Information in Written Directions," *Journal of Memory and Language* (Vol. 26, 1987)

Each of these can be oriented in a goal-based or a task-based manner. Goal-based instructions give the end product. Task-based instructions give the steps that will move you toward the goal. "Increase sales by 20 percent" is a goal-based instruction. "Schedule a meeting," "hire a consultant," "write a report," are task-based instructions.

Goal-based instructions tend to inspire imagination. They allow the taker to invent the tasks that might realize the goal.

In a task-based instruction, the goal is implicit, but the steps are spelled out. The goal can be played down, existing only as a implicit objective. In a fax manual, the goal is to make the user proficient with the technology, but what the user needs are the steps to make this possible.

Task-based instructions limit imagination by defining the path to the goal, but they also give necessary information. The information to be delivered should determine the orientation.

Depending on what you need to do, a goal-based instruction can be inspiring or frustrating; a task-based one can be helpful or humiliating.

Certain tasks call for certain instructions. If you are going to bake a cake, you probably want step-by-step instructions. You want to know that you should preheat the oven to 425 degrees and whether the butter should go in before the baking powder. You wouldn't be too happy to open your recipe book and find an instruction to "Combine tasty ingredients to bake a delicious cake," with only a photograph of the final product.

In other realms, step-by-step instructions can be stultifying. A photographer working for a client doesn't want to hear what f-stop and shutter speed he should use. He needs to have the goal. "Take a picture of this interior so that it shows off the built-in furniture."

Takers tend to respond to a goal-based instruction by developing their own mental plan composed of tasks that might be expected to accomplish the goal.

"Whether they are aware of it or not, most people began to make a mental plan to execute any instruction, breaking it down into a hierarchy of tasks. Let's look at a fairly simple task like changing a tire. At the top of the list is the goal, which is to have a working car. That means changing a flat tire. That can be broken down into: taking the old tire off of the car and putting the new one on. Within each of these tasks are more specific ones—jacking the car off the ground, unscrewing the lug nuts," said Peter Dixon, Jeremiah Faries, and Gareth Gabrys in an article, "The Role of Explicit Action Statements in Understanding and Using Written Directions," in *Journal of Memory and Language* (Vol. 27, 1988).

This plan hierarchy operates at more complex levels of accomplishments. When your boss tells you to tighten up spending in the advertising department, you begin to translate the goal into a plan based on performing certain tasks—reviewing current expenses, assessing the value of certain media, making plans to cut back spending. Then you might turn each one of these into a subgoal, from which you might develop more specific tasks.

The goals focus on states of being and the plans focus on actions that might produce these states.

If you are giving a goal-based instruction, keep in

**IF YOU WRITE OR USE
ERASERS AND DRIVE TO
WORK DAILY OR
SOMETIMES HAVE
HEADACHES...THEN READ
THIS...MAYBE**

Often instructions are
made confusing because
the conditions are
delivered before the actual
instruction and the taker
gets bogged down by ifs.
According to an article in
Simply Stated, a newsletter
published by the American
Institute for Research
(9/82), "Complex condi-
tional instructions are one
source of obscurity in
many public documents,
particularly in instructions,
forms, and regulations....
The example below is from
a form for people immi-
grating to the United
States. This instruction
would be difficult for even
native English speakers to
unravel:

"If you are the spouse or
unmarried minor child of a
person who has been
granted preference
classification by the
Immigration and
Naturalization Service or
has applied for preference
classification and you are
claiming the same
preference classification,
or if you are claiming special immigrant classi-
fication as the spouse or
unmarried child of a
minister of religion who has
been accorded or is
seeking classification as a
special immigrant, submit
the following."—(INS Form I-485)

mind that the taker will start to formulate a plan, so make sure that the overall goal is delivered up front.

Assuming that mental plans are constructed from the top down and that mental plans are formulated as the directions are being given, then "the comprehension of directions typically will be most efficient when the directions begin with the high-level information. If readers identify the information that begins a sentence as being relatively low-level information, they may either buffer that information (thereby giving up immediacy of interpretation) or incorporate the low-level information into their plan without benefit of high-level information that might be found later in the sentence," said Dixon, Faries, and Gabrys in the article.

In delivering instructions, you should keep in mind how you orient your own instructions. Task-based ones yield more uniform and predictable results (although this depends somewhat on their quality). As the margin for interpretation widens with goal-based instructions, so do the possible results. Often, instructions contain both goal-based and task-based messages.

Both goal-based and task-based instructions can be either implicit or explicit. "Get George Sherman on the phone for me" is explicit and task-based. "When you've got George Sherman on the phone, tell him that the meeting has been rescheduled" only *implies* an instruction to call him. It is the measure of explicitness that determines the clarity of an instruction, not whether it is goal- or task-based.

Goal-based instructions aren't bound by definition to be vague; they can be quite explicit. One of the most complete extensive examples of goal-based instructions are architectural drawings.

Architects work with ideas of space, color, materials, and joinings, and transform them into goal-based instructions. The working drawings don't tell the contractor how to dig a hole or make the concrete forms; they show him what the goal is—through the use of words, pictures, and numbers. Every element of the building is defined by size, shape, and material. The building is shown at different scales and from different vantage points—the section, plan, elevation, axonometric, and isometric. A full set of construction documents also includes specifications for measuring quality and spelling out how much stress particular elements should be expected to bear. Architects give their plans to craftsmen/carpenters who in turn develop more detailed instructions in the form of shop drawings outlining the specifications of how something will be built.

Contractors are then free to use their own knowledge and imagination on how the goal is to be accomplished, how the production should be staged, what the timing should be, how equipment should be brought to the site.

Architectural instructions are a model for all kinds of instructions. They define a goal, and then offer the components that will help people to realize it.

BUILDING BLOCKS

All instructions should be built with certain components—or structural members, to use the vocabulary of architecture—to enable the takers to use their own skills in following them. No matter what form the instruction takes or what kind of instruction it is, including these components will facilitate understanding by minimizing the general problems of communication and enabling the taker to visualize the instruction.

"Before beginning, prepare carefully."—Cicero, *De Officiis* Book I

The components are:

Mission

Destination

Procedure

Time

Anticipation

Failure

To define these components, I am going to use the example of instructions to go someplace because

**The rule of the road
is a paradox quite,**

In riding or driving along;

**If you go to the left,
you are sure to go right,**

**If you go to the right, you go
wrong.**

—Rule of thumb for driving in
Great Britain

**❶
MISSION
❷
DESTINATION
❸
PROCEDURE
❹
TIME
❺
ANTICIPATION
❻
FAILURE**

we've probably all had experiences where we gave instructions to someone else who promptly got lost trying to follow them or where we tried to follow someone else's directions, cursing all the way. The principles of geographic instructions work for all kinds of instructions, though.

Mission. The mission is the purpose or the aim of the instruction. What do you hope to accomplish? You want to invite someone to your home for dinner, so you extend an invitation and give them your address. The mission of the instruction may be to enjoy the company of that person, perhaps even to do business. Dinner at your house—how far you decide to go to accomplish your mission. The mission should be given first and it should be distinguished from the destination. In this way the takers know what to expect, they know why they are being asked to reach a destination. This sounds really simplistic, because in giving road directions, the mission is usually implied, but it's surprising how often the mission is left out of other instructions or confused with the destination.

The mission should inspire how the instruction-taker performs. In the crash of the Avianca jet liner (*See Chapter 2.*), the pilots didn't make it clear to the air-traffic controllers that the *mission* of their request to land was to avert a catastrophic situation (running out of fuel). The air-traffic controllers—assuming that all pilots have a safe landing as their mission—made them wait because of crowded skies. The controllers didn't recognize that the Avianca pilots had an emergency, special request.

Hearing the mission first will diminish the tendency of people to confuse the channel or form with the content, to become distracted by the forms and neglect the spirit of the instruction. Let's say that you own an advertising firm and are asked by a museum to publicize a new exhibit of beer steins. When you are instructing employees, tell them that their work should be focused on bringing people to the exhibit and insuring that their tour through it is pleasurable, instead of saying, "We have to design a poster or some advertising for a beer stein exhibit."

This already orients them toward a destination—the specific production of a poster or print ad. Maybe the best solution would be to send up hot-air balloons or produce radio ads or sponsor beer tastings. The mission or purpose could be accomplished in a variety of ways, so predisposing employees toward a particular destination will limit the imaginativeness of their solutions.

Destination. The destination is the end-result of your instruction—the point you have chosen to be the culmination of your instruction. If the mission is the intangible aim of your instruction, the

destination is the graspable objective of it. All instructions should have an end-result that is made clear when the instruction is given. If you were giving someone directions to your house, you would tell them the address—reaching that address is the destination. This defines the scope of the instruction and helps the taker make necessary decisions along the way.

Shad Northshield, a seasoned instructor as the senior executive producer of CBS News, stressed the importance of the destination or objective in empowering instruction-takers. "You don't tell people to do something unless you make it clear what it is you want to achieve. That takes into account their own creative facilities. Instruction-giving should be a kind of enlightened autocracy. Let them make an investment; out of that comes great respect and affection. When I ask an editor to do something, I'm dealing with a person who is very creative. At the same time, he is a technician. My instructions work best when they understand what I want and why. Often, they don't do what I suggested. Very often they do something better, but it still fulfills a need I had."

Procedure. This is the heart of the instructions, the actual directions toward which all the other components are oriented. "Drive three miles, then turn north. Take the Eisenhower Expressway for about 10 miles, then turn off at the first Oak Park exit..." The type of instruction influences the significance of the procedures. In a task-based instruction, all other components serve the procedures. In a goal-based instruction, they may only be suggested.

Time. The estimated time it will take to carry out an instruction should be built into an instruction, whether it be how to get to Grandma's house or how to load a communications program on a computer. This gives the follower an indication of possible errors and will lessen the investment in fruitless or misguided attempts. If you have an idea of the time an instruction will take, you reduce the anxiety of feeling like you are wasting your time on the wrong path.

You are in Los Angeles and some friends invite you over for dinner at their house in Santa Monica. They give you directions. They tell you to take the San

Diego Freeway and get off at the Santa Monica Freeway. If you have no idea how long you should drive before your exit, you could wind up in La Jolla before realizing you have overshot the mark (although your error might be somewhat tempered by southern California traffic). However, if your host tells you that the Santa Monica Freeway should appear after about 45 minutes of driving in moderate traffic and you have driven on the San Diego Freeway for 1 hour, you will be alerted to the fact that something may have gone wrong.

Unfamiliarity breeds anxiety. Most people are apprehensive about going someplace they've never been. My wife, Gloria, sits next to me in the car and asks, "Did you ask them how long before the Santa Monica Freeway? Did you bring their telephone number? Are you sure? Are you sure?" Of course I'm not sure, I've never been on this road in my life. How do I know whether I've gone too far? It drives me crazy, so the ride seems like it takes an hour. Then coming home seems so fast. It's because I don't have the anxiety of wondering how long the ride will take. You can never completely remove the anxiety of going to a place for the first time, but you can reduce it.

Of course, you have to keep in mind that familiarity alters time perception—especially in Los Angeles, where everyone will tell you that the drive takes 20 minutes no matter where you are going. Then it usually takes about three times as long, so the newcomer gets nervous.

Estimating the time a task takes also influences the importance an instruction-taker will give to a task. "Will you write a report on what happened at the meeting in the next half hour?" will be accorded less weight than "Write a report on the meeting and I want it in a week."

Anticipation. Anticipation is the reassuring element of instructions. This is what the taker can expect to encounter along the way of carrying out the instruction. Anticipation helps correct misperceptions in time and ill-defined goals. Knowing what you can expect to see along the way

"There is the issue of how Americans give directions. Let's say the basic directions to a location are as follows: 'Go straight for four blocks.' Here's how many Americans will give these directions: 'OK. You see this street? That you're on? OK, you just stay on it, and you just go straight, and, let's see, you're gonna come to a restaurant on your right, it's called Bud Looberman's House of Good Chewing, but the sign fell down, in 1981 I think, when the oven exploded and the Virginia baked ham came through the front wall, must have been going 200 miles an hour, and destroyed Eldorina Glandell's new Toyota Tercel and put her in a coma, which thank goodness she came out of fine except for sometmes when she makes that kind of barking sound. Anyway, you go right on PAST THAT. Then you come to...' And so on. So we should not be surpised that Americans are only dimly aware of where anything is."
—Dave Barry, "A Solution for Moscow: Turn It Into a Shopping Mall," *International Herald Tribune* (9/20/88)

reassures you that you are proceeding correctly. You should drive until you see the red brick church and take a right. When someone has told you that the drive will take 20 minutes and you drive for 30 before seeing the first landmark, you shouldn't panic about the time estimates.

Road instructions are usually good in the anticipation department. You will pass Sam's Feed Lot and when you get to Belly-Up Savings and Loan, turn left. Even electronic equipment manuals often tell you what to anticipate along the way. "If a red light flashes, then you have installed the battery correctly." The lack of anticipation is most often found in informal instructions. If you tell your secretary to "Get Snead on the phone for me," and neglect to tell her that Snead doesn't want to hear from you, she may give up with the first call. If she anticipates his reluctance, she might call again or try another route.

Failure. This is what is often missing from directions, yet is probably the most effective way of reducing frustration on the part of the follower. All directions should have in them the indications that you have gone too far, the warning lights to turn back. In other words, if you see a second Mobil station, you have gone too far.

> "At the University of Houston, Jack Matson runs a course the students have nicknamed Failure 101. They are encouraged to build the tallest structure possible out of ice-cream-bar sticks, then to look for 'the insight in every failure.' Those who end up with the highest projects went through the most failures. Whoever followed a fixed idea from the outset never finished first.'"—Jay Cocks, "Let's Get Crazy!" *Time* (6/11/90)

These components apply to all instructions. Most people are anxious about doing something they have never done before. If they are told how long the task is expected to take, they have some measure against which they can compare their own efforts, and they are more likely to realize when they may have taken a wrong turn and are investing too much time and effort going in the wrong direction.

The following conversation breaks down a simple dinner invitation into its instruction components.

Mission

"We'd love to see you and your wife."
(Implicit mission is to nurture friendship.)

Destination

"We'd like to invite you for dinner this Friday
night at 7 PM. Our address is 1015 Shady Lane."

Procedure

"Get on the Gloria Expressway. You will need to
get off at Exit 17, Normandy Drive. Turn right at
the stop light. Take Normandy Drive for about 2
miles until you come to Shady Lane. Turn left."

Time

"The whole drive should take about 35 minutes
in moderate traffic."

Anticipation

"You will spot Shady Lane because it's right after
the Shady Grove Water Tower and there is a
Burger Bonanza on the southeast corner of the
intersection. Our house is the third one on the
left. It's white, with blue shutters, and it's the only
one on the block with a circular drive."

Failure

"If you pass the Valhalla Shopping Center on
Normandy Drive, you have gone too far. Turn
around and take a right on Shady Lane."

The mapping metaphors extend beyond geographical directions. The same building blocks can be used to compose wildly diverse instructions: telling someone how to fly a kite, program a VCR, or develop a business plan. The following diagram breaks down the instructions for changing paper in a fax machine and assigning a task to an employee, illustrating how the same basic components are translated into different kinds of instructions.

Replacing paper in fax machine.	Instruction Component	Telling employee to make a phone call.
Communicating information.	Mission	Communicating information.
Changing paper.	Destination	Making appointment.
Press cover release button. Remove old roll (note direction). Install new roll with leading edge at top. Run edge under green line in front of the roller. Close cover.	Procedure	Call Johnson at his office. Tell him I want to meet for lunch on Friday at 12:30 at the Talman Grill.
This should take about 2 minutes.	Time	Try to reach him in the next hour.
The paper will automatically advance one cycle after the lid is closed.	Anticipation	If he wants to know why, tell him I want to discuss the new baseball guide.
If the paper doesn't advance automatically, check to make sure it was installled clockwise or is not jammed.	Failure	If you can't reach him, let me know.

SEQUENCE

Attention should be paid to the order in which the instruction content is given, for it will affect the order in which it is followed. You probably wouldn't give someone road directions in random order, but you might give an assistant instructions for the day without thinking about their order. This applies to the building of a particular instruction, as well as to offering several instructions at once.

Your directions will be understood more easily if they are given in sequence—the mission or purpose of the instruction, the desired destination, the procedure, the estimated time it should take, what can be anticipated along the way, and the signals that indicate mistakes or failure. Each step will add to the taker's ability to understand and make decisions about the next step. The mission will help the takers see how the destination was determined and maybe even inspire them to suggest other destinations that might accomplish the same mission. With an awareness of mission and destination, the takers can isolate procedures that don't make sense in light of the purpose and seek clarification.

GREAT EXPECTATIONS

In formulating an instruction mission and destination, you have to develop a sense of what you can expect from an instruction versus what is beyond the bounds of communication. How far can you reasonably go toward accomplishing your mission? Messages are limited by the understanding level of the giver and the taker, by the limits of communication, and by the limits of knowledge available.

> "While Michelangelo's work ['David'] *inspired* countless artists, he couldn't *instruct* others to create comparable masterpieces. Artistic genius still defies codification. On the other hand, once the first Western mathematician learned how to do long division, it was only a matter of time before that capability spread to every corner of Europe. After all, people can only instruct others in what they themselves know how to do at a conscious level, the explicit (as opposed to the intuitive) portions of human cognition. Explicit processes (like playing tic-tac-toe or doing long division) transfer easily from one person to another or from people to machines. Just write out the instructions. But how do you instruct someone (or some computer) to recognize caricatures in a magazine, let alone find a human figure in a misshapen piece of rock?"—Arno Penzias, *Ideas and Information: Managing in a High-Tech World*

The mission and the destination of the instruction prepare the taker for the procedure by giving a frame on which to organize them. They can either limit or expand the imagination of taker.

CLARITY VERSUS CONSTRAINT: RELATIVE AND ABSOLUTE MESSAGES

In the same way that words can be placed on a continuum from concrete to abstract, instructions can be plotted on a line from relative to absolute depending on their degree of specificity. The instruction "Let's get some light in here" could be interpreted to mean "Open the drapes," "Turn on all the lights," "Turn on a particular light," "Let's call in some experts to shed some light upon a subject." The performance of the instruction is highly relative to the taker's interpretation.

The range of possible interpretations increases as the instructions move toward the relative end. Depending on the task at hand, the width of the interpretation range can be either desirable or deadly. If you are trying to put together a futon bed, you need a high degree of specifics. You want to be told in no uncertain terms. If you are a competent salesperson, you might be insulted if a sales manager starts specifying how you talk to a potential client on the phone. A more relative instruction to "Increase sales" might be more effective, for it could inspire a variety of actions. On the other hand, a highly relative order to "Work harder" might not give you enough clues as to how the goal might be reached.

The chances for clarity increase as a message becomes more absolute, but so do the contraints. The search for the perfect instruction content requires finding the balance between clarity and constraint, between the relative and the absolute. There is magic in the ambiguity of the relative, but there is also confounding mystery.

You can spell out all of the details of what you want at the expense of stifling the imagination of your employees. You can also be so vague that they have no idea what you want.

> "I've a set of instructions at home which open up great realms for the improvement of technical writing. They begin, 'Assembly of Japanese bicycle require great peace of mind...'

"At first I laughed because of memories of bicycles I'd put together, and, of course, the unintended slur on Japanese manufacture. But there's a lot of wisdom in that statement....'Peace of mind isn't at all superficial, really,' I expound. '....What we call workability of the machine is just an objectification of this peace of mind. The ultimate test's always your own serenity. If you don't have this when you start and maintain it while you're working you're likely to build your personal problems right into the machine itself.' "—Robert Pirsig, *Zen and the Art of Motorcycle Maintenance*

The level of control and dependency varies among different types of instruction. Assembly instructions involve careful adherence to each step. A dictionary on the other hand is an instruction book for words, but it is not necessary to read it cover to cover.

I want people to feel a sense of propriety in their work, the freedom to create, to do things beyond my suggestions. I don't want someone to feel constrained by what I'm asking. I want them to go beyond, but not impinge upon, my vision. I define only the boundaries in which they can work.

Instructions should be like mental Sherpas, helping you to find your way, but not constraining what you see along the path.

The following are questions to ask yourself while composing the content of an instruction:

- Have you made it clear to the taker that you are giving an instruction?

- Have you explained the mission or the purpose for the instruction?

- Are you clear on the desired destination? What is it that you want to get done? Don't answer too quickly. It's easy to say, "I want a report on the return of merchandise." But maybe what you really want to know is how well our products compare to other products as far as returns go. Maybe you don't need a report, maybe a table or chart might better answer your questions.

● Have you identified the items to be covered by the instruction? Don't just tell someone to plan a meeting; include the ancillary instructions—who should be notified, what special considerations there are, what kind of record you want for the meeting.

● Have you ordered the instruction in such a way that the taker will understand the sequence in which it should be carried out? What are the most critical aspects of it? What could be ignored if time and resources are constrained?

● Have you included what the taker might anticipate finding as he or she performs the instruction?

● Have you allowed for failure? Takers need to know the signs that they have gone astray in following the instruction. The sooner they understand the mistakes, the sooner they can correct them.

THE TREASURE HUNT APPROACH

The instruction-giver should also account for what happens after the instruction has been delivered by building in ways that compliance can be monitored. The giver's responsibility is to follow the stages of action and specify at what points the takers should report their progress.

They must let the takers know that they are available for clarification and for reassurance. When you go on a treasure hunt, you are given a first clue or instruction. When you solve the first clue, you get an affirmation. "You did a great job. Now you can proceed with step two." Most instructions don't give you this kind of encouragement along the way.

No one pats you on the back and tells you, "You're going to fall off the bike a number of times before you learn how to ride it, so learn to fall without hurting yourself." Instruction reassurance makes you comfortable; you know that the failures are necessary. It gives you a sense of humanity in sharing the burdens.

Reassurance should be an aspect of every instruction. Instructions to perform a task or find a place can be constructed with affirmations along the way. "When you go under the turnpike, you are halfway there; when the screen says *Transmit,* the fax is being sent." Any kind of instruction will benefit from this approach. Let the instruction-takers know that they are on the right course and they will pursue the task or goal with more joy and diligence.

The anxiety of feeling that you are on the wrong track can be alleviated, if not eliminated, by getting a pat on the back as you reach points in the process.

SURROGATE FINGERS

An image to think about when you envision the components of an instruction is the pointed finger. Each component should lead you to a specific place along the path to comprehension. When you ask someone how to get to someplace and they point their finger, that is an unmistakable direction. When someone is describing a place to you and they point to it on a map, you know exactly what they mean. There is nothing better than a finger for pointing out people and locations, for identifying, for stressing a point. In a written text, highlighted paragraphs, bold type, arrows, etc., all act like fingers to point the way. Instructions should be like surrogate fingers. They should offer the security of being able to have a point clarified, to have something repeated, to know that there is somewhere to turn for more information.

I've been doing consulting work for the American Association of Retired Persons. I found that 85 percent of their phone calls have to do with three or four subjects—availability of senior citizens' discount on a particular product or service, renewals or inquiries about membership, requests for health insurance information, and questions about social security. So we put this information on one page that says, "Here is what you probably want to know." You don't have to wade through a lot of complicated instructions about what you don't need at the moment. People want assurance that there's somewhere to go for basic information about their concerns—be it a person, a manual, or a technical support department—to point them in the right direction, solve their problems, and encourage them along the way.

The time spent crafting an instruction will be compensated for by takers who can follow it with more ease, make fewer mistakes, work faster, and perhaps follow your instructions beyond your own ability and imagination.

Unfortunately, instruction-givers too often direct their focus on choosing the channel of an instruction instead of building the content. The content of an instruction should determine the channel.

RIGHT OF WAYS

"The simplest explanation is not always the right one, truth is very often not simple."

Sigmund Freud, *New Introductory Lectures on Psycho-Analysis*

I know a man who taught his son to tie his shoe in five minutes. He tied the shoe-lace into a bow, then untied it one step at a time. He taught his son by doing it backwards.

His son instantly grasped the relationship of each step to the tied bow. He showed his son the goal (the bow), then showed him the steps leading up to the goal.

I learned how a piano is put together by taking one apart. If I had to put one together from the parts, I wouldn't know where to start, but after I had disassembled one, I could put it back together.

I used to operate under the notion that people are basically the same and that there was always a "best way" to communicate information to be understandable to most people. I thought if I could just formulate an instruction in the perfect form, if I could find the right words and pictures, and make sure that the context was appropriate, I could come up with the best solution. But that implies an arrogance, as well as an ignorance, of communications. This implies that understanding is a specific point. Understanding is a path, not a point. It's a path of connections between thought and thought; patterns over patterns. The essence of leaps of understanding relates to connections. Understanding is not about simplification and minimalization; it's about organization and clarification. It is about seeing relationships.

LIMITED MANNERS

"It is always with the best intentions that the worst work is done."—Oscar Wilde

After constructing the content of an instruction, you must choose the channel in which to present it. This means choosing both the form and the dressing of it.

While technically the choice of channel shouldn't alter the message itself, the way instruction-takers will respond to it will be influenced by the form and dressing in which it is delivered. They will influence how the instructions are treated and will influence the taker's performance. An imposing 8-inch-thick manual will lead a taker to the assumption that he or she is dealing with a complex or difficult subject. A professionally printed document might be accorded more respect than a note scribbled on the back of a bar napkin—even if the content suggested otherwise.

The trouble is people rarely distinguish the choice of channel from the message itself. Confusing the content with the forms makes all of the choices more difficult.

While the choices of dressing or materials are infinite, you have only two choices of form: words and pictures. (Numbers can be a subset of either category depending on whether they are spelled out or in numeric form.) Of course, these can be used together. That brings the total number of combinations to three.

The choices are limited, but they are not simple. There has been little conclusive evidence as to the superiority of words versus pictures or symbols in communicating different kinds of information. Information and instruction designers have set forth various theories, but usually they are *ad hoc*, specific to certain fields, such as computer documentation or traffic signage.

I DIDN'T READ THE BOOK BUT I SAW THE MOVIE: WORDS VERSUS PICTURES

Debating the superiority of words versus pictures to communicate information has provided ample fodder for behavioral scientists, who sometimes arrive at contradictory conclusions. It's hard to measure whether pictures are better than words, because it's next to impossible to formulate a word instruction that is identical to a pictorial one—a comparison essential to a valid measuring of comprehensibility.

New computers programs can reproduce your handwriting when you want a more personal look. You simply type onto a keyboard and your own handwriting appears on the screen.

"Perfection of means and confusion of goals seem, in my opinion, to characterize our age."—Albert Einstein

Pictures are rising in stature as means of communicating, perhaps because TV babies have grown up to expect images to tell the story. Newspapers use more charts and graphs; advertisers fewer words and more images, and movie scripts have more action and less diaglogue than they did in the 1940s and 50s.

"The pre-TV adults are the one-thing-at-a-time generation. **They read a magazine article straight through from beginning to end; then they make a phone call or watch TV. The TV babies, by contrast, seem to be happy processing information from different sources almost simultaneously. They really can do their home-work, watch TV, talk on phone, and listen to the radio all at the same time. It's as if information from each source finds its way to a different cluster of thoughts."**—Robert W. Pittman, "We're Talking the Wrong Language to TV Babies," *The New York Times* (1/24/90)

There is some consensus that pictures about concrete objects and events are understood more quickly, while words are favored when depth and clarity of comprehension are demanded, such as communicating abstract ideas. But this isn't enough to decide between the two.

A rule that could be applied to information in general just doesn't exist. What has come through in many studies is that combinations of pictures and words are more effective than either alone.

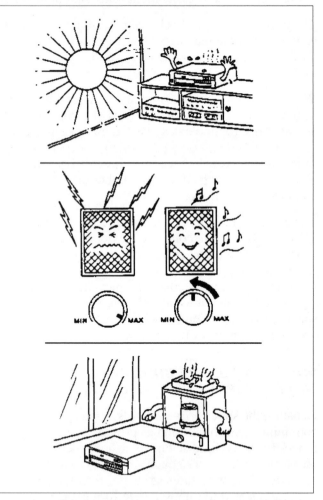

Sometimes pictures can't stand alone. These might benefit from some verbal assistance. Adapted from a pictures-only portion of the owner's manual for a TEAC PD-700M Compact Disc Multi Player.

One such example is a study of the comprehensibility of procedural instructions that was conducted with Navy personnel. Harold R. Booher discussed the study in an article, "Relative Comprehensibility of Pictorial Information and Printed Words in Proceduralized Instructions," in *Human Factors* (Vol. 17, No. 3, 1975). It investigated "the importance of multiple channels, redundancy of information between channels, and type of information in channels." Subjects were given 6 picture-word formats to solve 24 problems that encompassed 3 different kinds of tasks. "The results showed pictorial information important for speed but print information necessary for accuracy." The comprehension of instructions on all three tasks was most efficient with combinations of print and pictures.

An experiment conducted by Christopher K. Riesbeck of Yale University measured the effectiveness of directions showing how to go from one place to another. After receiving printed directions to a post office in San Diego, people were asked to reconstruct the layout of the corner where they were directed to turn. The layouts varied. Riesbeck concluded that:

❶ "Natural language is not very good at describing even fairly simple layouts.

❷ "People will use specific knowledge that they have, even to the point of rejecting what they are told.

❸ "People perceived ambiguities in the description and invented resolutions of them only when asked to draw a picture of the layout and not when they were told just to read over the directions and see if they seemed all right."—"You Can't Miss It?: Judging the Clarity of Directions," *Cognitive Science* (Vol. 4, 1980)

As long as the superiority between words and pictures can't be determined, it makes sense to use both, where applicable, when communicating information.

In a world increasingly dependent on visual communication—graphs, charts, tables, icons, etc.— the subject has been neglected sorely by the school system. Children are taught art and design as free play, not as a basis for the communication of information and ideas.

CHOOSING THE DRESS

After the form or forms have been chosen, the next step is to determine how the instructions should be dressed. Should they be given privately or publicly? Should they be on paper or on film? Do you need a conference, a casual chat, a memo, or a formal manual? The content and form of the message should be the determinants.

"There is nothing so useless as doing efficiently that which should not be done at all."—Peter Drucker

Poor choices result when people choose the dressing before they have decided upon the content. I tell people that if they have an hour to do something, they should spend 58 minutes deciding what they want to do and only 2 minutes deciding how they want to do it. I bet most people operate closer to the opposite. People who develop annual reports seem to be more concerned with the way (or the how) the information is presented rather than asking themselves what it is they want to present.

A simple instruction to "Turn on the phone machine" hardly needs to be delivered in a formal memorandum. A complex instruction that the follower may need to refer to often will dictate a written form. Certain instructions are better communicated one-to-one. Let's say you suspect that one of your vice presidents is carrying on a torrid affair with one of your competitors and may be leaking company secrets in the throes of passion. You wouldn't send a memorandum to the entire company instructing them to report to you any evidence of this. You would quietly instruct a trusted employee to keep his or her ears open.

If you want specific figures on the sales of Chevrolets in the last 10 years, perhaps a memo outlining just what you want is appropriate. If you are trying to instruct a difficult employee in the ways of getting along with people, a face-to-face private meeting would be in order. If you want to launch a new product, mentioning it to someone around the water cooler would be inappropriate. The mode and the personalities involved should be considered.

Remember, the manner in which an instruction is presented will influence the taker's perception of its importance and will figure in how well it is followed. The giver needs to be aware of these perceptions and make the choice of channels accordingly.

To search for the perfect channel for an instruction is pointless. There is no such thing. The way to instruct people is to offer a variety of forms. The perfect instruction manual is perfect only if the reader thinks in the same patterns as its writer. To someone who needs to be told how to operate something, a clear, easy-to-read manual is just one more dust-gatherer.

> **"While few modern builders would attempt even a small chicken coop without first doing a few calculations, the creators of Notre Dame could barely multiply two small numbers together, and had no means of doing long division."**—Arno Penzias, *Ideas and Information: Managing in a High-Tech World*

DO THE RIGHT THING

The same instructions mean different things to different people. The best we can do is try to match up the manner of instruction to the manner of the taker. Variations in technique shouldn't be just acceptable, they should be mandatory. Variations can be programmed into instructions—both formal and informal. Computer documentation can be offered on-line and on paper. It can be created with up-front directions, such as "Experts can turn to page 75; novices should read chapters 1 and 2." In informal settings, instruction-givers can offer the -takers a choice, "Can I tell you about the article assignment or would you rather I wrote it down?"

When I was asked to redesign the Pacific Bell Yellow Pages, my work was prompted out of the desire to give people alternative ways of searching for things. Most phone books include only an alphabetical listing. You have to know that auto insurance is found under the category of "Insurance." (Less than half of the listings that pertain to cars are listed under "Automobiles.") My office went through the phone book and came up with categories under which the specific listings could be grouped. Now people can look under "Automobiles" and find all of the listings that have to do with their cars.

Clients come to me and say: "We want to find the best way to do this manual or directory or publication." It's not an acceptable defense to say, "I did the right thing." That might not be enough. There can be many ways to do something. If someone gave you directions for the scenic route between two locations and you were driving a Mack truck and weren't allowed on the roads, it wouldn't matter how good the directions were.

"In politics, religion, and even in elephant identification, what we proclaim is a manifestation of where we stand and what we perceive. So it is with training....[This] point was dramatically demonstrated at a Dallas American Society for Training and Development (ASTD) national conference during a session entitled, 'Needs Analysis: What's the Best Way to Make Tomato Soup?' As the participants in the packed room laboured through a series of group activities, they discovered there was no best way to approach needs analysis, only many good ways, depending on perspective. Unfortunately *correct* turns into *right* and dividing lines get drawn. Ensuing camps create rules, absolutes, and dogmatism, all the while forgetting that their stance began with a point of perspective."—Chip R. Bell and Fredric H. Margolis, "The Practice of Training: A Matter of Perspective," *Journal of Management Development* (Vol. 8, No. 1, 1989)

If you want to go from San Francisco to New York, you can go many different ways. You can plan your trip to take the least time, see the most historic sites, follow the back roads, take only interstate highways, go on truck routes, or have the best scenery. Or you can make combinations—the fastest trip with the best scenery.

All roads might lead to Rome, but each one would make for a different trip.

Everybody needs a different level of information. Many people want only to play movies on their VCRs. Some manufacturers make a model that does only this for less than $100. The people who

purchase it don't feel guilty about not using all the features. Most of us live lives loaded with features and abilities we can't use. VCRs can now be set to record programs two years in advance, but you can have trouble finding out what's going to be on television next month. I have never programmed a song on my CD player. I know that it can be done. I could play the third song on a CD twelve times or play only the odd number cuts. Even if I knew how to do this, I probably wouldn't.

Everyone wants to know about a machine at a different level. I don't care about the internal workings of my fax machine. I don't need to know how or why it operates. I just want to know how to turn it on, send a fax, and change the paper roll. I

For those who don't want to know what goes on in their VCR, there's a product called VCRPlus that enables you to record programs by punching in code numbers printed next to every show in television program guides. Of course, you have to figure out how to read the guides.

don't want to know how to build a fax machine. Someone else might want to know what goes on inside the machine.

We are taught that there is a single way of learning—wholesale memorization, whether you are interested or not. So students just regurgitate the information on a piece of paper called a test and soon forget it. Fortunately, there are alternatives; there are even opposites, such as empowering yourself to learn, making your own choices based on your own interests.

DOGMATIC REITERATION

The trouble with most instructions is that they are presented as if there is only one way to put anything together or only one way to operate any piece of equipment, and people become obsessed with finding this "right way." There are often many ways to follow and to give instructions, depending on your preference for learning. There is no one right way or best way.

Instructions have to allow for different needs and different levels of explanations.

There's a lot of different ways to say the same thing. Some people like to get their explanations verbally, others like to read them, others like to learn by example.

It's okay to be redundant. To insist that it's not is a defensive posture. We have a perfectly good manual. It's all there if you'll just look for it. The phrase that should run through your mind is "in other words." When you experience some frustration at not being able to communicate an idea to someone else, don't stubbornly repeat yourself in a voice that gets louder and rises in pitch. Instead, try to communicate the same idea in a different way. Use different words and try to say the same thing. Perhaps the new set of words will mean more to the receiver.

"What's really angering about instructions of this sort is that they imply there's only one way to put this rotisserie together—their way. And that presumption wipes out all the creativity. Actually there are hundreds of ways to put the rotisserie together and when they make you follow just one way without showing you the overall problem the instructions become hard to follow in such a way as not to make mistakes. You lose feeling for the work.

"....Technology presumes there's just one right way to do things and there never is. And when you presume there's just one right way to do things, of course the instructions begin and end exclusively with the rotisserie. But if you have to choose among an infinite number of ways to put it together then the relation of the machine to you, and the relation of the machine and you to the rest of the world, has to be considered, because the selection from among many choices, the *art* of the work, is just as dependent upon your own mind and spirit as it is upon the material of the machine. That's why you need the peace of mind.

"....This divorce of art from technology is completely unnatural. It's just that it's gone on so long you have to be an archeologist to find out where the two separated. Rotisserie assembly is actually a long-lost branch of sculpture, so divorced from its roots by centuries of intellectual wrong turns that just to associate the two sounds ludicrous."—Robert Pirsig, *Zen and the Art of Motorcycle Maintenance*

In reality, there are many ways. You can put together a futon couch without setting all the screws and dowels out on the floor in the recommended pattern. You can fasten the arms to leg pieces first, the back to the seat, the seating unit to the arms. And not only are there many ways to put something together, but the instructions you have may not even be the best way. The person who gets stuck writing the instructions may be the most brilliant mind in the company, but he or she could also be some third-rate engineer who couldn't cut the mustard. And independent of his or her capabilities, the instructions are bound to be biased by that person's experience.

Money magazine asked 50 tax preparers to do a sample tax return for a hypothetical family of 4 and got 50 different answers. According to an article by Denise M. Topolnicki, "The Pros Flub our Third Annual Tax-Return Test" (3/90), only 2 came back without errors, and even those arrived at different conclusions. The preparers included certified public accountants, store-front chains such as H&R Block, and enrolled agents who take IRS-administered examinations. The amount of tax estimated by the preparers ranged from about $9,800 to $21,200 and the fees they would have charged ranged from $271 to $4,000.

> "The right answer, says *Money:* $12,038. 'When they say correct, they mean correct by their interpretation,' says Don Skadden, vice-president of taxation of the American Institute of CPAs. 'There may be 15 other equally correct solutions.' *Money* admits the return wasn't simple. It involved 23 tax forms and such intricacies as self-employment income, rental property and income from limited partnerships." —Harriet Brackey, "A Taxing Test," *USA Today* (2/23/90)

The point is not to simplify, but to clarify.

There is room for redundancy. In fact, if you think about offering a variety of instructions, your chances of being understood and having your instructions followed will increase. This works whether or not you are giving or receiving them.

AGE OF ALSO

We are a culture obsessed with absolutes—a phenomenon manifest in many different areas. Who is the best and the brightest? Who is the fastest? Who are the 400 richest? What are the top 10? These distinctions may make for amusing magazine covers, but they have little to do with the way we live. We live in an age of alsos.

Each new technology that comes along is touted as the best that will replace the rest, but most predictions haven't come to pass, and each technology

"I don't believe less is more. I believe that more is more. I believe that less is less, fat fat, thin thin, and enough is enough."—Stanley Elkin

"In laboring to be brief, I become obscure."—Horace, *Ars Poetica*

"Newness does not equate with utility, and simplicity is, more often than not, at odds with credibility."—Jay Hall, president, Teleometrics International

seems to get added to the rest. The computer was supposed to make paper obsolete, but it has done just the opposite. Computers have been a bigger boon to the paper business than the Gutenberg press. The ability of computer printers to crank out paper and copiers to copy has us all drowning in it.

Prediction: Computers to result in the "paperless office."
Reality: Paper-handling has become a number-one office problem.

We live with alternative versions, ersatz and originals, all in multiple copies. Personalized news services will not replace newspapers and magazines. Scanning articles isn't the same as flipping through a newspaper or magazine. With a service, you can't tear out an article, nor happen upon the article you didn't know you were looking for. And you can't cover as much territory as quickly as you can with the real newspaper or magazine. Many have claimed that newspapers are dead. But they are still the cheapest, most efficient way to get in-depth news on a daily basis.

Prediction: Television and now home videos will be the death of the movie industry.
Reality: More films are being produced than ever before and are making more money.

Prediction: Faxes will take the place of phone calls.
Reality: Many people now make a phone call just to tell someone they are going to send a fax. Then they call again to find out if the person has received it.

In much the same way that each alternative provides its own particular benefits, each way of giving an instruction can serve to clarify the goal. A picture can illuminate a written instruction, just as words can make a picture comprehensible.

Let's say you were putting out mouse traps and had only this drawing:

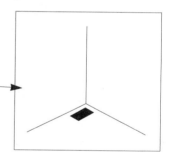

Most people would have a hard time figuring out where they were supposed to put the traps. The sentence "Place in the corner of a room" would make the drawing clear.

While many things depend on following instructions exactly, the instructions themselves still can be presented in a variety of ways. If you are trying to make *pommes soufflées*, you have to slice the potatoes with a mandolin for an exact thickness, then fry them for exactly 45 minutes in oil that is exactly 350 degrees Farenheit, then fry them again for two minutes in clean oil heated to exactly 380 degrees. Only then will the potato slices puff out into the round shape that inspired their name. (Recipe is from *La Varenne Practique*.)

"The USA Today weather map says that tomorrow will be yellow with a touch of red in the Northeast."
—Frank Romano

But the recipe could be composed of pictures instead of directions; it could be on audio or video tape. It

could describe what happens if the oil isn't hot enough or what happens if the potatoes aren't cooked long enough.

Hodding Carter IV, a staff writer at *M inc.* magazine and authority on okra, created a new format for recipes in the following article. Instead of listing cooking times in minutes, he gives them in music selections. The instructions are just as specific, but must certainly add to the experience of cooking the dish.

ALTERNATIVE RECIPES: "A MAN AND HIS VEGETABLE"

"Buy seven pounds of okra (one pound for making a poultice, five for pickling, and one for cooking gumbo), return home, and wash the whole lot. Put on some Cajun fiddle music and move every part of your body. Then begin your poultice.

"Okra has a long tradition as an anti-inflammatory agent, and seven pounds of the slimy stuff is bound to cause some slipping and sliding, which inevitably leads to bruises and burns. Chop up a pound and simmer in three quarts of water. Throw in some elm or white bark if you happen to have any lying around.

"In a large pot, sterilize some jars. (Look in *The Joy of Cooking.* No room to explain it here.) You need them for pickling. On another burner, make a brine of white vinegar and water at a three-to-one ratio, respectively. Add two teaspons of pickling salt for each pint of brine, and turn the burner off as soon as the brine begins to boil. Then fill the jars with the five pounds of okra, fresh chili peppers, sprigs of dill, pearl onions, sliced celery, garlic cloves, and peppercorns....

"Finally, begin your gumbo. Cut the remaining pound of okra into quarter-inch rounds. In a large soup pot, stir one half cup of flour into three quarters of a cup of olive oil and cook over low heat until it begins to brown. Throw in the okra, two chopped onions, five stalks of celery, and season with one tablespoon of cayenne pepper, five cloves of minced garlic, and salt.

"While this is cooking on extremely low heat with a closed lid, put the Neville Brothers album *Live at Tipitina's, New Orleans, Louisiana* on your turntable, but start with the second side. Stop dancing from time to time, lift the lid, and quickly stir the simmering concoction. After nearly an hour, when 'Why You Wanna Hurt My Heart' drums to an end (last song, first side) and you hear the crowd at Tipitina's whistling and whooping, you've made a gumbo roux. It should look like mush.

"To this pasty roux add two quarts of chicken stock and three quarts of water. Pour in a lot of hot sauce (at least three tablespoons of Tabasco, Crystal, Panola, or Trappey's—all from Louisiana), four tablespoons of Lea & Perrins, and salt and black pepper. (There ain't no such thing as a mild gumbo in the middle of the winter.) Toss in two or three halved blue-claw crabs, three bay leaves, and three large, sliced tomatoes. Simmer three to four hours, lidless, adding a pound of kielbasa in the last hour. Somewhere after the first two hours, okra's viscous powers will have taken effect, and your runny soup will be transformed into a thick, cohesive gumbo.

"Five minutes before you plan to eat, add a pound of peeled medium shrimp and two pints of oysters. Serve in bowls over rice to twelve people."—Hodding Carter IV, *Esquire* (2/90)

A more industrial example of variety of instruction was constructed by Textron Aerostructures, which manufactures parts for both military and commercial aircraft. Textron developed an on-line computer program called "Product Integrity Instructions (PII)." The program uses bar codes to provide detailed explanations and graphics as an addition to the existing work instructions.

Existing work instructions may state: "Drill (40) each 1/16 holes, from Station X to Station Y at

WBLZ per engineering drawing." On the planning paper, an employee finds a bar code and by simply scanning it, the PIL program displays a picture showing the exact hole locations, the tool required, the stock number for the drill, how the part or parts locate the tool, any hole reamers required, and every other step necessary to build the product. "Every step is detailed so that questions and the potential for errors are virtually eliminated," said Gary L. Smith, vice president of production operations and plant manager.

The demand for details is high in a company whose product line includes missile case assemblies, tailbooms, intertank structures for NASA's Space Shuttle Program, and structural assemblies for the U.S. Air Force's airlifter fleet, as well as parts for commercial aircraft. The benefits of the program range from fewer defects in the products to increased productivity. Textron pioneered the concept, which has already attracted the attention of other aerospace manufacturers.

The applications of such a program are infinite. In this way, individuals can find their own level of explanation without having to wade through interminable instructions that do not apply to their needs.

Even with machinery, there is more than one way to make it work. Most computer software programs, for example, have many different ways to accomplish the same formatting. Often the manuals are structured in such a way that they are divided into varying degrees of detail. Some equipment manufacturers provide a short manual for basic operations for those who can't wait to get the machine out of the box. Then there is full-scale manual devoted to the complete range of operations possible. Many software programs, such as Microsoft Word, provide such a guide. "Type W-O-R-D and then depress the Return key to start the program." This gives you the freedom of options.

Apple Computer has built an empire on offering a variety of ways to perform the same function. You can use the mouse, the keyboard, screen menus, or quick keys to perform the same functions. Recorded voices are being worked into more programs.

This concept of redundancy reassures.

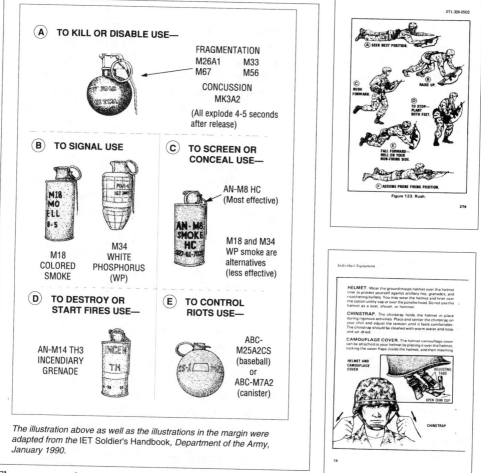

The illustration above as well as the illustrations in the margin were adapted from the IET Soldier's Handbook, *Department of the Army*, January 1990.

The army understands this well. A basic rule in boot camp is to tell you what you are going to do before you do it, what you are doing while you do it, and what you have done after you have done it.

TAKE CONTEXT INTO ACCOUNT

Some people who would spend hours agonizing over the right way to present an instruction might not give a thought to the setting in which it is delivered. Most people give instructions when the thought crosses their minds, rarely taking into account the particular context or environment. Like the choice of channel, the physical setting in which the instruction is delivered will affect the taker. Highly delicate or complex instructions require a more serene setting. If you are in your office trying to explain a new marketing campaign to a buyer, and you are interrupted by phone calls, your fax machine is running in the background, and you are having your beard trimmed, you can figure that the buyer is going to misunderstand you. In the same setting, you might be able to tell someone to call a cab for you—and have the instruction successfully carried out—but don't count on it.

Inspirational instructions designed to motivate people are delivered most efficiently in the context of a group or meeting, which stimulates the exchange of ideas as well as enthusiasm.

Many people don't look at meetings as instruction interchanges, but that is exactly what they are. Perhaps, if they were viewed as such, they could be made to produce higher value for dollars spent.

"Corporate expenditures for meetings rose from $2.4 billion in 1974 to $7.1 billion in 1987; associations' spending went from $700 million to $10 billion during the same period. A survey by the Convention and Visitors Bureaus indicates that almost 67 million delegates attended 271,000 meetings in 1988, a 37 percent increase over 1987."
—Paulette Dininny, "Meet the Meeting Planners," *USAir* (2/90)

These are figures tallied from formal meetings and conventions and don't include the infinite water-cooler confabs and coffee-machine conferences.

Marvin Cetron, author of *American Renaissance: Our Life at the Turn of the 21st Century* and president of Forecasting International Ltd. in Virginia, predicts that "Communications is pushing the growth of the meeting business....Most technology and information transferred is not from academic journals, not from colleges and universities, and not from books....Technology builds on technology, and new ideas and systems are generated when you can share ideas and share the pitfalls. It takes place from person to person. It's not strictly something you can do on the phone, facsimile machines, or the computer. You've got to have time to get together."

Meetings and conferences happen in a variety of settings. They don't take place only in the Grand Ballroom or the Empire Room. Coleman Finkel, an authority on the design of conference rooms and learning environments, cites eight separate environments in which meeting activities take place: the principal meeting room, the "break" room, the place where participants work on team projects, the sleeping rooms, reception areas, dining rooms, recreation and exercise rooms, and the overall facilities.

At a convention, each one of these settings can help or hinder the exchange of information, the instruction-giving and -taking, that occurs. In the article, "The Total Immersion Meeting Environment," in the *Training and Development Journal* (9/80), Finkel called for helping meeting participants to "become learners again. From the time they arrive at the meeting site, we must encourage these busy, pressured, action-oriented men and women to relax; to forget about the difficult, competitive world of business; to become thinkers, listeners, probers. Here environment has a transitional role to play: arriving participants should immediately feel a difference. The mood that is engendered should be calming, reassuring, conducive to introspection, contemplation, and openness to new ideas."

With corporate expenditures for meetings over $7 billion, meetings are perhaps one of the most institutionalized settings for instruction-giving. The money is wasted if the settings aren't conducive to the exchange of information. Participants who are watching people in the swimming pool, narcoleptic from uncomfortable furniture, near blind from low light, and suffering hearing strain from faulty public address systems aren't going to benefit from the expenditure.

The purpose of meetings, like the purpose of most business activity, is to communicate instructions that will inspire employees to creative performance.

RADICAL ALTERNATIVES

The imaginativeness of a solution can be inspired by the instructions given. Numerous studies demonstrate that people can be motivated to creativity simply with the addition of an instruction to "be creative."

The tendency of people to accept obvious solutions sometimes prevents them from performing up to their ability. Instructing them to look for novel solutions can surmount this.

"Discoveries are often made by not following instructions; by going off the main road; by trying the untried."—Frank Tyger, "Thoughts on the Business of Life," *Forbes* (5/15/89)

"The trait most likely to accompany an extreme is its opposite," said the character Chick Swallow in *The Tents of Wickedness*, by Peter De Vries.

"Whether revered or reviled in their lifetimes, history's movers framed their questions in ways that were entirely disrespectful of conventional wisdom. Civilization has always advanced in the shimmering wake of its discontents."—Garry Trudeau, commencement address to the Class of 1986 at Wake Forest University in Winston-Salem, North Carolina

"How can an ability to develop high quality solutions be brought to performance economically? Gagne (1962) holds that instructions may be viewed as attempts to establish sets to guide thinking within a given situation. He believes that suggestions or instructions limit the number of inaccurate solutions to be considered....Most investigations have focused on the inhibiting effects of the way a student sees a problem. For example, Maier (1933) increased the problem-solving performance of his students by instructing them to avoid obvious approaches to the problem. Thus the inhibition of habitual approaches facilitated the discovery of unusual ones.

"....Increases in the production of unusual, original, novel or clever responses have been reported by researchers who have instructed students to so respond."—Melba A. Colgrove, "Stimulating Creative Problem Solving," *Psychological Reports* (Vol. 22, 1968)

Rather than accept the first solution, ask yourself what would be the opposite way to solve a problem. Never stop with your first answer or alternative.

The next page shows one interpretation of an assignment I used to give design classes to demonstrate that we all have a sense of visual logic that can be used to communicate. I told the students "You all have 40 pieces of paper that are 8 1/2" square. On the first page you must have 3 one-inch squares. On the last page, you must have 11 squares—either black or white or in combination—to be placed wherever you want. Now you have to get from page 1 to page 40 in a visually logical way." Without words, they discovered that they could recognize logical progressions with a visual language based on placement, size, and time.

Melba A. Colgrove conducted a study at the University of Michigan with 475 students who were asked to find solutions to time-scheduling problems on a subassembly line. They were given a situation

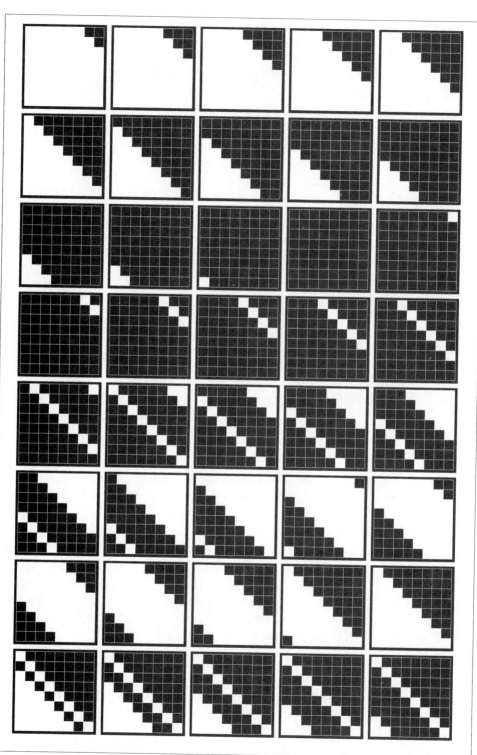

in which a foreman calls in three workers to discuss the results of a consultant's time study. The subordinates, who currently rotate positions on a hourly basis, resent the interference of the outside consultant and distrust management's motives.

The students were divided into 2 groups and were both given identical instructions to suggest a work schedule that would produce the best results. One group received an additional instruction—"You have the reputation of being a very original person and of being good at coming up with answers to difficult problems. That's why [the foreman] came to you. Keep this in mind while studying the problem."

The solutions were categorized into 3 groups—

❶ Old solutions with minor variations.

❷ New solutions, such as each person working his best position, adding rest pauses, music.

❸ Integrated solutions, which were combinations of the above.

"The integrative solutions are regarded as having the highest quality because they combine the results of the time study and means for avoiding the workers' feelings of boredom.

"In the group given the standard instructions, only 39 percent arrived at the integrative solution. In the group that received the suggestion to be original, the rate was 52 percent.

"The results of this experiment demonstrate that the mere suggestion that a person has the reputation of being an original thinker creates a mental set that upgrades his problem-solving performance. Thus it follows that more students can generate innovative solutions to a problem than ordinarily do. This suggests that the tendency to develop rather obvious solutions prevents indviduals from performing up to their capacity."—Melba A. Colgrove, "Stimulating Creative Problem Solving," *Psychological Reports* (Vol. 22, 1968)

WAITING FOR CREATIVE SOLUTIONS

"An act that produces effective surprise—this I shall take as the hallmark of a creative enterprise," Jerome Bruner stated in his book, *Beyond the Information Given: Studies in the Psychology of Knowing.* Then he further defined it as "the kind of surprise that yields high predictive value in its wake—as the instance of the formula for falling bodies or in any good theoretical reformulation in science." Creative enterprise can also be found in "an ordering of elements in such a way that one sees relationships that were not evident before, groupings that were before not present, ways of putting things together not before within reach." It can also be produced through "metaphoric effectiveness...by connecting domains of experience that were before apart."

"In the creative state a man is taken out of himself. He lets down...a bucket into his subconscious, and draws up something which is normally beyond his reach. He mixes this thing with his normal experiences, and out of the mixture he makes a work of art."—E. M. Forster

> "Generally speaking, it is inhumane to detain a fleeting insight."—Fran Lebowitz, *Metropolitan Life*

> "The creative act is not an act of creation in the sense of the Old Testament. It does not create something out of nothing; it uncovers, selects, re-shuffles, combines, synthesizes already existing facts, ideas, faculties, skills. The more familiar the parts, the more striking the new whole. Man's knowledge of the changes of the tides and the phases of the moon is as old as his observation that apples fall to the earth in the ripeness of time. Yet the combination of these and other equally familiar data in Newton's theory of gravity changed mankind's outlook on the world."
> —Arthur Koestler, *The Act of Creation*

> Einstein said his most original ideas came to him in mental pictures, not in words or numbers; Aristotle said that thought is impossible without images.

If you think of one idea, think again. There is a tendency to get stuck on first solutions. The first idea is not necessarily the best idea. It may just be the most common idea. In a word association study conducted at Stanford University, students were divided into groups and given different instructions to respond to words. Some of the groups were told only to respond to the word, with no instructions to be original or to take a certain amount of time. Other groups were told to wait several seconds before responding. The most original responses came from this group. "The associations which students took longer to produce also tended to be the more original responses. It may also be assumed that it is necessary for a student to inhibit his earlier responses to a stimulus in order to produce an original response," said John C. Masters and Gary W. Anderson in "Delay and Instructions as Determinants of Originality in Word Associations," *Journal of Verbal Learning and Verbal Behavior* (Vol. 7, 1968).

Visual imaging can be used to inspire imaginative solutions. Recent research into such imaging suggests numerous possibilities for exercising this miraculous capacity of the mind.

Dr. Stephen Kosslyn, a Harvard University psychologist who has done much of the new research, and one of his students, Carol Seger, completed a project that established the importance of certain images in daily life by asking people to report on their mental images every hour in a diary. They found that people predominately used mental pictures to make decisions (such as imaging food when deciding what to eat), to solve problems by imagining different solutions, to understand verbal descriptions, and to distance themselves from painful situations. Psychlogists believe the skills involved in the creation of imagery can be sharpened to expand mental endeavors beyond visual activities to problem-solving and logic.

FAITH IN FORM

We all need more faith in the solutions we develop. The trouble is that schools teach most of us that the best ideas are somewhere else, so we spent most of our energy looking for them. We need to develop faith in our own ideas and this faith will lend us more patience in communicating them.

By improving your communication habits and building your instructions with the essential components, you will be able to form your instructions with more confidence and ease.

Expect diversity. Expect confusion. Expect chaos. But don't accept them without making some effort to turn them into productive agents for creative instruction-following.

"At some point, the virtue of patience degrades into the law of delay....Learning all the details is too time-consuming, and not necessary anyway. What has to be available to inform decisions is the pattern, the overview, or the trend. Beyond that we simply get onto the slippery slope of detailing ourselves to death, on making okra gumbo."—William Sheridan, a research officer at the Library of Parliament in Ottawa, Canada, in a paper, "Developing a Personal Information Strategy"

DESTRUCTIONS

"In 1988, when speaking to a meeting of the Economic Club of New York, Mr. [Alan] Greenspan, now Federal Reserve chairman, said, 'I guess I should warn you, if I turn out to be particularly clear, you've probably misunderstood what I've said.'"

William Lutz, "The World of Doublespeak," *The State of the Language*

Instructions are what you spend 30 minutes giving someone else because you don't have the 10 minutes it would take to do it yourself.

"I make it a rule only to believe what I understand," said Proserpine in *The Infernal Marriage* by Benjamin Disraeli.

At voting precincts around the country, a sign mandated by the federal government can be found plastered on the walls, informing people that if they cannot read, someone will help them vote. I always wonder how many people benefit from this assistance?

YOU CAN BE ASSISTED IF:
You cannot read.
You cannot see the names printed on the ballot.
You cannot operate the levers.
You cannot enter the voting booth unless aided by another person.
You speak Spanish and need an interpreter.

From a poster outside of a voting booth in New York

Sometimes, poor instructions are easy to spot, but much of the time, their shortsightedness is not so apparent. Instruction-takers sometimes blame themselves for a failure to understand when the fault lies in the presentation of the instruction.

GIVING BETTER THAN YOU CAN TAKE

"After he had worked one year for [a] company, a recent MBA graduate was asked by a consultant, 'How are things going?' He replied, 'Well, it's been a hard year. When I was working on my MBA, everybody taught me how to be a good leader; nobody ever talked to me about how to be a good subordinate.' "—Cal W. Downs and Charles Conrad, "Effective Subordinacy," *The Journal of Business Communication* (Vol. 19, No. 2)

The role of the takers in an ideal instruction system is to identify inadequate instructions, to point out what the problem is, and, wherever possible, to ask for additional information or clarification that might improve the instruction. This can be challenging when the instructions appear outwardly adequate or even comprehensive.

To assume an active role in the process of communicating instructions, takers must learn to look beyond the surface for weak points in the system. Instructions don't work because of failed connections in the instruction system. At each step in the system errors or omissions can short-circuit the message.

An inability to follow instructions doesn't necessarily mean that you have limited mental capacity. It could mean that you're surrounded by bad instructions. Staying on the lookout for egregious errors might stop you from blaming yourself when you cannot follow an instruction. Also, it can provide evidence of how your own instructions are hard to follow.

You don't have to look far or wide to find an instruction that goes awry in its mission to clarify, fails to recognize the needs and abilities of the follower, contradicts itself, or doesn't make sense. These are *destructions*—instructions that hinder instead of help or just plain don't work. Destructions are only parodies of instructions.

Marshall Brickman, who wrote the screenplay for *Sleeper,* must have been overwhelmed by them when he composed the following ultimate instruction parody in *The New Yorker* (7/5/76).

INSTRUCTIONS

By Marshall Brickman

"Congratulations! You are now the owner of a new Simplex automated timesaving miracle Fletch-o-mat, designed by space-age scientists specifically to remove the drudgery from tiresome daily fletching. To operate, unlock the safety grommet (G) and loosen knurled screw (B) by turning in a clockwise direction, bringing the elbow directly in line with the lower back. Now touch the bottom of the heel with the chin, exactly as in *Mayurasana,* 'the Peacock' *(figure 5),* concentrating on the White Spot, or Source of All Being. Repeat the mantra for the count of ten, meanwhile mixing 1/4 tsp. nutmeg with the melted butter and the shallots. Now slowly add the iron filings, brine shrimp, and a pinch of matzo meal (for needed nitrogen) and, using a rubber spatula, smooth the mixture *upward* on your face, especially remembering the oily areas around the nose and forehead. Once those dead skin cells have been sloughed off and your pores can *breathe* again, the soft cartilage may be carefully planed away until the desired shape is obtained.

The flap of skin is then folded back over the bridge and sutured in place with three or four common roofing nails or a stapling gun. A dressing of hydroxyzine suspension (1 mg. per 5 ml.) may be applied topically to prevent redness, scaling, rot, mites, motes, bloat, crabgrass, or Murray face (a postoperative symptom in which the patient's visage is seen to resemble that of a man named Murray). For three to ten days thereafter, cover everything with a sheet of clear plastic wrap to help the seedlings retain moisture and grow to full maturity. Later, after the plants are dried and crushed, you can separate the seeds and twigs by forcing the material through a strainer, which will avoid a paranoid, or 'bad,' trip. A much more pleasurable trip is obtained by taking the auto ferry directly to Capo di Gallo, near Palermo, and boarding the charming funicular railway, which starts at the base of the scalp and works its way forward, massaging the entire area and stimulating circulation where it is most needed, at the gumline. A brisk up-and-down rather than a to-and-fro motion is what most dentists recommend. A series of rapid contractions also has a delightful effect; your wife can develop her ability in this area by practicing just a few moments a day, using a strumming motion, striking the low E string down (*oom-*), followed by a glissando up (*pah!*), tightening the embouchure for crescendo and relaxing the lips for diminuendo. In no time you'll be playing such old favorites as 'Bile Dat Cabbage Down' and John Blow's 'Elegy on Queen Mary.' If, after six lessons, you remain a social pariah, remember that a simple implosion device may be fashioned using a discarded length of two-inch pipe and materials available from any scientific supply house. The energy released by such a reaction is equal to the explosive force of 30,000 tons of TNT, or seven forty-year-old men riding a bicycle up a flight of stairs, or a child skipping rope for a hundred years (which burns up 750 calories but does nothing for that flab around your middle). The easiest exercise is one you can do while sleeping at your desk: (1)

Tense the diaphragm muscles. (2) Grasp the Flex-
o-toner in the middle. (3) Snap the lever around
quickly. Now measure your arm. You'll be
astounded at the results you will get in only three
seconds. If you want even better results, H. P.
Whitebait, leaders in the investment field for
years, recommend tax-free municipals or C.D.s,
which yield a smaller return but follow a pattern
you can sew yourself with just scissors, a pot of
glue, and an astrolabe. Simply compute the
volume of the room, which is the width times the
length times the height divided by a simple
Chinese screen or potted plant, which maintains
the traffic flow without distorting the ambience.
An understated Parsons table or lovely hand-
rubbed Shaker gibbet completes the decor, *and
will cost less than ten percent of what you would
pay a professional decorator!* Everyone agrees:
Mister Cork-Board (reg. U.S. Pat. Off.) takes you
step by step and eliminates the anxiety-producing
guesswork associated with linoleum installation or
any other creative undertaking. What's more, the
accompanying diagrams (reprinted from *Creative
Undertaking*) reveal the ancient secrets of the
Egyptian embalmers and show you how to turn a
nice dollar by winding cadavers in strips of old
percale. It's *so* easy. (1) Open the packet of
powdered grout and empty into a coffee can or 60
mm. shell casing. (2) Add just enough water to
make a thick paste. (3) Apply to the armature,
shaping carefully until the amorphous mass
resembles a horse or other object of your fancy
(suggestions: wolf, nude boy, bunch of pears). (4)
When dry, place the completed work under a good
strong light, pausing briefly to examine your chin
in a magnifying mirror. See those thousands of
giant gnarled tree trunks sticking up out of the
blighted terrain? That's your beard! That's why
we coat each and every razor blade with a thin
film of Silislide, the incredible new friction
retardant that adds literally years to the life of
your dog, because it contains not only a natural,
organic *moisturizer* but a set of hex wrenches, a
soldering gun, six terminal lugs, and a melding

tool. Even a woman or child can follow our simple
schematic drawing and learn how to make BIG
MONEY in your own home by going down to the
basement after dinner and practicing the kind of
personalized, demanding craft that made this
country what it is. Using a jeweler's loupe and a
No. 4 Superfine needle, start by engraving the face
(Andrew Jackson if it's a twenty), remembering
that most beginners slip up by omitting the little
chimney on the left side of the White House.
Work carefully. Write clearly. Do not look at your
neighbor's paper. When you are finished, remain
sitting quietly. Speak to no one. Anything you say
may be taken down and held against you. You are
entitled to one telephone call. If you have never
been impanelled (and under no circumstances
remove panel: there are no user-serviceable parts
inside), please familiarize yourself with this
simple time-honored trial procedure: (1) Place
suspect in ducking stool *(figure A)*, making certain
straps (b) and (c) are secured. (2) Lower witch
into pond *(figure B)* for period of not less than five
minutes' duration. (3) Watch carefully: those
bubbles on the surface of the water mean that all
the goodness is being extracted, while the bitter
oils and acids are left trapped *inside* the hair
follicle, leaving the fingernails soft and shiny!
Now buff to a high lustre. There's nothing more to
do; nothing to learn, assemble, or understand.
Simply roll the doubling cube, adding the number
of points to your Master Score—unless you have
previously acquired a Hazard card, in which case
you must advance to the penalty booth. Once
inside: (1) Draw the curtain closed. (2) Examine
the sample ballot. (3) Pull down all levers marked
'Ausgezeichnet.' Remain calm. Do not panic.
Place your head between your knees. Pull the two
yellow tabs down smartly to inflate the vest. Step
out of the booth. Once in the water, obey the
stewardess. If a shark appears, remain perfectly
still. Have your main points in mind. Speak
clearly and in a loud voice. Use simple words. The
repellent will last approximately one hour. After
that anything left over may be frozen for reuse in
small plastic containers."

TAKER RESPONSE MODES

Takers make choices about how they will respond to an instruction, which will affect their relationship with the giver. If they understand the instruction, their responses will have fairly predictable outcomes. (If they don't, God knows what can happen.) Essentially, they can choose to:

❶ Ignore the instruction.

Result: Frustrating the giver.

❷ Deliberately follow it incorrectly.

Result: Making the giver mad.

❸ Perfunctorily do only what they think will keep the instruction-giver at bay.

Result: Maintaining the status quo.

❹ Earnestly do what they think will please the instruction-giver.

Result: Maybe making someone else happy.

❺ Earnestly try to satisfy themselves by looking upon the instruction as a means to reach new understandings and acquire new skills.

Result: Making themselves happy and probably making someone else happy as well (at least their mothers).

Obviously, the first 3 responses do not produce desirable outcomes, at least not from the giver's perspective. The 4th approach of trying to make someone else happy may have beneficial effects in the short run. However, only the 5th response will produce the most creative instruction performances. Only by satisfying yourself can you go beyond the restraints or limitations of the giver's perspective.

This kind of response requires that takers participate in the instruction process, recognize problems, and communicate what they need to respond in a way that will bring them satisfaction. It's not enough just to be able to recognize a bad instruction when you see one. You have to understand why it failed.

NONCOMPLIANCE BY INVITATION OR ACCIDENT

Bad instructions can be divided into 2 categories: those that can't be followed and those that are constructed in such a way that people rebel against following them. The first category is more likely to occur in instructions that involve assembly or operation of equipment or anything in which the users have either an assumed or expressed willingness to follow instructions if only because they purchased the product. When you set out to put together a barbecue grill, you probably want to follow the directions. They may be presented in a way that makes this impossible, but by virtue of your buying the grill in the first place, you would like to follow them if you had the choice. If you consult a cookbook for a chocolate cake recipe, you are demonstrating at least an implicit willingness to follow the directions.

The instructions that invite noncompliance usually come from the category of instructions that you perceive as foisted upon you from the outside, such as those from superiors, signage in buildings, and implicit instructions in social intercourse. When your boss tells you to reorganize the file room before you go on vacation and you are on your way to the airport, you are likely to rebel. Although instructions in both categories fall victim to the same short-comings, inadequate instructions in this category aren't as obvious and are more difficult to pinpoint, owing to their often more implicit nature.

The following are the most common causes of instruction breakdown.

> Failure to translate the instruction to the perspective of the taker.
>
> Failure to take into account the understanding level or the needs of the taker.
>
> Messages phrased in abstract terms that defy mutual interpretation.
>
> An excess of information that obscures the intent of the instruction.
>
> Hiding the clear intent of the instruction under allusions and veiled references.
>
> Omitting essential pieces.
>
> Unnecessarily threatening enforcement of compliance with the instruction.
>
> Lack of context.
>
> Choice of an inappropriate channel to convey the content of the instruction, so the taker confuses the message.
>
> Departure from accepted custom without adequate warning.
>
> False claims or promises.
>
> Lack of attention paid to human behavior.
>
> Evoking the parent-child rebellion response.
>
> Self-destructive instructions.
>
> Time lapse problems.
>
> Inadequate incentive to follow.

LACK OF TRANSLATION

"Communication is what people with nothing to say do with people who won't listen."—P. J. O'Rourke, "How to Success in Business? Here's the Secret," *The New York Times Book Review* (10/29/89)

Like communications in general, instructions have to be translated by the giver into a language that can be understood by the taker. Certain words may have a different meaning to the person you are instructing. (*See Chapter 7.*)

Translation takes care and attention to language on the part of the giver, a care that is woefully absent from many instructions. Even the simplest instructions can be misinterpreted.

DO YOU TAKE WATER IN YOUR COFFEE?

Rumor has it that Braun manufactured a coffee maker on the back of which was the simple instruction:

"DO NOT PUT IN WATER."

The company started getting calls from disturbed customers who couldn't get the machine to make coffee. In talking the customers through the process, the company discovered that the customers had interpreted the instruction to mean that they shouldn't put water into the machine. In the next batch of coffee makers, Braun changed the instruction to read:

"DO NOT IMMERSE THE COFFEE POT IN WATER."

While enrolling for college, Loring Leifer saw a sign on the double-door administration building, "Please use door on other side." To her, the double door constituted only one door, so she translated "side" as the side of the building, so "other side" meant the other side of the building. She walked around to the west entrance and found the same sign, so she tried the north entrance. The only thing that kept her from trotting around to the east side was that several students walked right through the door on the left as she stood there reassessing the situation. Fortunately, after her inglorious start, she did manage to graduate.

While it would have been impractical for Loring to ask at the information booth for clarification of the sign (given the trouble she was having just getting into the building), she could have saved herself some trouble if she had first asked herself, "Is it possible that this sign could have another meaning?" She then could have tested this hypothesis by tentatively pushing the door adjacent to the sign.

When instruction-takers are confronted by a message that doesn't seem clear, that isn't presented in a language they can understand, they must seek clarification—either from the instruction-giver (if possible) or by asking themselves questions about the instruction.

NO ACCOUNTING FOR NOT-KNOWING

Once you learn something, you tend to forget what it's like not to know. I remember distinctly the moment I understood reading. I was in the first grade and the teacher was holding up flash cards.

After several cards, it dawned on me that the green-colored card in her left hand corresponded with the combinations of letters—GREEN—in her right. I understood that the word GREEN was a code for the color. It was an important moment, but I immediately forgot what the mystery of not knowing how to read was like.

As instructions are often formulated by people who know for the people who don't know, this inability to remember what it's like to not know results in instructions that don't give essential information to the taker.

The New York Times ran an article about the complicated new statistics for baseball (4/30/90). Imagine trying to follow these instructions for *runs created:*

> "**Runs created**, devised by Bill James, is a measure of total offensive output. It is computed as follows: Hits plus Walks and Hit By Pitch minus Caught Stealing and Grounded Into Double Plays times Total Bases plus .26 times Hit By Pitch and Unintentional Walks plus .52 times Sacrifice Hits plus Sacrifice Flies plus Stolen Bases. Divide this by At Bats plus Walks plus Hit By Pitch plus Sacrifice Hits plus Sacrifice Flies."

Sure Bill, no problem.

The understanding level of the taker should always be figured into the instruction. Because this is so hard to do, it's up to the taker to remind the giver what it's like not to know. While this is easier to do in conversational instructions, it can also be done with manufacturers' instructions. Write a letter to the company that made your VCR and tell them what you need to know.

"It's what you learn after you know it all that counts."
—John Wooden

INSTRUCTIONS LOST IN ABSTRACT CONCEPTS

As I discussed in Chapter 7, all words have either an abstract or concrete value. Highly abstract words widen the margin for interpretation and thus misinterpretations. This applies to instructions that are expressed in words with a high abstract rating. If a woman hires a cateress for a party and tells her to "really let yourself go with this one," the cateress might assume that the woman wants her to spend lots of money, dye all of the food different colors, or drop acid before cooking it. "Letting yourself go" is an abstract concept that demands individual interpretation.

Individual interpretation is a given in all communications; it doesn't need encouragement. So when you see an instruction that seems abstract to you, ask the giver, if possible, to replace some of the vague terms with more specific ones or warn the giver that your interpretation may go beyond his or her wildest imagination.

Great Moments in the HISTORY OF INSTRUCTIONS

1842: COMMODORE THOMAS A.C. JONES, U.S.N. PACIFIC FLEET, HAS INSTRUCTIONS TO SEIZE CALIFORNIA **IF** WAR BREAKS OUT. BUT HOW TO KNOW? MESSAGES FROM WASHINGTON TAKE 4 MONTHS TO ARRIVE! SO — ON OCT. 19, JONES INVADES MONTEREY, ARRESTS EVERYONE, REALIZES HIS ERROR, AND LEAVES AFTER 30 HOURS.

SO SORRY... I COULDN'T KNOW... LET'S HOPE I DON'T HAVE TO REPEAT THE BLUNDER...

"OOPS, NEVER MIND," SAYS COMMODORE JONES AFTER TAKING MONTEREY DURING PEACETIME

Commodore Jones, "on his cruise to California in 1842, made a spectacular blunder. As the ranking United States naval officer in the Pacific he seized Monterey, California, from its Mexican sovereigns during peacetime. True, he held the Mexican provincial capital for only thirty hours, and then realizing the error of his judgement he dusted off the disgruntled *oficionados* and tried to restore their dignity.

"....Jones was immediately relieved and ordered to return to the United States, which he did—two years later. Commodore Dallas was sent to Callao early in 1843 to take over Jones' command, but there is no record that he ever caught up with the 'disgraced' commander. Jones had been ordered independently to return home 'in such mode as may be most convenient and agreeable' to himself. It was 'most convenient' for him to sail from the California Coast to Hawaii followed by a leisurely cruise in the Pacific. He finally put into Valparaiso, but in the meanwhile Dallas had died in Callao in 1844, never having met his predecessor.

"It is a commentary on the time only a little more than a century ago. Communication was slow and faulty. National policy might be one thing, but if the men in the field did not know what was happening they had to do the best they could with the materials at hand.

"....Jones was not ordered to commit war-like acts, but on the other hand he was not forbidden to seize foreign territory if circumstances warranted such a thing."

Commodore Jones's instructions were as follows: "Increasing commerce of the U.S. within the gulf and along the coast of California, as far as the bay of St. Francisco, together with the weakness of the local authorities and their irresponsibility to the distant government of Mexico, renders it proper that occasional countenance and protection should be afforded to American enterprise in that quarter. You are therefore directed to employ either a sloop of war or a smaller vessel, as may be most convenient, or both if necessary, in visiting occasionally or cruising constantly upon that line of coast.

"The order seems legitimate enough, and it certainly had enough latitude implied so that the commander's judgment could be exercised."
—James High, "Jones at Monterey," *Journal of the West*

Commodore Thomas Ap Catesby Jones was a military master at the creative interpretations of instructions—first in getting himself into trouble, then in backing out after having overstepped the bounds of military manners.

THE FACT SIEGE

Overloaded with instructions, the communication system will invariably go haywire. If you want to take the ferry to Provincetown, you don't need instructions on how to build a boat. And, if you are given them, you will be bound to misunderstand or miss altogether the information that you need.

When you are trying to negotiate a new city and ask someone for directions to a particular place, the reason you can't remember anything past the instruction to "walk three blocks" is probably that you are being overloaded with new information. I remember once in Rome I stopped to ask a man directions to the Piazza Navona. He looked me over and said in heavily accented English, "You walk down to the corner, turn right, walk straight for three blocks, and then ask someone else." Here was a man who understood information overload.

Recognizing when you are being overloaded with information requires making a judgment on the complexity of the task at hand. If you ask which way to the train station and someone pulls out

TURKISH PUZZLE RING
(Illustrated on the next page)

"Legend has it that this ring signified betrothal, and that if taken off—for obvious reasons—would fall apart and be impossible to fit together again. I've never fathomed how someone thought of it, as the intricacy of the design is impossible to picture in the mind. Perhaps the three rings, sometimes there are more, were forcibly overlapped and hammered together at that point. Alternatively, a solid ring could have been partially cut into bands and the remaining portion elaborately carved into interlocking forms. Whatever the answer, with the help of baksheesh, I passed an hour at the bazaar in Istanbul learning how to take them apart and put them together. I also bought an instruction booklet.

"Of course, I soon forgot the sequence of moves. The instructions, I later discovered, were written and illustrated with a Byzantine sense of humor. No doubt with the intention of reinforcing the moral of the legend.—Alan Fletcher of Pentagram

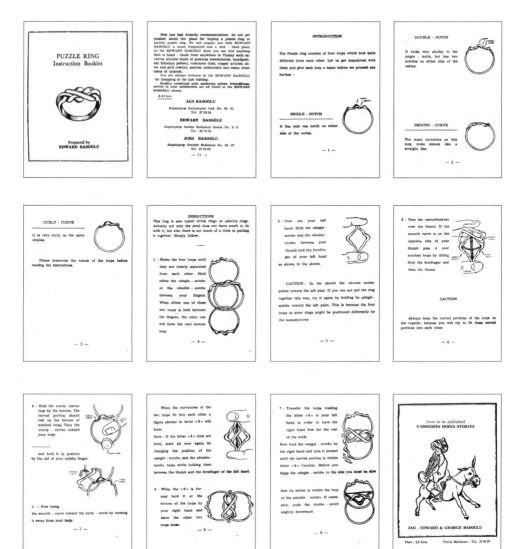

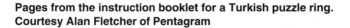

**Pages from the instruction booklet for a Turkish puzzle ring.
Courtesy Alan Fletcher of Pentagram**

topographic reports and construction drawings, obviously you are getting more information than you need. Before you tackle instructions, think about how much time you imagine the job should take. Ask the giver for an estimate. Specify how much you need to know.

"Don't build a cathedral when a chapel is all you need."—Brian Currah, theater design professor

"The hazards of one-by-one enumeration have never been so plain as in the 1990 census, now consuming the labor of a record 350,000 workers. Over the last four months, the census has been staggered by a rate of noncooperation that exceeded the estimates of the most severe critics. Nearly twice as many Americans as ever before either failed or refused to mail back census forms. In some large cities, the response rate fell below 50 percent."

—James Gleick, "The Census: Why We Can't Count," *The New York Times* (7/15/90)

Often too much information increases the likelihood of contradictions and ambiguities of interpretation. You can't believe that you are getting so much instruction for such a simple task. The 1990 U.S. census form was a masterpiece in its earnestness to overwhelm you with information. Even the first sentences in the guide were confusing. It told you to "Please use a black lead pencil only," then followed it with "Black lead pencil is better to use than ballpoint or other pens." The first instruction forbids you to use anything other than a pencil and the second tells you that it is only *preferable* to use it.

The government seems to be afflicted with this condition at all levels of business. A sign in the Civil Courthouse in New York City politely requests that potential jurors "Answer to Your Own Name." Imagine that you are a potential juror who is spending two weeks on a hard wooden bench. You'd probably start to wonder just what this meant. It seems too obvious and unnecessary to mean what it said. You'd ask yourself, "Why would somebody answer to another name? Why would they want to? What would happen if I answered to another name?" You'd probably start listening to other names as they were called, and pretty soon you'd be tempted to respond, just out of boredom or contrariness.

Your Guide for the

1990 U.S. Census Form

This guide gives helpful information on filling out your census form. If you need more help, call the local U.S. census office. The telephone number is on the cover of the questionnaire. After you have filled out your form, please return it in the envelope we have provided.

On the inside

How to fill out your census form	Page
Example	
Your answers are confidential	2
Instructions for the census questions	2
What the census is about	2
Why the census asks certain questions	3–5
	5
	5

CENSUS '90

U.S. DEPARTMENT OF COMMERCE
BUREAU OF THE CENSUS

D-3

ICEBERG INSTRUCTIONS

Subtlety can be effective in getting along with people, but it is not what you need in an instruction. Instructions that appear to be complete, but contain ambiguous information or implications can be more insidious because the giver may assume that the instructions are adequate, but they are not. A dearth of information can be as maddening as an excess, or as Siegfried said in the opera of the same name, "Between east and west lies north."

Imagine you are one half of a young couple that has just moved to New York. On your way to the

grocery store, you pass this flyer. You see this as a golden opportunity to get acquainted with your neighbors. Imagine your chagrin when you show up with your wife/husband bearing a tuna casserole and discover that it was potluck for homosexuals. There were clues in the flyer, two symbols for males entwined together on one side; two for females on the other. The word lavender also has homosexual connotations, as does the inverted triangle. However, these clues are just too arcane in an instruction that is there for the world—or at least the neighborhood—to see.

Iceberg instructions arise out of an impatience on the part of the giver or a reluctance to delegate tasks. They can also be born out of a fear of insulting the intelligence of the receiver.

This fear must plague the manufacturers of those little packages of shampoo, soap, and hand lotion that you get in hotels, because a lot of them don't

Portion of the 178-page *Tax Guide For Small Businesses*

Start-up expenses do not include any organizational expenses for a corporation or a partnership. These expenses are discussed next.

Organizational costs for a corporation. Corporate organizational costs are those that are incident to the creation of the corporation. They include the cost of temporary directors, organizational meetings, state incorporation fees, and accounting services related to setting up the organization. They also include the cost of legal services, such as drafting the charter, bylaws, terms of the original stock certificates, and minutes of organizational meetings.

However, costs of issuing and selling stock or securities, such as commissions, professional fees, and printing costs are not organizational costs and may not be amortized. Costs connected with the transfer of assets to the corporation also cannot be amortized.

To qualify for amortization, an organizational cost must meet all three of the following tests:

1) It must be incident to the creation of the corporation. The cost must be incurred before the end of the first tax year in which the corporation is in business. A corporation using the cash method may amortize organizational costs incurred within the first tax year even if it does not pay them in that year.

2) It must be a cost that is chargeable to a capital account.

3) It must be one that could be amortized over the life of the corporation, if the corporation had a fixed life.

Organizational costs for a partnership. Partnership organizational costs are those that are incident to the creation of the partnership. To be amortizable, an organizational cost must be one that is chargeable to a capital account, and it must be one that could be amortized over the life of the partnership, if the partnership had a fixed life.

Partnership organizational costs do not include syndication fees. That is, they do not include costs connected with the issuing and marketing of interests in the partnership, such as commissions, professional fees, and printing costs.

How to amortize. The costs that qualify in these three areas are deducted in equal amounts over a period of not less than 60 months. You can elect a different period for start-up and for organizational costs, as long as each is 60 months or more. Once you elect an amortization period, you cannot change it.

To figure your deductions, divide the total of your start-up or organizational costs by the number of months in the amortization period. The result is the amount that can be deducted each month.

The amortization period starts with the month you begin business operations. (You can amortize only if you actually go into business.) For the amortization of organizational costs, a partnership or corporation is considered to begin business operations when it starts the activities for which it is organized. This can happen either before or after the corporate charter is granted or a partnership agreement is signed. A partnership or corporation will be considered as having begun business if its activities have reached the point where the nature of its business operations can be established. For example, if it acquires the assets it needs to operate its business, this

Page 46   Chapter 13

may constitute the beginning of business activities.

Making the election. If you want to amortize your costs, you must attach Form 4562 to your income tax return. If you elect to amortize both start-up and organizational costs, in addition to furnishing all of the information that is required in Part II, Form 4562, you must attach a separate statement to your return for each type of cost. Each statement should:

1) Show the total amount of the start-up or organizational costs you will amortize,

2) Describe what each is for,

3) Give the date each cost was incurred,

4) State the month your business began operations (or the month you acquired the business), and

5) Specify the number of months in your amortization period (not less than 60).

Each statement must be attached to your return for the tax year in which the amortization period starts, the first tax year that you are in business. Both the statement and the return must be filed by the due date for the return (including any extensions of time).

Partnerships and corporations. If your business is organized as a partnership or corporation, only the partnership or corporation can elect to amortize its start-up or organizational costs. A partner or shareholder cannot make this election.

If you incur costs in setting up your partnership or corporation, you cannot amortize them. If the partnership or corporation does not reimburse you for these costs, it cannot amortize them either. These costs then become part of the basis of your interest in the business. You can recover them only when you sell your interest in the partnership or corporation.

However, you, as an individual, can elect to amortize the costs you incur to investigate an interest in an existing partnership. These expenses qualify as business start-up costs if you succeed in acquiring the interest.

Construction period interest and taxes. You are not allowed to deduct real property construction period interest or taxes that are paid or incurred in the tax year on property that is used in a trade or business or in an activity conducted for profit. Instead, these amounts must be capitalized. However, for amounts paid or incurred before 1987, these costs could be amortized over a 10-year period.

For more information, see Publication 535.

Research and experimental costs may be amortized or they may be deducted as current business expenses. You have the choice to deduct the costs currently as business expenses or to treat them as deferred expenses and amortize them in equal amounts over a period of not less than 60 months. See Chapter 5 for a discussion of the choice to deduct the costs.

The amortization deduction is an election that applies to those costs that are: (1) paid or incurred by you in connection with your trade or business, (2) not being currently deducted, and (3) chargeable to a capital account. If the costs are chargeable to a capital account and they have no determinable useful life, you may elect the 60-month amortization. However, if they are chargeable to a capital account and have a determinable useful life, you must capitalize the costs and depreciate them over their useful life. An example is your expenses for investigating and acquiring a license. These

expenses must be capitalized and depreciated over the determinable life of the license.

Your costs that you elect to amortize are accumulated starting with the year you make the election to amortize. You should select an amortization period at the time you make the election. If you have two or more separate projects, you may elect a different amortization period for each project. Your amortization period begins with the month in which you first realize benefits from the costs.

You may not only amortize costs paid or incurred by you, but you can also amortize expenses paid or incurred on your behalf by another person or organization. However, costs incurred on your behalf do not include those expenses for acquiring or improving land or depreciable property used in relation to the research or experimentation if you acquire the rights of ownership.

Research or experimental costs are those expenses incurred in relation to your trade or business that are research and development costs in the experimental or laboratory sense. Such expenses include costs incident to the development of an experimental or pilot model, a plant process, a product, a formula, an invention, or similar property, and the improvement of already existing property of the type mentioned. Costs incurred in the ordinary testing or inspection of materials or products for quality control or those for efficiency surveys, management studies, consumer surveys, advertising or promotions are not qualifying costs.

Bond premium is the amount you pay for bonds that is greater than the face value of the bonds.

You must amortize the premium on tax-exempt bonds, but you may not deduct the amortizable premium in figuring your taxable income.

You may elect to amortize the premium on taxable bonds. If you do not elect to amortize the premium, it will be treated as part of your basis of the bond.

You decrease the basis of the bond by the amortizable bond premium in all cases in which you are required, or elect, to amortize the premium. This will give you the adjusted basis you will use to figure the correct gain or loss on the sale or redemption of the bond.

A dealer in bonds or anyone who holds them mainly for sale to customers in the ordinary course of a trade or business and who would properly include bonds on hand in inventory at the close of the tax year cannot claim a deduction for amortizable bond premium. Instead the premium is part of the cost of the bonds.

Bonds acquired in an exchange after May 6, 1986. If you receive a bond after May 6, 1986, in exchange for other property and the basis of the bond is determined (in whole or in part) by reference to the basis of the other property, then for purposes of determining the amortizable bond premium, your basis for the bond cannot exceed the bond's fair market value immediately after the exchange.

This treatment does not apply to an exchange of a bond for another bond if the exchange is part of a corporate reorganization. However, if any part of your basis in the bond transferred in the exchange is not taken into account in determining bond premium because of these provisions, the same portion is not taken into account in determining the bond

---

have any instructions about how to get inside. You never know where to tear them or where the contents are going to wind up when you do.

The trouble with both technical and general instructions is that most of them are implied. When the manual says "Press the Playback button," it is implied that you have already located the cord, plugged the machine in, pressed the "On" button, and understood that *play* is the same as Playback. The same goes for oral communications, which depend heavily on nonverbal signals that have a myriad of interpretations.

While there is no need to talk down to people, you can usually find a way to explain something clearly without getting pompous about it.

MISSING PIECES

For one reason or another, essential pieces are often left out of an instruction, whether by oversight or incompetence. This wouldn't be such an overwhelming problem if the instruction taker were able to recognize the omissions. When you are holding a computer manual in your hand, there is an assumption that therein lies everything you need to know if you could only understand it. The tendency is to blame yourself if you cannot find or follow the instructions.

Often when experts design instructions, they lose sight of what a novice needs to know. It's almost impossible to know something and to imagine what it's like not to know. The experts' minds become crowded with related problems and issues, with an acute awareness of detail, with sophisticated processes and possibilities. What is most likely to get obscured in this mass of information is the basic material essential to a novice who might want to follow the instructions.

Sometimes pieces are left out because the instruction-giver doesn't connect one piece of information to another. For example, Napoléon instructed his fleet to attack whenever the French had more ships in an area than the British. From a superficial standpoint, this order makes sense. If the French had more ships, they might have a better chance against the British. But essential information was missing from this instruction. Owing to more advanced machinery, the British soldiers could fire twice as fast as the French. Napoléon's troops followed his orders—and lost the Battle of Trafalgar in 1805. Rigid instructions that don't permit flexibility invite inferior solutions. For another example, the fixed buy-and-sell computer programs were instrumental in the stock market crash of October 1987.

OVERKILL

When the penalty for noncompliance of an instruction grossly exceeds the perceived importance of the instruction, a revolt is bound to result. People do not like to be threatened—especially when they are opening bottles, riding escalators, or drying their hands.

In a Newport, Rhode Island, restroom, there was a sign on the cloth towel roll that read: "Intentional misuse of this apparatus could result in fatal injury." This is a clear case in which the severity of the instructions go so far beyond the real consequences of disobeying that the taker is teased into proving them wrong.

What about the tags on mattresses: "Do not remove under penalty of law." Someone once applied for a job and put on his resume after a question about his criminal record that he had been "arrested in a hotel with a suitcase full of DO NOT REMOVE tags." He was hired on the spot.

When someone threatens you with an "over my dead body will you do this," don't you have an overwhelming impulse to push them over and do it anyway?

Sometimes, drastic threats can be effective. I was on a plane to Singapore with my wife, Gloria, when airline personnel passed out cards that visitors must fill out before entering the country. The cards asked for your name, the purpose of your visit, where and how long you would be staying, etc. In red ink emblazoned on the card were the words: "WARNING: DEATH FOR DRUG TRAFFICKERS UNDER SINGAPORE LAW." My wife turned to me and said, "Now that's a little more effective than 'Just say no,' don't you think?" However, you must be wary of giving instructions that you can't back up with actions.

NO CONTEXT

An instruction that is given without its context is like peanut butter and jelly without the bread. Including the the applications and effects of an instruction gives it shape and meaning—and it's a lot easier to eat. Most people wouldn't think of telling someone to send a letter to 700 Walnut Street without giving the city and the state in which this address is located. Yet these people often instruct their employees to do tasks without describing the larger mission to be accomplished.

Let's say you are having a party and the party planner you have hired asks you about music. You say you want classical music. To you, this means a small chamber orchestra group playing Bach, Handel, Vivaldi, Corelli, and Mozart. You can't imagine any other interpretation. The party planner hires a band that plays the music of Tommy Dorsey, Lionel Hampton, and Count Basie. You are furious. "I was perfectly clear. I said *classical music*," you say with menace. "But, I thought you wanted a band that plays the *classics*," says your party planner, also annoyed because she thought she was following your instructions. To her the classics mean "Stormy Monday." If you had put your request in context and told her that you were trying to create the feel of an 18th-century salon, she would have understood that you both had different ideas about classical music.

"Habit is habit, and not to be flung out of the window by any man, but coaxed downstairs a step at a time."—Mark Twain

"The largest single investment that almost every company makes is in its employees working in particular ways, protocols, and cultures. A small part of this investment is called training expense, but the larger costs are normally not accounted for— 'untraining expenses' and the costs and benefits of the momentum, inertia, and commonality generated when a group of people grow accustomed to working together in particular ways with particular tools."—Fernando Flores and Chauncey Bell, "A New Understanding of Managerial Work Improves System Design," *Computer Technology Review* (Fall 1984)

A VICTIM OF HABIT

Be careful of habit. If your employees get the idea that you prefer a certain approach to situations and then you instruct them otherwise without adequate warning, they may interpret that instruction based on the existing protocols. If every morning, you pass your secretary's desk and say, "Good morning, call Lou in Los Angeles and ask him what ads aired last night," he or she will start to make the call without thinking. So if one day you say, "Call Sam in Saskatchewan and ask him to send the paper samples," your secretary might assume you mean Lou in Los Angeles. When you break a pattern or habit, you should stress that you are doing it, unless you want to run the risk of having your instruction reinterpreted by historical precedent. By saying, "Instead of calling Lou, I want you to call Sam," you highlight a departure from the convention.

I have offices in New York and San Francisco. In sending material between the 2 offices, we usually use Federal Express for priority overnight service and UPS for 2-day service. I asked my San Francisco office to "ship me some books and papers by 2-day express." I needed them sometime the next day, because I was leaving town in the evening. Well, Federal Express calls this "standard overnight service," which we rarely use. However, this was what I wanted. The office reasonably assumed that "2-day" meant UPS, which is how the package was sent. They made a decision based on past experience because I didn't make it clear in my instructions that I was departing from custom.

"Habits are the indispensible core of stability and ordered behaviour; they also have a tendency to become mechanized and to reduce man to the status of a conditioned automaton. The creative act, by connecting previously unrelated dimensions of experience, enables him to attain a higher level of mental evolution. It is an act of liberation—the defeat of habit by originality," said Arthur Koestler in his book, *The Act of Creation.*

People in an office develop patterns and habits in the ways that they work based on the company history of how work gets done. They respond to instructions according to these patterns. When managers want something done in a different way from company custom, they must stress the departure or bear the consequences of having the instruction ignored.

FALSE PROMISES

The late John Muir wrote and published a book, *How to Keep Your Volkswagen Alive: A Manual of Step-by-Step Procedures for the Compleat Idiot.* Have you ever thought about what the person who couldn't figure it out felt like?

Often, instruction-givers are tempted to couch their instructions in reassuring phrases like "It's so simple, a two-year-old could do it," "It won't take any time at all," "It's as easy as pie." These phrases are harmless enough if the taker has no trouble with the instructions, but they can do severe damage to the self-esteem of someone who does.

It serves the taker well to keep in mind that instructions are often not what they appear or what they may claim to be. Just because you can't follow the instructions designed for a "2-year-old" doesn't mean that you lack the intelligence of one.

Some instruction-givers can't resist making false promises. They are only guilty, though, of trying to make the taker feel more confident, however misguided their attempts might be.

How to Keep Your Volkswagen Alive, **or the VW "Idiot Book" to insiders, is hardly guilty of false promises, though. The book, which has sold over 2,000,000 copies since it was first published in 1969, is a compendium of everything you might want or need to know about the VW Beetle, as well as information on several other VW models. In addition to maintenance and repair instructions, it contains information on VW clubs, shows, parts catalogs and wholesalers, and the history of the company. It has served as required reading for university technical writing courses, and *Car and Driver* calls it "the king of automotive how-to-do-its."**

THE PARENT-CHILD SYNDROME

Giving instructions always smacks at least a bit of pedantry. I, the smart informed one, am going to serve up my knowledge and superior information to you, the bumbling clod who can't seem to get it right. Most people don't like to be cast in the receiving role, perhaps deciding that it is an inferior position. It reminds us all of the powerlessness of childhood, when we had to accept "Because I said so" as a reason for eating broccoli. We couldn't wait for the day when we could foreswear it forever.

"When a colleague was opening his mail the other day he came upon two packages each holding an identical book and letter inviting him to review it. The letters were signed by someone styling herself Marketing Co-ordinator."—
Michael Dixon, "The Tell-Tale Gap between Deeds and Words" *The Financial Times* (6/1/90)

I was on a plane with my brother, Eric, an associate professor of sociology at Columbia University who has an articulate and plausible explanation for almost any form of human behavior. We were talking about why passengers don't follow this instruction as the plane landed. Eric explained that this instruction seemed so inconsequencial after the perceived risk of flying that passengers didn't think it was necessary to comply with it. I, who can't resist contradicting my brother, countered that in reality accidents often occur during this part of the flight, having known several people who sustained injuries from wayward carry-on luggage. My brother said, "That's ridiculous," at which point 2 tennis rackets fell on his head.

—LL

Instruction-givers should take this into account when phrasing messages, but too often they don't. (*See Chapter 5.*) This means that instruction-takers may be unnecessarily resistant to an instruction. Most of us like to think that maturity has erased this petty rebelling, but we are probably wrong. Takers need to keep this rebellion response in mind. Anything that smacks of parental restraint may raise the recalcitrant child in us.

The classic example of this is the instruction delivered on airplanes immediately after the plane has landed: "Please remain seated with your seat belts fastened until the plane has come to a complete stop." Okay, clear enough. At this point, half of the passengers jump up and dive into the overhead storage compartments in a panic to retrieve their carry-on luggage, leaving the seated and rule-following other half vulnerable to head contusions, neck fractures, and possible paralysis as the heavy luggage falls on them from above.

Why don't people remain seated? It has been my experience that no one's carry-on luggage has ever left the plane without them. So what's the rush? I think that the instruction sounds like something a third-grade teacher would say to her class. There are no explanations, no reasons, just a rule to be followed.

The only way to get passengers to follow the instruction to remain seated is to communicate the dangers involved in noncompliance. A flight attendant could tell the passengers that "there have been many injuries from luggage falling on seated passengers; the passengers are responsible for this. We suggest that you don't get up until the plane has come to a complete stop. I assure you that you will get off the plane just as quickly."

SELF-DESTRUCTIVE DIRECTIONS

Some instructions contradict themselves, leaving the instructee completely baffled as to how to act. When someone stands in a doorway and tells you "You go first then I'll precede you," what do you do? Who goes first? I was in a restaurant restroom and saw a sign on a hot-air hand dryer that said, "Do Not Push Button When Hands Are Wet." While I was pondering this instruction, my hands dried.

A notice outside the Hotel Emporio's Mandinga Disco in Mexico informed patrons that the club was for "Members and Non Members Only." Who else is there?

If takers don't have the option of asking for clarification, they must make a judgment on what the giver meant to say and act accordingly. The rules of etiquette would suggest that the person motioning you through a doorway means for you to go first.

TIME LAPSE

Sometimes, perfectly good instructions don't work because people don't have cause to follow them often enough. This is sometimes the reason people can't seem to program their VCRs; they don't do it often enough. We all have trouble with the tasks that we don't perform on a regular basis. You learn to use your microwave because every morning you heat reheat coffee in it. The process becomes second nature. Setting the clock on the other hand is done only twice a year. You forget because you don't do it often enough to embed the instructions in your memory. Many people are reluctant to look up the details in the manual because after you have owned a product for a while, you like to feel that you know it. Having to look up the way to reset the clock reminds you that you don't. Maybe you would be willing but you threw the manual out or can't remember where it is.

In the best possible world, industrial designers and instruction-writers take this into account and incorporate memory joggers into the product—either by printing instructions on the product or by making its operation more self-evident, or by designing on-line assistance.

In this imperfect world, instruction-takers can compensate for memory lapses by creating their own memory-joggers, such as writing down the basic instructions for recording a program on their VCR.

Overcome with frustration at files, which were over-running his office, Samuel Goldwyn ordered his secretary to "Get rid of all this."

"I can't," she replied. "Some of those are important papers."

He replied, "All right, then, make a copy of everything before you throw it out."

"Last week the Commander in Chief tapped on his first personal computer, hooked up in a study near the Oval Office. Bush will take lessons from a White House expert at least once a week, and has made learning to use his own computer a personal goal. 'to prove no one's ever too old to learn.' But he hasn't set his sights too high. 'I don't expect this to teach me how to set the clock on the VCR or anything complicated,' says the President."—Wendy Cole, *TIME* (5/6/91)

WHERE'S THE HUMANITY FACTOR?

At the heart of many of these destructions is the sad fact that the instructions were created based on considerations other than what might work best for the people who are supposed to follow them. Maybe the instruction-givers were driven by time constraints, maybe by ignorance of the followers needs, maybe by money.

Many signage programs are a case in point. They are designed by graphic designers who are paid based on a percentage of the cost of the signs. If you want to show someone in the pediatric department of a hospital how to get to the cardiac care unit, paint a yellow line on the floor and tell them to follow it. People by nature look straight ahead and slightly downward when they walk. If we didn't, we'd fall down every time they came to a curb or a stairway.

Where are all the signs? Over our heads is the most popular place. Here you get the flashing lights, the clever icons, the brushed aluminum panels. But this is not where most people look when they are trying to get somewhere.

I have an airplane with a 12-foot wing span hanging upside down from the ceiling just outside of my office. All day people come in to talk to me and no one yet has noticed the airplane. They are all looking down to make sure they don't trip over anything.

The decision to hang signage is based on that fact that the ceiling is the largest expanse of space from which the most amount of information can be attached without impeding circulation through the space. It has nothing to do with where people look for information.

Examples of architecture that doesn't take into account human needs stand painfully evident in every city. The State of Illinois Center in Chicago is one such building. In order to maintain the integrity of the design in the glass building, all windows were supposed to remain bare, without any blinds or draperies. The direct sunlight pouring through made it almost impossible for the hundreds of word processors who worked in the building to even *see* their video terminals. Human ingenuity prevailed and office workers brought in large patio umbrellas, which they set up to shade their computers. A news report of this provoked the mayor to issue instructions that the umbrellas be removed at once. A victory for aesthetics; a defeat for the building occupants. The word processors started wearing sunglasses on the job.

Too little of what we produce has to do with real-life human interaction/behavior. The humanity factor should determine the design of instructions.

Electronic equipment and household appliances hit closer to home as evidence that the user isn't always the deciding factor in the development of products or their instructions.

"We are in great haste to construct a magnetic telegraph from Maine to Texas; but Maine and Texas, it may be, have nothing important to communicate....We are eager to tunnel under the Atlantic and bring the old world some weeks nearer to the new; but perchance the first news that will leak through into the broad flapping American Ear will be that Princess Adelaide has the whooping cough."—Henry Thoreau

As takers, there is little we can do about this except try to make the instruction-givers—the product designers, technical writers, graphic designers, architects, etc.—understand that taking into account the human factor in developing instructions will benefit everyone in the long run.

In the meantime, takers can try to understand why they are too often neglected in the instruction-construction process.

FIE-TECH OR MAN VERSUS THE MACHINE

Any sufficiently developed technology is indistinguishable from magic.
Arthur C. Clarke

*I*n New York, no one has time to sit down and drink a cup of coffee, so many New Yorkers resort to buying a cup of coffee from a deli to drink on the run. Well, these cups all have plastic lids that are supposed to make the coffee easy and spill-free to drink on the run. (There will be time-share vacations on Neptune before this is accomplished.) The lids used to be simple plastic cylinders with a molded edge to fit snugly around the rim of the cup.

In the never-ending quest to create the first drip-free coffee cup, the plastic lids have become complicated affairs requiring pushing here and pulling there, a little tearing, a little punching, and some folding, all of which usually results in much coffee-spilling on you before you have even tried to drink it. And this is only a coffee cup lid. The packaging industry has created a new generation of containers that require instructions just to get to the product inside.

Adult-proof packaging is only the most superficial aspect of contemporary complexity. We have gotten farther away from the workings of the devices that run our lives. Before, when tools were simple, we had a sense of how and why an object worked. We used to be able to see the way things were made. Goods were purchased from the establishments where they were made so we could see them at different stages of development. We bought bread from a bakery, where dough could be seen rising on sheets and loaves baking in the ovens. Shoes were purchased from a shoemaker. It was easy to see what went wrong when a wheel fell off a Conestoga wagon.

Even the mechanical devices that assisted us were easy to understand. You depressed the key on your manual typewriter that pulled a wire that was connected to a hammer that popped forward and struck an inked ribbon. Simple. But then came the electric typewriter, and we could no longer feel what was happening with the pressure of our finger. The hammers were replaced by a ball that moved too fast to see, and then the electric typewriter was replaced by the even more unfathomable word processor.

THOSE THAT NEW TECHNOLOGY LEFT BEHIND

"Millions of intelligent people—people who manage to drive cars to work every day and read a book a week—are stopped in their tracks when faced with programming their VCRs. They can argue fine points of law, but can't boil water in the Microwave oven. They can calculate taxes for major corporations, but can't change the message on their answering machines. They're the technologically disabled of our society. And they are us."

According to Link Resources, a market research firm:

● "Almost a third of VCR owners never set the timer to record from the TV.

● "Of the 20 million households that have personal computers, 2.2 million (11 percent) use them less than once a month. Another 2.2 million use them once or twice a month.

"These are not stupid people. They're uninformed, intimidated, confused and overwhelmed. They use their electronic devices; they just don't use them fully. People buy $3000 computer systems because they need a super typewriter.

"Experts worry that a society of techno-idiots can't make informed decisions. How can we understand global-warming when we can't come to grips with call-waiting?"—Anita Manning, *USA Today* (1/16/90)

"It seemed easy enough when Eddie explained it at the shop. 'All you do,' he said, 'is connect the converter box to your VCR and the VCR to the TV set.'

"I labored for two hours trying to hook into the system. Cable from wall to box input. Cable from box output to VCR input. Cable from VCR output to TV antenna input (VHF). It should have worked. It didn't.

"....The next morning, I called Falcon Cable...'I'm sorry, Elmer,' the lady who answered the phone said, 'but there's no one here. I'll take your number.' I tend to mumble at times of stress. She thought I had said my name was Elmer Teenez. No one called back.

" 'That's because they checked their records and they have no Elmer Teenez as a customer,' my wife said. 'I've never met anyone else who couldn't say their own name. Let's try it together. Al (pause) Mar-teen-ez.'

" Eddie had made the off-hand comment that if I needed help, just call. So I called....Eddie is one of those nice guys who can't say no. Guys like me who whine to get our way count on that.

" 'You have no pride,' my wife said when I hung up.

" 'Pride goeth before the fall,' I said." —Al Martinez, "Hooking Into a Converter," *Los Angeles Times* (4/8/89)

Nowadays a lot of electronic equipment doesn't get repaired, but gets replaced instead. The cost of repair is often as great as the cost of a new model.

We have grown farther from the process of manufacture. We can't see how things are working. With the technology of today, we can't see the relationship between the thing and its operation. Everything is concealed in intricate circuits and memory boards. There is no way to visualize failure because the failure is now invisible. In the old days, when the light went out you shook the bulb and if you heard a rattle, you knew it was burned out.

The alienation of man from his environment affects everyone differently.

VOYAGE TO THE BOTTOM OF THE PC

"At Boston's Computer Museum, a 50-foot-high mock-up combines bits-and-bytes realism with animation to demystify the arcane world of computers. 'Lots of people use computers without knowing how they work. This makes those workings understandable,' says Executive Director Oliver Strimpel, who dreamed up the $1.2 million Walk-Through Computer and won funding for it from software pioneer Mitch Kapor, the Sloan Foundation, and Digital Equipment."
—*Business Week* (7/9/90)

"In the early fall of 1983, I hauled off and punched a computer. It was two months after I'd purchased my first machine, and ten minutes after I'd somehow relegated an entire chapter of a book I was writing to the eternal limbo of the data void. My work was gone forever, vaporized because in my abiding naiveté, I'd relinquished control to a machine I didn't understand."—Donald R. Katz, "Don't Be Mean to Your Machine," *Esquire* (5/90)

Our machines come to us enclosed in their inviolate temples. We are warned: "CAUTION: TO PREVENT ELECTRIC SHOCK, DO NOT REMOVE COVER. NO USER-SERVICEABLE PARTS INSIDE. REFER SERVICING TO AUTHORIZED SERVICE PERSONNEL." And further depressing is that even the authorized ones don't seem to understand how the machine works. When one of the computers broke down in my office, we called our repair service, who sent someone to fix it. The repairman took the computer apart and then started replacing the parts. Each time he dropped in a new card or circuit board, he tested to see if the problem was corrected. He never figured out what went wrong or why it went wrong. He just corrected the problem by trial and error. Machines are black magic to most of us, but I find it disturbing that they might be magic to the technicians as well.

According to a survey we conducted of business people, 92 percent owned equipment that they couldn't use to its fullest. In rating their own ability to use certain equipment, over 40 percent claimed that they either couldn't operate or could perform only basic operations on an office phone, a computer, a fax machine, or a VCR. Sixty percent of the respondents possessed over 30 instruction manuals; 10 percent said they had more than 100. Some estimated the number of manuals by the amount of space they took up, such as a "folder full," "a drawer full," "a file cabinet full." Others too overwhelmed to count used expressions like "too many," "tons," "countless." The higher up they were in the corporate echelon, the more manuals they seemed to possess. Robert E. Horn, chairman of Information Mapping, Inc., claimed his office has "one of the world's largest private collections."

Unless you happen to be trapped on an island, your life is dominated by equipment, and it all comes with instructions.

You need at least a basic proficiency with a dozen appliances just to make it to work in the morning— an alarm clock, an electric razor, electric toothbrush, a hair dryer, iron, refrigerator, coffeemaker, toaster, microwave, electronic security system, a garage-door opener, and an automobile. Then, when you get to work, the equipment really gets complicated— computers, fax machines, copiers, and, perhaps the most telling example, office phones.

Nothing symbolizes the complexity of modern life like the office phone, the repository for a host of incomprehensible functions and paraphernalia like call-waiting, auto-redial, conference-calling, speed-dialing, paging, and voice mail. This innocent-looking device has also spawned a host of auxiliary equipment like answering machines, beepers, and paging systems. Yet most people I know can't even put someone on hold and transfer a call. Just making a phone call has become a complicated ordeal.

PRESS ONE

For example, in an attempt to save employee time, more and more companies are using recorded messages to sort calls. These elaborate phone triage systems rival the complexity of Red Cross operations during wartime. Just getting a live person

LIFE WITH A COPYING MACHINE

The copying machine gets jammed, so you call the service representative to fix it. And it gets jammed, so you call the service representative to fix it. And it gets jammed, so you call the...

"The goal of all inanimate objects is to resist man and ultimately to defeat him."
—Russell Baker

"Speaking of telephones, we have some of the best technical people in the world at Apple and most of us haven't a clue how to use our telephones."—John Sculley, chairman of Apple Computer

YOU WANT YOUR TONSILS OUT, FINE, BUT DON'T EXPECT ME TO TRANSFER A CALL TOO.

I was talking to my doctor, who suggested that I call back to make an appointment with his receptionist. Trying to avoid spending more time on hold, I asked if he could just transfer the call. He laughed ruefully and said, "I'll try, but don't expect much. They didn't cover transferring in medical school." Sure enough, a few clicks and clunks later, I heard the old familiar dial tone.

on a telephone involves careful adherence to a complex set of directions. What started with the airlines has mushroomed to many other industries and new levels of sophistication. The recorded messages used to have just one tier of instructions; after pressing one button, you were likely to get a human voice. In researching this book, I found that one tier is now positively primitive and companies seem to compete with each other for the most elaborate systems. I came across 5-tiered messages. The first tier goes something like this: "If you are calling to order a Supersonic product, press one. If you are calling with a problem on a piece of equipment, press 2. If you are calling for directions to our dealership, press 3. For customer service and back orders, press 4. If you are calling for a particular person and know their extension, press it now." Once you select one of the options, you are confronted with a new level of instructions. "If you want directions to our Sheboygan store, press 3."

The options increase exponentially. One begins to wonder how far someone will have to go to get a person on the other end of the line. And, God forbid, you should get to tier four and hit the wrong button, it's back on hold for you buddy.

Think of how many sales are lost, clients made angry, and customers frustrated at having to go through this lengthy, humiliating ritual just to ask a simple question. Imagine what will happen when the rest of the world jumps on the bandwagon of this technology. Right now this phenomenon has been somewhat limited to big business, but the day cannot be far off when you will call you lawyer and get the following message: If you are calling about divorcing your spouse, press 1. If you are calling about a malpractice suit, press 2. If you want to sue someone, press 3. The possibilities are endless. How about your psychiatrist? "If you are depressed, press 1. If you are obsessing, press 2. If you need to renew you prescription for Thorazine, press 3..."

A device that was first conceived to help human beings stay in touch has become buried under a host of special features and options—all designed to avoid human contact.

OPTION OVERLOAD

Many are beginning to question the American way of equating the number of choices available to people with personal liberation. Acts that were performed without thought 10 years ago now require numerous decisions and specific instructions. Take water in restaurants, for example. It used to be something that was set down in front of you—whether you wanted it or not. With the popularity of bottled waters, now you have to decide. Do you want Pellegrino or Perrier? Ramalosa or La Croix? Evian or Naya? Would club soda be all right or are you trying to cut back on sodium intake? With gas or without? Do you want a lemon, or a lime? Do you want ice? Is the water chilled? The routine that once took a split second now can involve a 5-minute conversation with a waiter or waitress.

Some of life's basic conveniences that we once took for granted now require assessing options, making decisions as to need, and following more complex instructions. Even turning on a light nowadays can require making many decisions—what level to set the dimmer, when to set the timer to go on or off. Should it be fluorescent, incandescent, or halogen? Lights now have different levels of meaning that require more sophisticated decisions.

"An increasing number of sociologists and other experts are beginning to believe that the marketplace may have outsmarted itself. Americans, they say, are becoming overwhelmed, even paralyzed by all these choices, and some experts say that the apathy is spilling over into other areas of daily life," said Lena Williams in an article, "Free Choice: When Too Much Is Too Much," in *The New York Times* (2/14/90).

You may be tempted to respond by withdrawing from the technology rat race to join the ranks of proud techno-dolts, that segment of the population that attempts to elevate electronic incompetence to some kind of beatific condition. After all, these are mere machines, and technological wizardry seems a skill incompatible with your highly developed sense of humanity.

THANKS, BUT NO THANKS

According to a publication, *Communications of the ACM* (12/89), "Twenty years ago, forecasters were envisioning U.S. household by the end of the 1980s filled with such futuristic devices as automatic bed-making machines, lawn-cutting robots, and garbage-vaporizing lasers. Now a collection of 1960s predictions gone awry has been compiled in a study entitled *Leading Technologies that Led Nowhere,* by Steven P. Schnaars. Another example of off-the-mark forecasting is the annual $5 billion AT&T hoped to be earning by now from its Picturephone. Price (and the potential of being broadcast coming out of the shower) killed that project. 'People won't rearrange their life style just to use a product,' says Schnaars."

Often, giving or receiving instructions means exchanging numbers, and every day it seems there are more numbers that you have to know about yourself.

A Deluge of Digits	
Typical numbers in a modern life.	**DIGITS**
Social Security	9
Zip codes	5 or 9
Addresses (home and office)	2 to 12
Telephones (home and office)	20
Checking account	9
Automatic teller machine	4 to 6
Bank credit cards	16
Driver's license	9 to 19
Automobile plate	7
Computer identification	4 to 9
Fax number	6
Home security system	4 to 6
Combination locker	4
Briefcase combination	3
Federal Express account	9
Cellular telephone	10
Telephone answering access code	3
Telephone calling card	14
Safe deposit box	4
TOTAL	**142 to 175**
May vary depending on occupation and residence	

The average number of digits people have to know. Adapted from *The New York Times* (5/24/89).

What you may not realize is that the skills required to assemble your kid's bicycle and program your VCR are the same ones needed in your interactions with other people. The same reasons that you cannot figure out how to set the clock on your microwave might explain why your employees don't perform up to their capacity— you don't understand their language. So you can't understand their instructions about what kind of direction they need to perform their jobs; you can't make the best use of the information they bring to you; and you can't use fully their abilities.

Operating and assembly instructions are a metaphor for the fallibility of human communication. Most of us are well aware of their shortcomings. We have all opened boxes to find machines that defy operation and toys that refuse to be assembled, yet we don't recognize the similarities between these situations and communication in the workplace. The instructions fall prey to the same shortcomings as company presidents and we have trouble following them for the same reasons.

A good manual should lead you through a machine, in much the same way a good boss leads you through work. Instead, more often, the language of the manual isn't translated into your language and you can't seem to reach what you need to know. The instructions seem contradictory and confusing; they are out of sequence; or they bog you down with intricate, elaborate instructions for every feature, but neglect to tell you the most essential information that would enable you to plug into those features.

Manuals should be the means by which we move between the world of art and science, between modes of understanding—classical and romantic. (*See Chapter 6.*) Instead, they are often a barrier instead of a bridge to activity. And they are getting harder to avoid. The complexity of today's communication systems and the pervasiveness of complicated machinery have made us more dependent on them.

Most of the informal instructions that we get everyday affect us in much the same way as the formal, written instructions. The instructions don't talk to us in a way that we can understand. They don't translate technical vocabulary into plain English. Many of them expect too much of our understanding; they don't tell us the signs that we have done something wrong or encourage us when we have done something right.

MANUAL RESISTANCE

Every week, machines seem to grow more stream-lined, smaller, lighter, and faster. The first answering machines weighed more than 200 pounds and took up half of a desktop. Now, some weigh less than a pound and record messages on a cassette that's half the size of a business card.

These machines sit on your countertops and creden-zas oozing ultra-thinness, ultra-lightness, ultra-chic-ness, and ultra-features. These are all desirable characteristics that you can grasp, because for years manufacturers have been using these adjectives to sell you everything from cars to VCRs. You have been convinced that these machines will liberate you

"Every time we ask one of our kids to set our VCR clocks, we display digital paralysis. Everytime we beg them to reset the buttons on our car radio, we diminish in stature.

"....I came by a story written by teenager Russell Jacobson in his school newspaper, *Tideline,* of Palisades High School in Pacific Palisades, CA, and it was enough to make your blood run cold. The thrust of this article was that shrewd teenagers can use their knowledge of tech-nology not only to impress and confuse parents, but eventually to make them dependent on their kids....'It used to be the only means of effectively disposing my parents to my case was to hold my breath until I turned blue,' he wrote, but now Russell gets what he wants by threatening not to program the VCR for his father so he can watch 'Victory at Sea.' "—Erma Bombeck, "Byting the Hand that Feeds 'Em," *Daily News* (7/25/89)

"Imagine dozens of landing craft, Marines rushing out on the beach carrying on their backs the latest, most compact, high-tech gear that we can provide. And following close behind, trucks carrying hundreds of looseleaf binders containing the maintenance instructions to repair this fancy gear, should any of it break."—"A Truckload of Paper onto a 5" Disk," *Data Conversion Update* (Vol. 3, No. 1)

from the dreary duties that are anathema to a life of pure bliss. Thus, you are lead to believe that every millisecond of efficiency will bring you that much closer to nirvana.

Understandably, you feel betrayed when you discover that you have to spend your time in paradise paging through operating manuals, because while the machines are shrinking, the manuals seem to be growing larger. Besides, how could such a streamlined machine have such a clunky, cumbersome, and incomprehensible manual, you ask yourself? When a computer took up an entire room, you were inclined to accept a manual the size of a breadbasket. Now that an equally powerful computer fits into an interoffice mail envelope, you wonder why the manuals for it need their own file cabinet.

Manual handling has become an expensive time- and space-consuming consideration for most businesses. The amount of money and resources poured into writing, storing, updating, and retrieving documentation for office equipment and computers is staggering, to say nothing of the cost of outdated, inaccurate, or misplaced materials.

A study cited in *Fortune* magazine found that paper storage costs corporations an average of $0.25 per page, with retrieval costing $1.50. A misfiled document is estimated to cost $120 in employee time. Do you know how much paper-handling costs your business? I bet you can't figure it out.

While you are looking at the machine itself, you can pride yourself that you are a model of the modern man or woman. This becomes a nearly impossible illusion to maintain when you have to tote around a five-pound manual in case you should need to do anything other than dust it.

Learning how to work something is like trying to learn music late in life. When you are young, you can thrill yourself with being able to play "Twinkle, Twinkle, Little Star" because your knowledge of the realm of music is so limited. As an adult your taste becomes more sophisticated. After hearing Chopin, playing "Chopsticks" isn't likely to provide much of a sense of accomplishment. The simple exercises that you must perform to become a musician won't keep you motivated the way they might a 5-year-old. Learning to operate machinery is the same. When you understand what a fax is supposed to do and have some familiarity with other electronic equipment, it becomes harder to focus on simple instructions like "plug the machine in." You can be easily distracted.

These responses may not be logical, but they are human. After you have agonized through a VCR manual to record a football game, you don't want to have to repeat the process every Monday night. It's humiliating; it reminds you of the discrepancy between the technology at your fingertips and the ability of your fingertips to operate it. The thought that modern conveniences may be making our lives

BUT WHERE DO YOU PARK THE MANUALS?

"If all copies of the OMIs (Operations and Maintenance Instructions) that were printed to support the first launch of the Space Shuttle were stacked atop one another, the tower of paper would rise 2,000 feet above the roof of the VAB (Vehical Assembly Building). It would be nearly twice as tall as the world's tallest building— the Sears Tower in Chicago....The weight of the paper used for the first mission's OMIs exceeded the dry weight of the orbiter Columbia by more than 7 1/2 tons."—"Out to Launch," *Space World* (4/82)

"Technology, almost by definition, is intimidating to most people. So, when you then tell someone that they have to go through a manual in order to be able to use the technology, instead of creating a bridge, you really create a barrier. With the Macintosh what we actually find is that most people who fall in love with the product delight in the idea that they never opened a manual. The goal for the designers is to design a product that never requires a manual." —John Sculley, chairman of Apple Computer

more inconvenient flies in the face of progress and in the face of how much money we are willing to plunk down for them.

> In the Preston Sturges movie, *Unfaithfully Yours* (1948), the main character, Alfred (played by Rex Harrison), cooks up a few plots to murder his wife after he suspects that she has been unfaithful. Part of the plans involve tape recording his own voice then running the tape at a faster speed to sound like a woman's screams. In his imagination, everything works perfectly. In reality, he takes out his Simplicitas Home Recording Unit and doesn't understand a word of the instructions after the message at the top of the page: "The first thing to remember about the Simplicitas Home Recording Unit is that it is *so simple it operates itself.*"

I believe people are intimidated by great technological leaps and will accept only a certain level of advancement. When video disks came out several years ago, consumers weren't interested because they couldn't be connected ideologically to any existing technology. Compact audio discs succeeded because they were perceived as a record that plays better and doesn't scratch. CDs didn't demand the acceptance of a new technology. Now video disks will probably be accepted because of their similiarity to CDs.

The disparity between us and our knowledge of what goes on inside machines is so much greater today. And to be reminded so continuously of the gaps in our understanding is depressing. I think this is why people get depressed while visiting museums or reading James Joyce. They realize the distance between the wealth of the contents and their own ability to comprehend it. The gap between human potential and actual ability can be a demoralizing expanse.

Depression aside, you are also wasting your money when you pay for features in equipment that you do not use. Rest assured, you are paying for that On-Hook-Voice-Request button on your fax machine. What use have you gotten from it? As long as consumers cast their vote for feature-laden electronic equipment simply by purchasing it, manufacturers will continue to think up new features.

The fierceness of competition within the manufacturing industry has produced a generation of products whose primary functions are virtually buried under a mountain of special features. Running machinery used to be a simple matter of making a choice between on and off. Operating instructions, sometimes known as "documentation," have become an industry unto themselves. Even turning on a light these days involves following sophisticated procedures and making numerous decisions. I know people who live in new houses where there are lights for which no one can find a switch. Switches are around the corner from the lights, in the next room, down the hall from the source, in configurations that have no bearing on the placement of the lights. How does the configuration of switches relate to the placement of lights? What about dimmer switches? Is the light really off or is the dimmer switch just turned down? What level of light do you want? How do you operate the timer? When do you want the lights to go on and off?

It used to be that you had to remember to wind your watch every day. Now watches come with instruction manuals. They can remind you when to take your medicine, calculate your taxes, and keep a list of telephone numbers.

RISE AND FALL OF DIGITALS

"Few objects are more symbolic of the onslaught of digital technology than those ugly, television-shaped, silicon-chip-laden computers for the wrist—tiny devices that only a few years before their appearance would have required a gymnasium full of vacuum tubes. These machines exploded on the material plane so powerfully that it seemed certain the analog sweep of a second hand would be relegated to the museum alongside pendulums and sundials.

"....But then—more abruptly than the transformation appeared—digitization stopped. In its place there arose a reaction so radical, and a resurgence of an analog aesthetic so powerful, that within the two or three years ending just a year ago, the bellwether digital watch and its industry disappeared.

"....Looking back at the vertical rise and fall of digital, it's clear that some of the public reaction had to do with 'interface' problems, poorly conceived applications, and the like. Who hasn't seen a digital clock flashing eternally on a VCR or

TELESCOPE INSTRUCTIONS SET SPEED RECORD

Tasco Sales, Inc., should be applauded for trying to save the customer time in putting together their Model 9F Telescope and for bringing the rat race into assembly instructions.

"READ THIS CAREFULLY; HI-SPEED ASSEMBLY INSTRUCTIONS ALLOW YOU TO ASSEMBLE THIS TELESCOPE IN LESS THAN 15 MINUTES. YOU MUST FOLLOW DIRECTIONS STEP-BY-STEP."

a coffee maker because the owner can't figure out how to program the thing? For many people, daylight saving time came to refer to the six months during which you had to add one hour to what it said on your watch."—Donald R. Katz, "Aren't You Glad You Use Dials?," *Esquire* (9/90)

WHAT ELSE IS NEW?

"The rapid advance in our modern 'conveniences' has left some men lagging. Meet the hindmost.

"....Just between you and me—I wouldn't want this to get back to [my wife]—I'm really not as clever at dealing with today's so-called 'conveniences' (even when they are already assembled, with batteries installed) as I would like [my wife] to believe.

"I offer as an example the headlights on the car I was recently sold. (I didn't buy the car—I was sold the car. I had driven to the dealership garage to have my radiator checked for winter, and this salesman said, 'Have I got a deal for you.' So I drove away with this Buick Century Limited. What it's limited to, I don't know, but it certainly wasn't the price.)

"Anyway, the first time I turned on the lights, they were on bright. I immediately fumbled around on the floor with my foot for the dimmer button, and there was no dimmer button. Now the cars were flashing their bright lights at me and honking their horns. Some, mostly truck drivers, were rolling down their windows and shouting unkind things at me as we passed.

"I'm sure by now you know how sensitive I am. So I pulled off the road, and after much soul-searching and car searching, I fastened an umbrella over one headlight, and I strained the light from the other one through an old 'M Go Blue' T-shirt I dug out of the back seat. The next day, back at Algoods, where I'd been sold the car, Tom, the patient service manager, showed me how to dim the lights by pulling back on the steering-wheel gadget that notifies opposing drivers of the direction in which you are planning to turn.

"Or take the two smoke alarms I bought last July....I installed one of the smoke alarms in the kitchen close to where my dear wife does the burning, and I put the other alarm in the bedroom. After hanging around for some months without action, the one in the bedroom became bored one night around midnight and began to emit a shrill chirp every minute or two. Well, I've slept through—and with—a number of disturbances, but I rose up on the fourth night of this infernal beeping and cleverly, for me, switched the raucous one for the quiet one in the kitchen. When this one, at exactly 3:10 AM, began trying to outchirp the one I had exiled to the kitchen, I banished both mechanical canaries to the trash. The next day I bought two new ones.

"Two days later a friend—whom I now hate—made an offhand remark that one of his smoke alarms had begun to beep to let him know that its battery was weak. Upon which I dashed home, but the trash had already been picked up.

"Have I told you that the first time I tried to get money out of one of those bank machines it nearly cost me at least three fingers of my best hand? I managed to get my card positioned in the right place without too much trouble. Then I was instructed to punch in my memory code, of course, which I had been cautioned to keep in a secret place known only to me and God. And I had followed the instructions so carefully that now maybe God knew where it was, but I certainly didn't. Thus I was required to take a shot at the number from memory. Which is tantamount to my chances of being appointed head honcho of NASA. But I would give it a shot.

"My first shot was 5352. The machine said I'd made a mistake and to try again. So I tried 3255. The machine wasn't any happier. Then I tried 2535. Still no money emerged. And I was reaching in to retrieve my card when this razor-sharp door dropped in front of it and nearly severed my three digits. And on the display panel I read, 'We'll contact you later.'

" 'You came close enough to contacting me then,' I quipped to the machine, loud enough so the first dozen or so bankees lined up behind me would appreciate my ready wit. Upon returning to my car I happened to notice that my license plate number was 60A3552. I've probably been putting my memory code number on motel registration cards ever since I've been involved with this banking-machine business."— Maynard Good Stoddard, "What Else Is New?" *Saturday Evening Post* (3/89)

Quietly, you blame yourself for your failure. You worry about how you will eat when your children leave home. You feel pathetic. You are overwhelmed by instructions.

MS. FAKE BYLINE WINS PULITZER

The New York Times ran an article on a Texas-Mexico ferry that was written "By Fake Byline." The newspaper uses a computer system that demands that all stories have bylines. In cases where a story is to run without one, the words "By Fake Byline" are typed in place, then later deleted. In this case, the computer operator didn't know how to delete the byline, according to Mike Pearl, in an article, "Byline Fit, So the Times Printed It," in the *New York Post* (7/21/90). But the real question is why couldn't the computer system be programmed to work with an article without a byline?

"All those wonderful features and functions there at the push of a button. But which button? As technology advances, we retreat—dumbfounded by the very innovations designed to help us," said Today show correspondent Mike Leonard during a segment on following instructions aired April 13, 1990.

Some respond by ignoring the instructions altogether. A study of product usage conducted in 1982 by P. Wright et al found that 34 percent of the subjects would not read any of the instructions that accompanied the 60 products used for the experiment.

Others content themselves with half-mast operation of equipment, using only the basic features and jerry-building ways around their lack of understanding. In essence, this means that the machines are running the operators.

SEX, DRUGS, AND MICROWAVES

"I mean what's a microwave oven, man? Everybody's got one, nobody knows what it does, nobody knows how it works, everybody's got one. Why? Why does everybody have a microwave oven? Think about it.

"Because the TV set told 'em to buy it.

"I'm telling you man, the government is building this computer, biggest computer they ever built. Spending billions and billions of dollars. It's a secret project but I read about it.

"....When they finish this computer we're all gonna be dead, man...'Cause they're gonna hook this huge computer up to everybody's TV set. Then they're gonna reverse the TV set so it can see you in your house doing your thing? Computer's gonna watch you, man, and if you do something the computer doesn't like, it's gonna send a message to the TV set. TV set's gonna send a message to the microwave oven, door's gonna pop open, you're gonna be ASHES, man...

"Don't believe me? Go in a store, pick something up, pick anything up, take a look...everything's got those little computer lines on 'em now. Everything. What do those little lines mean, man?

"Nobody knows. Nobody knows what they say, it's not English, it's computer. All these computers are talking to each other man, nobody knows what they're saying. It's like we're living in an occupied country.

"All day and all night long, the computers are talking to each other on the modems and the fax machines and the satellite link-ups? All day and all night. What are they talking about? What are they talking about? I'll tell you what they're talking about, they're talking about you and me...how to use us more efficiently.

"See they don't have feelings, man, they're just machines. All they care about is efficiency.

Mitch Kapor, creator of Lotus 1-2-3, said that the requirements for good software design are firmness, commodity, and delight. "Firmness represents the notion that the program should work well without any inconsistencies or cracks in its operation. Commodity represents the notion that the program should be useful and worthy of the user's time and effort in understanding it. And delight represents the notion that the program should engage the user and make the experience of using the program actually fun."

Code-a-Phone receives between 2,000 and 3,000 calls a week on its toll-free help line to answer questions from distributors, dealers, and customers.

ONLY A CELLULAR PHONE CALL AWAY

Do you know what long-tone DTMF signals are? Have you ever operated in the manual peripheral mode, used automatic pause (memory-linking), switchhook, and enhanced system service?

"The worst human being who ever lived had feelings, man. Genghis Khan had feelings. Adolph Hitler had feelings. Every once in a while he'd get a little bummed out. Computers never get bummed out man, never."—Eric Bogosian, *Sex, Drugs, Rock & Roll*

INSTRUCTION PERMISSION

Some people buy equipment, then are so afraid of not being able to use it that they never unpack it. They blame themselves. Code-a-Phone, one of the largest manufacturers of telephone answering machines, said that the main reason people return their products is they can't figure out how to use them.

In much the same way that general instructions should offer built-in reassurance that takers are on the right track, equipment instructions should reassure users. Manuals should remind users that they don't have to be able to use all the functions to operate a machine. People want to take the camera out of the box, drop in some film, and start taking pictures. They want reassurance: "You've done it. The camera is working now." Some people will want to go further. "Okay, I can take pictures. Now I want to use the manual override." You want to know how to operate it from a basic level. But the way most instructions are structured, people get overwhelmed before they start.

My family and I went to Italy last Christmas. I thought it would be nice to get a video camera for the trip. Sharper Image advertised a little camera made by Sony. I equated little with simple. Little turned out to be big squeezed into a little package, at least as far as the product special features were concerned. The feeling I had when looking through the manual was that after putting in the battery and the videotape, I should learn how to do "lap-dissolve titles." I don't even know what a lap-dissolve title is, but it doesn't sound like something I'd ever want to do. What I really wanted to hear was was, "Congratulations, you have made a good choice and have bought a wonderful camera. Now make sure the battery is charged (look for the red light), put in the film, and push Play. Take a picture. Play with it. Push Rewind, then see what you have done. There, you did a great job. We suggest you practice taking pictures. You might find that the camera works better when you move it slowly from one scene to the next. After a month, if you want to come back and visit this manual and learn to use the special features, we'll be here. But it's fine if you don't."

Manufacturers are starting to respond to the cry for simplicity. WordPerfect Corp., the makers of the number one selling word-processing software, recently introduced LetterPerfect, a modified version of its signature program. LetterPerfect includes most of the original features of its parent, but has eliminated some of the sophisticated layout

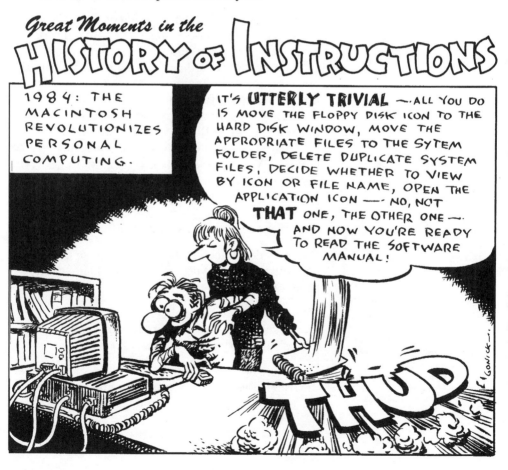

functions, whose operation demands more memory—on the part of the user as well as the computer.

People don't want to conquer a machine, they want to use it. Total mastery is not what most people want from their fax machines. They want to send a memo to Joe in Toledo.

Instructions should be developed that give people permission to operate the fax machine at a basic level. With clear focused instructions, they will get the message: "You did it. That's great." With this kind of reassurance they will be more inclined to proceed, to move on to more sophisticated usage of the equipment.

CUE CARDS

Instructions can't bear the burden of reassurance alone. Machines must be designed with clues or reminders as to what buttons perform what function so that one glance at the operating panel will spark your memory. For example, the instructions for performing basic functions on Phone-Mate answering machines are printed right on the machine. You can flip up the top and read step-by-step instructions on how to record a greeting or reset the time. Very simple. When you call in to get your messages, a recorded—but still human—voice talks you through the process and will tell you how to perform each of the features on the machine. You don't have to carry the manual with you at all times.

Batteries don't need instructions because most equipment comes with a diagram that shows the proper position for them.

This concept can be applied to the design of machinery to incorporate features that might trigger a user's memory as to its operation.

Designers have to decide how much responsibility the user should have for programming functions. Theoretically, a machine could be designed that had

"Design is the key factor that is going to separate high-tech company survivors from losers in the next 20 years....The company that can put out a product that is most easily understandable in terms of the consumer, no matter where he lives or what language he speaks, is the company that is going to come out better in the world market," said Charles Owen, a professor at the Illinois Institute of Technology, in an article by William Mullen, "The Low Side of High-Tech," in the *Chicago Tribune Magazine* (2/11/90).

one button for every function. Each would be labeled according to its function. You wouldn't need a lot of instruction, you would just need to find the right button. But the keyboard might have 2,000 keys and the computer would be cumbersome.

On the other hand, most functions on a computer could be performed with only a few keys—and an on-and-off switch. But this would require the user to program most functions. Often, the easier the operation, the more complex the machine.

Donald Norman, a California psychologist and author of an extraordinary book called *The Psychology of Everyday Things*, criticizes industrial designers for ignoring basic patterns in people's expectations of products. Well-designed products contain clues to their operation and facilitate the mind's "natural mapping"—the process of making physical analogies between equipment and previous knowledge. To make a right turn in a sports car, you can use the steering wheel in the same way that you did on a tricycle.

"Computer technology has shifted the responsibility for many decisions directly onto the designer. Before the Macintosh, the typesetter, color separator, reproduction house, and photographer were delegated responsibilities by the designer. Now the designer, through the computer, assumes these responsibilities."—Adam Kalish, "Computer Literacy Without a Shared Context," *Statements* (Fall 1989), published by the American Center for Design

---

FUZZY LOGIC

For several years, the Japanese have been at work developing machinery that operates in ways more compatible with the way the human mind works. They manufacture washing machines with optical sensors that with the push of one button determine how much detergent and water are required at what speed and time. They have cameras that adjust themselves to unusual lighting situations. The design of the software that runs these appliances is based on a principle known as *fuzzy logic.*

Unlike the classic artificial intelligence of most U.S. computers that rely on data fed into a fixed system, fuzzy-logic computers are based on neural networks that can learn from experience. Classic artificial intelligence depends on yes–no responses. Fixed rules are programmed into the computer; then data is fed into it and coded or sorted accordingly, always by the same rules. Neural-network computers can reprogram themselves based on new information. While fuzzy-logic computers can't reprogram

AMERICA DROPS THE BALL AGAIN

"[Fuzzy logic] is the latest in a long line of technologies—from robotics and VCRs to solar cells—that Americans invented, only to see savvy Japanese manufacturers take the lead in finding commercial applications. For Japanese firms, fuzzy logic may prove even a greater coup than the VCR: within a decade, everything from cameras and elevators to toasters and automobiles will probably incorporate fuzzy logic computer chips. 'In 10 years,' says Sheridan Tatsuno, principal of NeoConcepts in Fremont, Calif., and an expert on Japanese technology, 'fuzzy logic will be a 2-to-3-billion-dollar business.'

"By then we may be buying fuzzy VCRs that come with only one button—to turn them on and off—and are programmed solely by voice commands. Fuzzy cameras will automatically and subtly compensate for tricky lighting situations. Fuzzy microwave ovens will watch over meals with the same sensitivity as a human cook."—Michael Rogers with Yuriko Hoshiai, "The Future Looks 'Fuzzy,' " *Newsweek* (5/28/90)

themselves, they are based on a neural-network concept and the fuzzy-logic software is flexible enough to respond to new information, much the way human beings can.

Fuzzy logic was actually developed in the United States in the 1960s by a professor at the University of California-Berkeley, Lotfi Zadeh. Owing to the dearth of software available, corporate America didn't show much interest—unlike the Japanese. They have found numerous applications for the concept—from household appliances to computers, such as a Sony computer that recognizes handwriting on its screen.

According to an article by Michael Rogers (with Yuriko Hoshiai) in *Newsweek* (5/28/90), Zadeh is philosophical about being a prophet with little recognition in his own land. Zadeh, who still teaches at the University of California, said, "In the U.S., there's a tradition for what is precise, for Cartesian logic. In Japan, there is more appreciation of the imprecise, of ambiguity. I've always been confident that people will come around to my way of thinking."

Zadeh may be right for interest has piqued of late in the United States. In California, a computer system designed to approve home loans alters its recommendations based on which loans go sour. A Kenmore refrigerator uses fuzzy logic to defrost itself and the Johnson Space Center has expressed interest in using fuzzy logic and neural networks in space vehicles.

Several industry analysts have predicted that the manufacture of fuzzy chips will spawn lucrative start-up ventures in the United States in this decade.

FUZZY IMPLICATIONS

The success of products driven by fuzzy-logic computers attests to the need for equipment that mimics the way users think. This need can also be applied as a metaphor for instructions as part of general communications as well. In the workplace, people need to be instructed in a language that mimics the way they speak and understand. They need focused directions that relate to their duties and to their abilities to complete work assignments, to provide a service, or to make a product. They need instructions that can be adapted to new circumstances and unforseen outcomes.

Needs are the same in all aspects of people's lives. Whether trying to do a favor for a friend, to understand someone else's feelings, or to find a new place, they need to speak in a mutual and adaptable language.

SPONTANEOUS GENERATION: THEORIES ON THE ORIGIN OF INSTRUCTION MANUALS

"First impressions can be lasting, and, if consumers have a problem following the setup directions for one of our products, you can bet they will carry those negative feelings with them as they start to use the product."

Charles Gange and Amy Lipton, "Word-Free Setup Instructions: Stepping into the World of Complex Products," *Technical Communication* (3rd Quarter, 1984)

*W*hen the average American home had only a few appliances, no one thought too much about operating manuals. But now that the consumer electronic age has made button-pressing the dominant indoor activity, the jumbled jargon of instruction manuals rankles on a new plane and the nontechnical consumer is further put off by the world of machines, finding the technical world all the more arcane.*

The reluctant electronic-agers are also wasting their money when they buy machinery with features that they won't or can't use. They are getting shortchanged by manufacturers who produce products without adequate manuals that would allow the consumer full use of the product.

I thought that the process for developing operating and assembly instructions might shed light on the problems of instructions in general.

After 6 months of calling manufacturers of electronic equipment, we came to the conclusion that manuals are produced by spontaneous generation. One day there is an empty box; the next day it is filled with manuals in a nest of Styrofoam pellets.

Trying to talk to someone who writes operating manuals can be more difficult than trying to follow one. No one seems to know who writes them or even where they come from. If you ever want to get rid of someone for about six months, tell them to try to get the person who wrote your fax manual on the phone. It can't be done.

IN SEARCH OF THE HOLY GRAIL

My associate, Loring Leifer, came back with the following report after I asked her to attempt to find a manual-writer:

> Most of the people I talked to had a different version of the spontaneous generation theory.
>
> - "Our manuals are developed by the individual manufacturers."
>
> - "They just come in a box. I don't know who writes them. We just distribute them."
>
> - "I have no idea. I suppose it's someone over in Korea. We just get them already written."
>
> - "Gee, I don't know. I'll see if can find out for you." Fat chance.
>
> My first attempt was with Sears, Roebuck. I figured everyone has owned some piece of equipment from Sears at some point in his/her life. I was transferred 6 times, from a Sears store in the Bronx, to the Parts Department in Mount Vernon, New York, to what I thought was the Sears executive office in the Sears Tower in Chicago, which turned out to be the real estate office.
>
> In Mount Vernon, a parts representative said that they are on a computer system and the only way she could order manuals was by the model number. (Sears must have taken lessons from the U.S. Army.) I explained that I was doing research for a book and was trying to locate the department where the manuals were produced. The determined and rather single-minded representative kept asking for a model number; I kept explaining that I was working on a book. She said, "Doesn't your mother have a Sears refrigerator?" Apparently, she thought Sears equipment was even more ubiquitous than I did.

The Parts Department didn't seem to have any idea where the manuals came from or who wrote them, nor did it have a desire to know.

Finally, I got in touch with Manny Banayo, manager of public affairs in the Chicago headquarters. He told me to write Jim Podany, who was the person in his department who could help me. On February 3, 1989, I wrote a letter explaining what I wanted. I am a patient person, but when he didn't respond by September 18 of that year, I decided to call him. A secretary told me that John Summers, the marketing manager for Sears appliances, was the man to contact. Summers returned my call promptly and even commiserated with me, saying that he was always buying appliances with manuals that were written by someone in another language and then translated into English by someone who didn't seem to be able to understand it. When I asked him where Sears operating manuals were written, he said he didn't know, but that he thought they were written by "different people," sometimes in marketing, sometimes by the individual manufacturers.

I asked him to send manuals for electronic equipment, such as a VCR and assembly instructions for a bike, which he did. Now optimistic, I decided to explore further. In February 1990, I called him back to ask more about the process for developing the manuals. He said that he was moving on to a new job and I should call Jackie Bitowt after the first week in March after she got back from her vacation. She was the new marketing/communications manager for home products. After three days of calling her office, I got her on the phone March 8. She said that she couldn't help me without a letter. I explained that I had written to other people in her office already. She said she would need to see a letter and that John Summers was out of the office until Monday. Then she said, "Since the reorganization, we're just trying to get the job done. It is unlikely that Sears would participate in your book."

I didn't need the entire Sears organization to write the book. I just wanted to talk to one person who had something to do with the Sears manuals. I explained this to her.

She answered politely, "There hardly is a department."

I gave up on Sears and decided to try Panasonic.

Panasonic has a phone system that makes callers feel like they are trying to break into Fort Knox. Its mult-tiered recorded instructions offer so many options and buttons to press that even the most focused individual is likely to forget why he or she called the company in the first place. If you are calling for information regarding a piece of Panasonic equipment, if you are calling for service, if you are calling for directions to our Secaucus store, there's a number to press. My index finger started to ache. Finally, I pressed the right series of buttons and Michael Maggio in customer service suggested that I call Ron Tomcyk in public relations. He said that he thought about 90 percent of the manuals were written in Japan and that a couple of engineers in the United States revised them for the U.S. market. For any more information, I would have to call Justin Camerlengo, the general manager of corporate communications, he said. I left 3 messages and he didn't return any of them. Apparently people can be just as impenetrable as recorded phone messages. A few days later, Ann Ballas called in his behalf. She said that the manuals were written in Japan, where the equipment was manufactured. She suggested that I might try calling Jerry Surprise, who was the product manager at the facility in Chicago or Mike Collichio in consumer relations.

The trail seemed to be disappearing, so I decided to try Sony.

Several calls later, I found Lloyd Barningham in Kansas City. He is in charge of distributing the operating manuals for Sony products. He says

Apple Computer once tried including credits on its manuals. According to Sue Espinosa, director of developer channels, in a company newsletter, the results were not always pleasing for the following reasons:

● Many believed, rightly or wrongly, that they made a valuable contribution, but got excluded from the list of credits.

● A few individuals who were listed requested to be removed from the credits. Perhaps the undeserved attention embarrassed them or they had moved on to other projects by the time the book finally went to print.

● Some writers were personally besieged by calls from customers complaining about something in the book or about the product.

they are written in Japan and get sent over in a box and that he just distributes them. He did send a few examples of operating instructions, but I decided such passive acceptance of life wasn't going to get answers to my questions.

I began to suspect that there must be a secret program to mask the identity of manual writers along the lines of the Federal Witness Protection Program. I imagined this Manual-Writers Protection Program was probably designed to protect the lives of the manual writers and their families from irate consumers who can't figure out how to record *Cheers* on their VCRs.

Suspicious, but still determined, I went on to General Electric.

I have a General Electric refrigerator and I always thought the manual for it was quite helpful. Not only did it include understandable information on the installation, use, and maintenance of the unit, but it had material on how long different animal products would last in the refrigerator or the freezer. There were even instructions on how to get the racks out of the unit if the door couldn't be opened all the way.

The manual even had a phone number to call for more information. It was in large type and on the first page. I am always suspicious of product manuals that have no phone number and sometimes even no address so that you couldn't possibly track down the company to ask any questions about its products. General Electric went out of its way to broadcast its accessibility.

I also thought the manual was particularly well-written.

So at noon on Friday, June 30, 1989, I called the GE Answer Center number to try to find the person who wrote the manual to tell him or her what a fine job I thought he or she was doing. To my great surprise, a live human voice answered after the first ring and identified himself as Mr. Miller. Explaining that the manuals weren't written in his office, he suggested that I write to the Customer Relations office in Louisville, Kentucky. I decided to call instead. Directory assistance didn't have the number for that department, but an operator connected me with Customer Relations, which was answered by a machine that informed me someone would call me back if I left my name and number. One hour and nine minutes later, a woman named Tonie Sullivan returned my call and promised to try to locate the author of the manual. At 3:22 PM she called to tell me that a Jean Hopwood would be able to help me, but she would be on vacation until July 24.

Meanwhile, I called the GE Answer Center to get other examples of GE instructions. An operator politely told me that I would have to have a model number, but that she would be happy to send me two catalogs of GE products. She explained that Thomson Consumer Electronics, Inc., had purchased the GE line of TVs, stereos, VCRs, radios, and telephones, but that GE retained the home appliance division. After receiving the catalogues, I called the answer center to order instructions, but they became suspicious when I wanted so many different model numbers and said that this service was for owners of GE appliances. The operator suggested that I call Thomson directly.

Someone in the Louisville office told me to call Edith Garrett in Customer Relations and gave me a telephone number that turned out to be that of TCE Technical Publications. An operator told me that for $3.50 a piece, I could order any manual that I wanted. I inquired if this was the department where the manuals were written; she said she had no idea where they were written, but I could call the RCA referral number. An operator, who identified herself as Rosemary, heard my questions and rather agressively wanted to know "Who gave you this number?" I think she was trained by the CIA. She said, with Secret Service pride, "I don't have any information." I didn't exactly threaten her with bamboo splints under the fingernails. Only my polite determination was able to get her to give me the Consumer Relations number, which was answered by a machine that offered me several confusing options. Number 4 was for operating manuals, but when I pressed the button, I got the same number I'd called before in Louisville. I had to hang up and dial again. I pressed 5 this time for customer service and got another recorded voice promising options for various appliances.

At a point of total discouragement, a sympathetic man in the TV division let me talk to Dan Romisher, who used to work in technical publications. Dan actually divulged the names of the 2 women who were responsible for RCA and GE electronic equipment manuals. Pay dirt at last.

I actually had an extended conversation with a real, live, articulate person who, while she didn't compose the manuals from scratch, was responsible for adapting them for American consumers. Suzanne Deem was an administrator for consumer publications at Thomson (which makes GE electronic equipment). "We are supplied with a draft of operation instructions. We have developed a format for manuals based on meetings with merchandising, marketing, engineering, and product planning people. We also use our common sense. When you receive a product, what is the first thing you do? You would open the package and take out the paperwork and read it. We start with the safety instructions first, followed by a table of contents, then a product features page, and then the operating instructions.

"Common sense tells us that this is the order of importance. But our vendors tell us that people don't read the manuals.

"Our manuals come in pidgin English. They are supplied by the manufacturers, who are often Korean or Japanese. It is a real headache. Because of the scheduling and the fact that the manual has to be ready in time to be packed

into the box, we have to write or rewrite a manual while they are still making changes in the product. Sometimes we don't even get a workable unit on which to write a manual. For example, we are working right now on instructions for a TV. The software is being developed in Germany; the parts for the TV are being manufactured in Singapore; and it is being assembled in Taiwan. Product modifications are possible at any of these points. We're pressed for time. This process depends on a high level of communication between all these points and that's not easy when you are dealing with different people in different parts of the world who all speak different languages. It's a lot of anxiety. We're ready to print the manuals and we find out that the software is incorrect. If the manual is wrong, it's my fault," she said.

"There are 14 people in the technical publications department, but only 2 of us who produce the owner's manuals. We do about 40 a year. The rest of the people work in technical training and service data.

"I have a bachelor's degree in business education with a minor in library science. Many in the tech pub field come from an English major background. The supervisor here tries to get nontechnical people because they are more likely to be able to communicate with consumers than the engineers who talk like engineers.

"In the first 5,000 pieces of equipment, RCA puts a questionnaire into the owner's manual. We are always open to suggestions and we review and modify manuals based on consumer feedback."

When asked if she was good at understanding manuals, she said, "I never read them. I always have my husband do it. I'm learning though. My brother and his friends, most of whom have master's degrees, couldn't figure out how to program a VCR and I was able to do it, but it wasn't easy.

> "Our warrantee department did a survey and found that 92 percent of the people could understand our VCR manuals. TVs got a slightly higher rating."

Some of the more conscientious manufacturers do have people who are responsible for making sure that these mysteriously appearing manuals conform to some standards of clarity. They will rewrite or edit the existing manuals, trying to correct translation errors, or explain parts or functions that might have been added after the original manual was written.

WHAT'S THE PROBLEM

Our attempts to locate manual writers for some common consumer electronic products brought us to the conclusion that companies don't set out to write shoddy instructions. You can't just blame bad translators either. Poor manuals are the result of many factors.

They happen because of the way products are designed, built, and assembled. Globalization has redefined the way companies do business. The software may be developed in Europe, the parts manufactured in Taiwan, and the product assembled in Japan. This creates mind-boggling communications problems for the person writing the instruction manual, especially when changes can be made to a product at any of these 3 points.

When you have a product developed in 3 different countries by people of 3 different cultures, it's no surprise that the manual is a bit befuddling. If people have difficulty translating each other's ideas when they are both speaking the same language, you can imagine the difficulty of translating among 3 different cultures. My uncle, Howard Friedman, understands German. He had a Japanese camera that had instructions printed in German as well as English. He looked at the German version and it was radically different from the English one.

"An increasing number of companies are beginning to realize that well-written product manuals help increase customer satisfaction and so are seeking user input to help evaluate their documentation. Current research clearly reveals the importance of evaluating all kinds of instructions, from policy and training handbooks to product manuals."
—Dana Gillihan and Jennifer Herrin, "Evaluating Product Manuals for Increased Usability," *Technical Communication* (3rd Quarter, 1988)

"It's an irony of the information age that high-tech products are usually better designed and better made than the manuals that accompany them....The reason, according to Irwin Steinberg, who directs Carnegie-Mellon University's six-year-old Communications Design Center, is that 'the last thing most project managers ever think about is the manual. They get rewarded for bringing a product in on time and under budget, not for producing accessible instructions.'

"....Functional writing and document design are intrinsically different from most other forms of communication, assert Steinberg and [information designer] Alan Siegel, because they require people to act and interact with things they don't really understand.

" 'There has to be a visible language, a merging of graphics and text,' said Greg Kroeze, who supervises manual production for Allen-Bradley, the machine-tool company, 'There's a delicate balance between being simple enough but detailed enough to be useful. The biggest thing is that the document is made not to be read but to be used.'

"....At the Communications Design Center, for example, documentation is tested by studying videotapes of individuals talking out loud as they try to get things to work according to the instructions. Using this technique, one of Steinberg's students discovered he had left out three important steps for a manual he had nearly finished explaining how to measure radiation leaks."—Michael Schrage, "Struggling to Understand Manual-ese," *The Washington Post* (12/26/86)

As long as products are developed by parting out the different aspects to different countries—software to one place, parts manufacturing to another, and product assembly to a third—you can't expect more sensible instructions. The increased reliance on computers for translation is going to make matters worse.

If you think the person who translated your VCR instructions did a lousy job, wait until you see what a computer can do.

"In machine translation...entire documents are translated electronically....Virtually every major electronics company in Japan is said to be working on translation software. Fujitsu America, for one, says it may soon introduce in America a system it has sold in Japan for five years. But the software may only be sold with a Fujitsu workstation. In Japan, the package sells for $34,000."—"Multilingual Software: Too Crude To Be Useful," *The New York Times* (11/19/89)

With the price of computer translation programs dropping and their ability to crank out translated documents at one page per second, compared with a human translator's 10 pages per day, more documents will be translated by computer. The trouble is that to date bilingual human beings can distinguish shades of gray and where the bilingual translation programs cannot. The programs have critical flaws. "I can fish" might be translated to "I work in a cannery."

I developed an ACCESS guide to Tokyo. It was a real education in cross culturization. After attending a few meetings there, I discovered that silence was often more important than speech. I would propose an idea and the others would say nothing. The Japanese don't want to disagree, so they say nothing. If you respond by trying to defend your position, you have lost face. So you have to return the silence. The person who breaks the silence loses. For an American, this can be an unnerving practice.

"Actually, Sony is regarded by many in the consumer electronics industry as having among the best documentation. In addition, the company maintains a telephone 'customer information center' in the United States that receives more than 1,200 calls a day.

"According to Sakae, there is a 'computer record which summarizes all the questions.' This information is 'sent back to Tokyo and often our documentation has to be modified as a result of this feedback.' "
—Michael Schrage, "Struggling to Understand Manual-ese," *The Washington Post* (12/26/86)

Companies are recognizing the importance of creating manuals that are universally understandable. "Standardization is very important from a cost standpoint," said Sashi Sakae, president of Sony Service Co., a part of Sony Corp of America. "That's why our instructions are written in four languages."

But let's be realistic. The translation of equipment documentation is never going to get the same attention that translating the *Iliad* does. Imagine a group of pipe-smoking scholars talking about the merits of the Fitzgerald translation of a camcorder manual. It won't happen. It's unreasonable to expect that equipment documentation will ever get that kind of attention.

The time schedules for product development don't allow for it. The documentation has to be printed and ready to go into the box as the product comes off the assembly line. This means that sometimes manuals have to be developed for products that do not exist other than in prototypical form.

But I think instructions should at least be produced by people in the country where they will be sold. Having a bilingual Japanese person translate a Japanese manual into English is not enough. The Tokyo ACCESS guide was first written in Japanese. This version was translated into English and fully rewritten. Then a bilingual person read both versions to make sure that one captured the flavor of the other. I don't think I did one step too many.

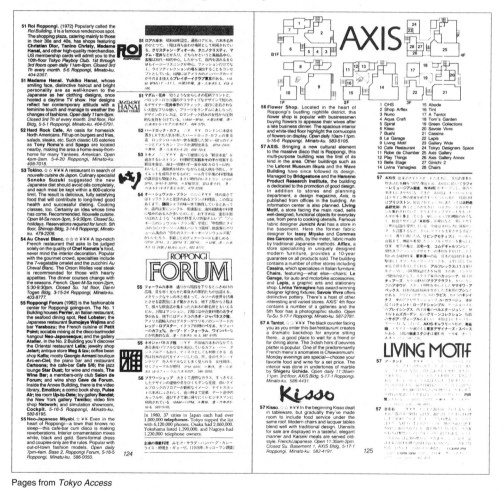

Pages from *Tokyo Access*

KNOWING TOO MUCH

(See the *"Disease of Familiarity"* in *Information Anxiety*.)

Bad documentation also happens because the person developing the manual knows too much about the product and can't place himself or herself in the mind-set of a novice. Expertise in a particular field sometimes precludes an ability to understand what the uninitiated user needs to know about a product.

According to Kerry Johnson, Ph.D., of the Omega Performance Corporation (a company that provides instruction-design consulting services), the principle reason operating instructions get so befuddled is that "the people who write them focus on their peers rather than on their audience. They don't look at the equipment from the point of view of the user. What people need to know to build a product is not necessarily what the people who sell it need to know [or the people who use it]. They each need a different level of information."

"The instruction writers have a private language. They have not adapted the language to that of the instructee, but have articulated in an inappropriate language. They refer to the 'response mechanism position' and you wonder what do they mean? They may mean the speaker."
—Publisher Jeremy Tarcher

Operating and assembly instructions attest to the phenomenon that once you learn something, you forget what it's like not to know. When someone knows too much, they are sometimes blind to the obvious, which is what the user probably needs to know.

"The field cannot well be seen from within the field."
—Ralph Waldo Emerson

This compounds the problems of translations because the language of the experts can't be translated into the language of the uninitiated.

Owing to the dichotomy in our education between hard and soft learning, not only do engineers and industrial designers forget what it's like not to know how to operate a piece of machinery, they may also lack training in basic communication skills.

DESIGNATED HITTER

It seems to me that most offices have a designated hitter, a person who has a knack for understanding how to operate equipment. These people must be examples of the techno-humanist, the person who can move comfortably between the world of technology and the world of communication, i.e., instruction. I talked to Olivia Harmantzis, a former employee in my office who used to figure out how everything worked.

"I wind up figuring out how to use things because I have the time to read the manuals and I have the patience to figure them out. Patience is essential. Sometimes I approach things as if I know how to operate them and that's when I make mistakes. With new equipment, you have to sit down, look at it, and read the manual from the beginning, correlating what you read against the equipment itself.

"Sometimes, there are pictures in the manual that don't correspond to the machine, which is very frustrating.

"In changing the bulb in the Artemide light, the instructions showed you how to change a bulb in three easy steps, but they never showed you what the bulb itself looked like. I kept trying to separate the glass from the metal housing, because I had an idea this is what constituted the bulb. It wasn't until I photocopied the bulb and sent the picture to an Artemide representative that he told me the whole apparatus was the bulb and all I had to do was plug it in.

"Once something is already operating, it becomes more frightening to make an adjustment. If you weren't there when the machine came out of the box, you are less likely to learn how to use it fully. Once it's operating, I don't want to try new things on it because I'm afraid I'll damage it.

"The equipment itself tells you a lot about how it operates without the instructions, if you stop and think about it. You have to have a willingness to learn how to do it and make sure that what you want to do is possible."—Olivia Harmantzis

LIABILITY OF MANUFACTURERS

Despite appearances to the contrary, product liability law requires manufacturers to instruct the user in how to assemble a product, to describe the main ways that the product might be used incorrectly, and to warn about foreseeable hazards arising from the ordinary use of the product.

Product manufacturers must test instructions and make them readily available and understandable to a person of ordinary intelligence. Failure to meet these standards can be grounds for a product liability case.

Of course defining just what constitutes ordinary intelligence is another problem. Take condom instructions for example. According to an article in *Science News* on September 17, 1988, a University of California study of the instructions for 25 brands of condoms determined that they all require at least a 10th-grade education, and most require some college-level reading ability for full comprehension. The instructions, which dealt with the use, handling, and storage of condoms, were analyzed based on vocabulary and word and sentence length to calculate their difficulty. The scientists who conducted the study claim that, "although little is known about the relationship between the condom user's comprehension of instructions for use and the condom's effectiveness in preventing pregnancy or disease, such a relationship seems reasonable." They further point out that young people as well as those who have failed to complete high school (13 percent of whites, 21 percent of blacks, and 42 percent of Hispanics between the ages of 25 and 34) could encounter difficulty with existing texts.

Clearly the manufacturers could do a better job.

Tampax is one manufacturer that shows sensitivity to potential problems of ignorance. What may seem ridiculously basic to some might be critically important to another.

TAMPAX®
Tampons | Flushable Applicator

If you're using TAMPAX® tampons for the first time please read these directions carefully.

TAMPAX® tampons provide a comfortable and discreet alternative to sanitary pads which are worn outside the body.

The TAMPAX® applicator has been carefully designed to fit your body and will not affect your virginity or internal organs. Because the applicator guides the tampon into proper position, it's easy to use and your fingers never touch the tampon. So TAMPAX® tampons can be used comfortably and with confidence, even by beginners.

How to insert a TAMPAX® tampon.

First, wash your hands before you begin.

Next, choose one of these positions for comfortable insertion:

• Sit on the toilet with your knees apart.
-or-
• Stand, placing one foot on the toilet seat.

Now, just relax and take your time.

1. Remove the TAMPAX® tampon from its protective wrapper. With your thumb and middle finger grasp the grooved center of the applicator (Diagram C). The removal cord should be hanging down outside the smaller inner tube.

2. With your other hand gently spread the folds of the skin in the vaginal opening (as shown in Diagram D). Insert the rounded tip of the TAMPAX® tampon into the vaginal opening. (If you are not sure where your vaginal opening is, you may wish to use a mirror to see, referring to Diagram E.)

Gently push and rotate the applicator until the outer insertion tube is comfortably inside the vagina and your thumb touches your body (Diagram F).

3. Keeping hold of the grooved rings on the applicator, use your index finger or your other hand to push the inner tube completely into the outer tube. This will place the tampon in the correct position inside you (Diagram G).

4. Now simply grasp the applicator and pull down gently to remove both tubes (one will be inside the other). The tampon will remain inside you, with the removal cord hanging outside your body (Diagram H). TAMPAX® tampon applicator tubes are made of paper, so just flush them away.

When a TAMPAX® tampon is properly inserted, you shouldn't feel a thing. If the tampon feels uncomfortable, it probably has not been inserted far enough inside you. If this happens, simply remove the tampon and try again with a new one.

How to remove your TAMPAX® tampon.

To remove your tampon, just pull down gently on the removal cord. Then simply flush the tampon away.

When to change your TAMPAX® tampon.

You should change your tampon every 4 to 8 hours, no matter which absorbency you're using, or however light your flow.

Be sure to remove your used tampon before inserting a fresh one. Always remove the last tampon you used at the end of your period. And remember, you should only use tampons during menstruation—never between periods.

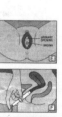

Just complying with their charge isn't enough, though. Manufacturers must fight the tendency of consumers to ignore the instructions—for whatever reason. A test of the product instruction habits of 48 literate adults, conducted by H. A. Simon and J. R. Hayes in 1976, found that in most product categories, the instructions were ignored completely at least 30 percent of the time.

The number of cases against manufacturers of products with inadequate labels has increased. The cases are easy to make and hard to defend given the low cost of warning labels, according to an article, "The Effectiveness of Warning Labels," by Mark R. Lehto and James M. Miller in the *Journal of Products Liability* (Vol. 11, No. 3, 1988). Warning labels aren't expensive special features; for a few pennies a label, manufacturers can deliver invaluable information to consumers.

IS TECHNICAL WRITING POSSIBLE?

An amusing 2-page advertisement for Toshiba appeared in *The New York Times Magazine* (5/16/90). To the right of a surrealist photo by Joseph Jachna depicting a giant hand holding a mirror is a quote from Jonathan Swift: "Vision is the art of seeing things invisible." This quote must have come to the mind of someone who was trying to figure out how to change the paper of a fax machine.

Developing operating or assembly instructions is no different than assigning a task in an office. Both require problem-solving and organizational skills— defining a need, assessing the understanding level of the taker, arranging information in an appropriate sequence. The content of both kinds of instructions should be based on the essential components of an instruction: mission, destination, procedure, time, anticipation, and failure. (*See Chapter 8.*) So who is best qualified to write operating manuals?

Owing to the way our educational system forces us to choose a scientific or a liberal arts orientation, where to go for instruction-writers becomes problematic. In fact, this dichotomy of education

Evidence of manual shortcomings can be found in the miles of shelf space that bookstores are devoting to books on how to use your computer.

Consumers have given up on the documentation that accompanies both hard and software and are ready to shell out more money on something they can understand. I am working with Danny Goodman on a book about how to use the Systems 7 operating system for Next computers. Bantam Books will be publishing it.

Danny Goodman wrote the best-selling book on how to use Apple's Hypercard. I think it shouldn't be that somebody outside the company created the best instructions for using the company's product.

P.S. The Whitley Group, a North-Carolina-based software company, developed a 45-minute cartoon video on the System 7 operating program which is now being sold by Apple Computer for $150.

Over 13,000 people belong to the Society for Technical Communication, an organization based in Washington, DC, that disseminates industry news, offers education and training programs, and provides scholarships and research grants.

The Rensselaer Poltyechnic Institute's technical writing program was one of the first of its kind in the country, graduating its first class in 1955.

Manual aficionado Robert D. Ingle, executive editor of the *San Jose Mercury News*, believes that "the best instructions are those based on a great deal of real-time observation of people using the product. Manuals must flow logically and must closely relate to the way people actually use the device or program."

makes the term *technical writing* almost oxymoronic, for how does an educational system that encourages animosity between science and the arts produce people who can be literate about technology?

The choice is between an engineer who can't write or a writer who can't engineer. It's no wonder instruction manuals are hard to understand.

Several schools are trying to correct this problem by setting up technical writing programs. To date, 70 schools have some kind of technical communications program. About 20 schools offer a master's degree program in technical communications. Boston University offers a master's degree in science journalism. The entrance and exit requirements vary widely from school to school. Some require a thesis, others do not. Some hold both oral and written examinations, some require knowledge of a foreign language.

The technical writing program at Rensselaer Polytechnic Institute in Troy, NY, is one of the few programs that offers a master of science degree in technical writing. Known as an engineering school, it attracts many students from nontechnical, liberal arts backgrounds, such as English and history.

Recognition of the schism between art and science has sparked several companies to try new tacks in creating usable instruction manuals. When Carl Sontheimer started Cuisinart about 12 years ago, among other duties, he wrote the food-processor instructions himself. Sontheimer, who has a Ph.D. from MIT, was flattered when he received two letters praising the "depth and thoroughness" of the manuals. But, when he called to thank the letter writers, he found out "they were engineering Ph.Ds. from MIT" as well.

According to an article by Michael Schrage, "Struggling to Understand Manual-ese," in *The*

Washington Post (12/26/86), "That was the moment when Sontheimer got himself out of the instruction business and turned over design of Cuisinart's manuals to professionals. The company has since made bright and accessible documentation a centerpiece of its marketing efforts."

A host of companies now offer training programs to companies interested in improving the quality of instructions. They offer advice on improving documentation for equipment as well as developing better communication skills between management and employees.

COMPUTER DOCUMENTATION

Computer companies in particular have shown an increasing interest in instruction manuals. The number of companies vying for a market share has increased exponentially in the last 15 years. Marketing the caliber of instructions is one way a company can define itself in a crowded field. As more and more techno-virgins are buying computers, manufacturers have to produce manuals that are understandable to a less sophisticated user.

Whereas manuals were once developed as an afterthought, companies are pouring more resources and attention into them now. And products are improving.

One innovator in the field of computer documentation is Hewlett-Packard. Their team approach to developing manuals relies on input from many different sources, and the technical writers get involved in the process while the product is still on the drawing boards. Their process for developing instructions serves as model for instructions in general. Information is tested on the users and may be presented in a variety of ways, so that users with different levels of ability can find their way through the manuals. Lisa Dearborn, an HP learning products manager who designs documentation for pro-grammers of computer languages such as FORTRAN, COBOL, BASIC, and ADA, explained the system that the company uses to design products and their documentation.

"Perhaps the most successful technical writer of all is Mr. [William] Crouse, who is said to have made several million dollars in royalties from almost 50 books, most of them on auto mechanics....'I do seem to have a mind that can page through a lot of technical material,' Mr. Crouse said, 'and when I'm writing, I think of an individual I'm trying to talk with, not talk down to.' "
—Edwin McDowell, "Publishing a Goldmine for Technical Writers," *The New York Times* (5/6/83)

"Technical writers. Do you know that you and creative writers have a common goal? That goal is information sharing, and how effective your information sharing is depends on your use of language—on the sound and sense of the words you choose, the organization and layout of those words, and whether the words are appropriate for your intended audience. The creative writers are aware of the effects of meter, rhythm, sound, layout, and figurative language on their readers; we technical writers should also be aware of these devices and their great potential for effective communi-cation....Effective use of language is the trick to turning on the lights."
—Susan Hennigan, "The Aha! Experience," *Petroglyph* (10/86)

"First impressions can be lasting, and, if consumers have a problem following the setup directions for one of our [IBM] products, you can bet they will carry those negative feelings with them as they start to use the product. The challenge is to develop clear, easy-to-follow, attractive setup directions that get consumers through setting up the product and leave them with their egos intact."
—Charles Gange and Amy Lipton, "Word-Free Setup Instructions: Stepping into the World of Complex Products," *Technical Communication* (3rd Quarter, 1984)

"Hewlett-Packard is spending nearly 2 years and $40 million designing a 'factory of the future' scheduled to open in Puerto Rico next year, where computer-systems employees will be hired on the basis of their creative potential."—Jay Cocks, "Let's Get Crazy!" *Time* (6/11/90)

"The goal is to help the team to design products that require less documentation.

"We use a team approach for every project. After we have determined a need for a new product or a modification of an existing one, we assemble a team made of people from research and development, technical support, marketing, learning products, and even finance. Everyone works together to meet their different needs. Someone from finance might say, 'I need to know the return on investment.' The learning products representative makes decisions as to what kinds of media are appropriate.

"After we develop a draft, we send it out to our internal users and reviewers. Usually, we send them to our response centers, where our technical support people look them over. They are the ones who talk to the users and have a good idea what the users want from a product. The R & D people also review the draft, as well as the marketing people, the support engineers in the factory, and our peers in the learning products area.

"After the internal comments have been received and incorporated, the product is sent to selected sites who try out the product and the documentation.

"After a product has been sent out, we use reader response cards, and user comments are incorporated into later editions. Usually, they send us comments such as 'This index could be better' or 'this doesn't give enough basic information.' We have a process for insuring that these comments get responded to and incorporated into the next edition.

"Our goal is to help people learn to use our products. We don't want to assume a certain media is the only way to present information. We want to be open. Should the documentation be presented on-line? In the classroom? In self-paced training? The answer may be all of the above. By blending responsibilities, you insure that the individual has a perspective on the whole project.

One factor in making decisions is how interactive is the program? If it's something that you will need to do often, it's disruptive for a programmer to turn back and forth from written material to the screen. Instructions flow more easily on-line. If it is a lengthy abstract explanation, a person can only absorb so much on a screen. Maybe a graphic would be appropriate."

Dearborn has a master of arts degree in English and taught composition at San Jose State University.

"This background is fairly common. The backgrounds are mixed in this department. We have people with computer science degrees and those with liberal arts educations. I taught technical editing and visited classrooms. I recall speaking to a technical writing class that was made up mostly of engineers. They were shocked at how much communication is involved.

"The field of documentation has grown in stature since then. In my experience, 10 years ago, there used to be more of an assumption that the customer will need to work a little bit to use your product. There was more acceptance of the difficulty in using computer systems. Now, there is an effort to make it simpler and more intuitive. This has affected documentation, making it easier to get at, putting more information on-line where appropriate, letting users have self-paced training or formal training.

"The learning products people get more respect, especially from research and development. They've improved during the four years I've been here as far as anticipating when things will be needed. It used to be, 'Oh, hey, we need a manual.' This year, we (the learning products staff) has been the focus of examining the ease of use of products. Learning products people are involved in the development of a product's usability. More and more, we get involved when the product is still on the drawing boards."—Lisa Dearborn

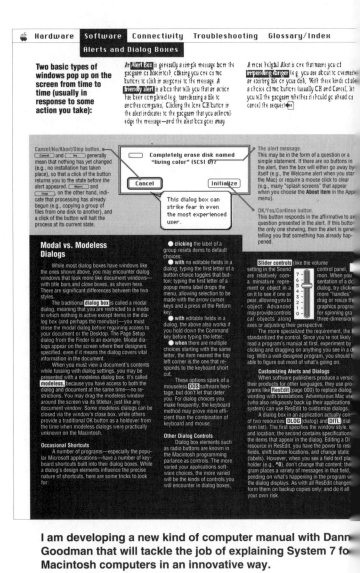

I am developing a new kind of computer manual with Dann Goodman that will tackle the job of explaining System 7 fo Macintosh computers in an innovative way.

Each 2-page spread will cover a single topic, but it will do in three levels—a simple, basic, "just get me started" approach, a more detailed explanation with "reasons why, and a full-on technical discussion. Users may choose thei own level of involvement with the material.

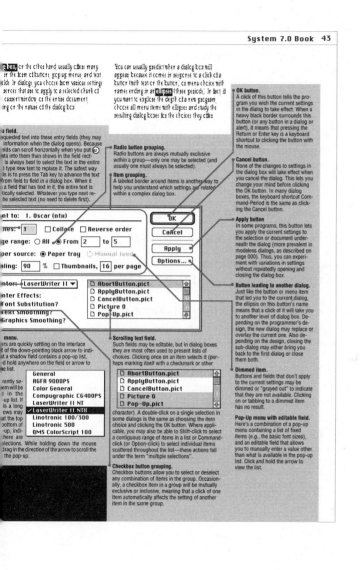

g box cr the cther hard usually cthes many
ir the item cf butter: pcp-up merus, and text
ields. Ir dialogs you choose them various settings
serves that ase to apply to a selected chunk of
current window, cr the entire document
ting on the values of the dialog box

You can usually predict when a dialog box will
appear because it comes in response to a click of a
button (with text on the button), or menu choice with
names ending in an **ellipsis** (three periods). In fact if
you want to explore the depth of a new program,
choose all menu items with ellipses and study the
resulting dialog boxes for the choices they offer

OK button.
A click of this button tells the program you wish the current settings
in the dialog to take effect. When a
heavy black border surrounds this
button (or any button in a dialog or
alert), it means that pressing the
Return or Enter key is a keyboard
shortcut to clicking the button with
the mouse.

a field.
equested text into these entry fields (they may
information when the dialog opens). Because
elds can scroll horizontally when you put
ata into them than shows in the field rect-
is always best to select the text in the entire
type new text to replace it. The safest way
is is to press the Tab key to advance the text
from field to field in a dialog box. When it
a field that has text in it, the entire text is
tically selected. Whatever you type next re-
he selected text (no need to delete first).

Radio button grouping.
Radio buttons are always mutually exclusive
within a group—only one may be selected (and
usually one must always be selected).

Item grouping.
A labeled border around items is another way to
help you understand which settings are related
within a complex dialog box.

Cancel button.
None of the changes to settings in
the dialog box will take effect when
you cancel the dialog. This lets you
change your mind before clicking
the OK button. In many dialog
boxes, the keyboard shortcut Com-
mand-Period is the same as clicking the Cancel button.

Apply button
In some programs, this button lets
you apply the current settings to
the selection or document under-
neath the dialog (more prevalent in
modeless dialogs, as described on
page 000). Thus, you can experiment with variations in settings
without repeatedly opening and
closing the dialog box.

nt to: 1. Oscar (ntx)

ies: 1   ☐ Collate   ☐ Reverse order

ge range: ○ All ⦿ From 2   to 5

per source: ⦿ Paper tray ○ Manual feed

ling: 90   % ☐ Thumbnails, 16 per page

OK

Cancel

Apply

Options...

Button leading to another dialog.
Just like the button or menu item
that led you to the current dialog,
the ellipsis on this button's name
means that a click of it will take you
to another level of dialog box. Depending on the programmer's design, the new dialog may replace or
overlay the current one. Also depending on the design, closing the
sub-dialog may either bring you
back to the first dialog or close
them both.

nter: LaserWriter II ▼

nter Effects:
☐ **Font Substitution?**
☐ **Text Smoothing?**
☐ **Graphics Smoothing?**

☐ AbortButton.pict
☐ ApplyButton.pict
☐ CancelButton.pict
☐ Picture 0
☐ Pop-Up.pict

Dimmed item.
Buttons and fields that don't apply
to the current settings may be
dimmed or "grayed out" to indicate
that they are not available. Clicking
on or tabbing to a dimmed item
has no result.

menu.
ers are quickly settling on the interface
t of the down-pointing black arrow to indi-
t a shadow field contains a pop-up list.
d hold anywhere on the field or arrow to
e list.

Scrolling text field.
Such fields may be editable, but in dialog boxes
they are most often used to present lists of
choices. Clicking once on an item selects it (perhaps marking itself with a checkmark or other

Pop-Up menu with editable field.
Here's a combination of a pop-up
menu containing a list of fixed
items (e.g., the basic font sizes),
and an editable field that allows
you to manually enter a value other
than what is available in the pop-up
list. Click and hold the arrow to
view the list.

General
AGFA 9000PS
Color General
Compugraphic CG400PS
LaserWriter II NT
✓ LaserWriter II NTX
Linotronic 100/300
Linotronic 500
QMS ColorScript 100

rently se-
em will be
1 in the
-up list. If
is a long
ows may
at the top
bottom of
-up, indi-
here are
elections. While holding down the mouse
drag in the direction of the arrow to scroll the
the pop-up.

☐ AbortButton.pict
☐ ApplyButton.pict
☐ CancelButton.pict
☐ Picture 0
☐ Pop-Up.pict

character). A double-click on a single selection in
some dialogs is the same as choosing the item
choice and clicking the OK button. Where applicable, you may also be able to Shift-click to select
a contiguous range of items in a list or Command-
click (or Option-click) to select individual items
scattered throughout the list—these actions fall
under the term "multiple selections".

Checkbox button grouping.
Checkbox buttons allow you to select or deselect
any combination of items in the group. Occasionally, a checkbox item in a group will be mutually
exclusive or inclusive, meaning that a click of one
item automatically affects the setting of another
item in the same group.

Many companies are looking for new ways to present instructions. Sony has a videocassette that demonstrates how to use a VCR. (This doesn't make much sense to me, because you have to know a lot about a VCR just to play a tape.) Cuisinart has sold over 100,000 videocassettes on how to get more out of your food processor.

According to information designer Alan Siegel in *The Washington Post* article, "Struggling to Understand Manual-ese," the issue is not whether efforts should be focused on improving manuals on paper or on film. "What it really boils down to is that there is a terrific amount of money poured into advertising to promote a product, but if companies would just take a little of that money and put it into instructional material, they would have better, happier and more loyal customers."

OVERCOMING MANUAL PHOBIA

It's up to the consumers to drive this message home. Don't put up with poor instruction manuals. Write the president of the company. Before you buy a product, ask to see the instructions. Ask a salesman to show you how to operate it. Refuse to leave the showroom until you understand.

How well a product sells is more important to the manufacturer than how well a customer learns to use it. Business is, after all, business. The responsibility lies with the consumer to tie product usability to product purchase. Ask to look at the instructional manual of a product before you purchase it. Ask yourself:

- Is it written in a language that resembles English? Can you understand it?

- Are the basic operations separated from the fancy features?

- Does the diagram in the instruction manual correspond to the actual product? (You would be surprised how many times it does not.)

This empty box was intended to contain an illustration from a Sony video camera, showing a "map" of a camera, with all the different buttons and parts numbered to correspond with a step-by-step description of how to operate the camera.

The problem with the diagram was that either the parts or the description was misnumbered. The two actually did *not* correspond. As a result, it was impossible to understand the instructions.

For any product manual, it is *critical* that the names or labels or numbers used in the diagrams be the same as the names or labels or numbers used in the written descriptions.

This particular video camera manual exhibited a second difficulty—it wasn't until page *36* that it actually told you how to take a video picture!

I can understand why Sony did not want us to portray this manual, even though, for the most part, Sony does a remarkably good job on instruction manuals.

● Are the sections of the manual organized in an easy-to-find manner?

● Is there a section on what to do if something goes wrong? Trouble-shooting or problem-solving sections are useful, because these tend to be the situations that send you to your manuals in the first place.

● Are the illustrations clear and can you see how they correspond with the actual product?

● Are the parts clearly labeled?

Adapted from assembly instructions for a Tasco Telescope.

● Is there a phone number to call if the manual doesn't answer all your questions? Any manufacturer who doesn't list a phone number or address up front for more information isn't really committed to customer service.

● Can you talk to a live person?

● Do the instructions tell you what is possible to accomplish by following them, what you can expect along the way, how long they should take to perform, and how can you tell when you've done something incorrectly?

Use your purchasing power to tell manufacturers that you expect to be able to use the features on the equipment you buy.

CUSTOMER SERVICE ISN'T A PUNCH LINE ANYMORE

The United States has learned some painful and expensive marketplace lessons. Before the avalanche of foreign products that hit the country in the 1970s, local manufacturers had a captive market for anything they produced. They didn't have to worry much about product durability or usability. The words customer service used to conjure up visions of grimy half-height windows in warehouses that framed 2 guys with name tags who resembled English bulldogs in uniform. The mention of *customer service* would elicit a nonplussed look on the part of the manufacturer and disgruntled snickers on the part of customers.

But in a field of cutthroat competition, technology customers can demand products that are designed better and are easier to operate; they can demand service as well. In a market that is saturated with similar products at similar prices and a slower-growing population that isn't producing as many new consumers, caring for customers makes sense.

> "The foundation for service excellence is culture. Culture is the invisible yet powerful code of conduct that exists in organizations. Culture defines the rules of the game, the essentials of winning behavior. Cultural change can be as much an act of undoing as creating. If an organization's existing culture is uncongenial to matters of service excellence, if the emphasis is on saving money rather than serving customers, doing what is convenient rather than being convenient, or emphasizing the sale but not the service to support it, then a cultural barrier—a service wall—exists that must be broken down to make way for new ideas."—Leonard L. Berry, David R. Bennett, and Carter W. Brown, *Service Quality: A Profit Strategy for Financial Institutions*

The Association of Home Appliance Manufacturers has established the Major Appliance Consumer Action Panel which mediates between disgruntled

Based on studies done by Technical Assistance Research Programs, the following findings were reported in the first issue of *On Track*, a newsletter published by CareerTrack in Boulder, CO:

● **The average business never hears from 96 percent of its unhappy customers. For every complaint received the average company has 26 customers with problems.**

● **Between 54 and 70 percent of those who complain will do business again with the organization if their complaint is resolved—95 percent will if it is resolved quickly.**

● **The average customer who has had a problem with an organization tells 9 or 10 people about it. Customers who have had their complaints resolved satisfactorily will tell an average of 5 people.**

consumers and manufacturers. Consumers who don't get a sufficient response from a manufacturer can write the panel and ask for a review of their complaint.

In Sweden, the post office sponsors an annual Golden Letter Day to promote the importance of customer satisfaction in doing business. One aspect of this is keeping in touch with the customer with the "golden letter."

"Consulting firm McKinsey & Co. reports that its customer-service work has tripled in the past three years, and consultant Bain & Co. has developed a model for measuring the dollars-and-cents value of retaining customers through better service.

"Extra service enables Armstrong World Industries Inc. to charge higher prices for floor tiles and Weyerhaeuser Co.'s wood-products division to command premiums for its commodity two-by-fours. Weyerhaeuser enhanced its service by developing a computer system for retail home centers and lumber yards so buyers can custom-design decks and shelving.

"....To learn more about service, executives are putting in stints at the front lines. At Xerox Corp., executives spend one day a month taking complaints from customers about machines, bills, and service.

"....To reward good service, Montgomery Ward and other companies are linking performance reviews and bonuses to customer-satisfaction ratings."—Steve Phillips and Amy Duncan, "King Customer: At Companies That Listen Hard and Respond Fast, Bottom Lines Thrive," *Business Week* (3/12/90)

"A growing number of equipment suppliers are diagnosing a wide variety of their customers' problems from service centers hundreds or even thousands of miles away. Increasingly, the remote diagnosis is followed up by a remote repair job. Among the companies that rely on long-distance telephone lines to peer into the software operating their equipment—and sometimes to change it—are Pitney Bowes for its facsimile machines, General Electric for its top-of-the-line body-scanning systems, and AT&T for business telephone exchanges....The Hewlett-Packard Company has begun using remote monitoring to spot malfunctions before they happen....For customers, it means that vital equipment often comes back on line in minutes instead of hours or days."—Barnaby J. Feder, "Repairing Machinery from Afar," *The New York Times* (1/30/91)

So many of our purchases are anonymous. We buy clothes through the mail and appliances from a discount outlet, with virtually no contact with the supplier. Even with our major purchases, such as a house or car, once the deal is done, we never hear from the agent or salesman again. I think it's reassuring to know that somebody is still there to answer your questions.

Articles and books abound extolling the financial prudence of courting the customer with postpurchase service, and manufacturers are heeding the lessons. Paying attention to what customers need after paying for the product makes particular sense with commercial consumers, who not only invest money in the initial equipment, but also must store, maintain, and update the documentation for it at phenomenal cost.

"Every department in an organization benefits by streamlining the useability of such documents as: telephone maintenance manuals, parts catalogs, FDA regulations, program specifications, transportation tariffs, MILSPEC documents, and 'hot-line' support documents.

"The latest technology lets you store a truckload of paper onto a single 5" optical disk. An optical disk "jukebox" holds in the area of one file cabinet, the contents of 200 file cabinets. The implications are staggering." —"A Truckload of Paper onto a 5" Disk," *Data Conversion Update* (Vol. 3, No. 1)

THE MORNING AFTER

Now what can you do about the products you already own but haven't figured out how to use yet? Maybe you got discouraged trying to read the manual; maybe you are afraid to take the product out of the box. What if it was manufactured by an unenlightened take-the-money-and-run kind of company—what can you do? (Let's not name names.)

(See Appendix.)

Look at the manual again. Try to distinguish confusing advice from errors of translation. If your camera manual tells you to "wind her crank," chances are the technical writer didn't know that in English inanimate objects are neutered. Photographer Herbert Keppler gives some practical suggestions in an article he wrote in *Popular Photographer* (9/88). They were developed for camera equipment, but can easily be applied to equipment of any kind.

- If [the manual] plows right into the main body of instructions, try to locate the parts that explain how to work with the equipment in its simplest mode. Mark these prominently with a colored pen.

- Once you've become familar with the [equipment], you'll find that the complete instructions will be easier to assimilate.

- If you find that your instructions are linguistically tangled, take the time to cross out all those in foreign languages.

- Look for the warnings in the instructions and take them seriously. Never fool around without first reading electrical or electronic equipment instructions.

- Are they up to date? Did you know that manufacturers periodically update instruction manuals, taking out erroneous information, rewriting unclear material, and adding information that has been learned since you bought your item?

Be patient. More manufacturers are bound to realize that good instructions can sell products.

THE MOST UNFORGETTABLE INSTRUCTORS

"If [an instructor] is indeed wise, he does not bid you enter the house of his wisdom, but rather leads you to the threshold of your own mind."

Kahlil Gibran, *The Prophet*

B

usiness, like sports, is all about making winners and losers out of apparent equals.

Most companies have well-defined, stringent requirements for hiring. Especially in management training programs, they tend to hire people with the same credentials, who come from similar backgrounds, who have similar levels of expertise, and who got similar grades in school.

Then, the company goes about finding the differences between them. Who will perform more effectively, who will bring in the most clients, who will make the decisions that result in higher profits, who is deserving of promotion? Who will rise in the corporate hierarchy and who will not?

In this kind of game, the distinctions between the two must be made with subtle differences.

Defining the qualities that make up a great leader is a popular hobby amidst business people. Everyone has his or her own list, made up of characteristics like vision, willingness to take risks, and strong people skills. But these characteristics depend on the ability to give and to take instructions—to translate vision into assignments that will realize it, to nurture talent among the work force, and to gain wisdom by heeding the advice and instructions of subordinates. How well an employer gives and follows instructions will figure in whether the company is a "winner" or "loser." And how well employees give and take instructions will figure in whether they are labeled winners or losers.

WHAT IS QUALITY?

What is quality? For centuries, this question has plagued everyone from philosophers to fur traders. How do you define that elusive characteristic that elevates one member of a type above another.

Without much difficulty, you can list the necessary ingredients of a successful instruction or even a successful instructor. But how do you capture the essence of a quality instructor, one whose instructions changed you in some way?

My own definition of a great instructor is someone who works in that margin of inspiration between one's own needs and the firing of someone else's creativity. That person for me was the architect Louis Kahn. I can't conceive of anyone being a better teacher. He was an extraordinary teacher. What made him an extraordinary person for people was that he taught 24 hours a day. And what he tried to do was to teach himself, and he did that so well that everyone around him learned. He allowed us to be more of ourselves.

If you consult literature on the subject of good instructors, you will find many vague generalities on the characteristics of a good instructor, such as:

- Enthusiasm for and familiarity with the subject.

- The capacity to incite the enthusiasm and interest of others.

- The ability to convince others that the instruction is necessary and consistent with corporate and individual goals.

- The ability to break down the instruction into bite-sized chunks and to organize them in an understandable order.

- The patience to allow the instruction-taker to carry out the task.

- Recognition of the hurdles to be faced along the way.

While the above are valid generalizations, they are not effective in pinning down the nebulous concept of quality. Our interest lies in the specific personality traits that inspire others to productive actions. So we conducted a survey of people in middle- to high-level management positions to find out who their roles models were, what they thought made a high-quality instruction. We asked them to list the most important things they learned from their model instructor and to give an anecdote or story to illustrate this. *(See Chapter 16 for a copy of the survey.)*

> "The origin of school was when a man was under a tree, who did not know he was a teacher, talking to a few little ones, who did not know they were pupils. They approved of each other, and the first classroom was built."
> —Louis Kahn

> "A teacher who can arouse a feeling for one single good action, for one single good poem, accomplishes more than he who fills our memory with rows on rows of natural objects, classified with name and form."—Goethe

The people who responded surprised us with their willingness to spend time and mental effort, to admit their own shortcomings, and to shed light on the subject. We heard from company presidents, media executives, creative directors, consultants, writers, and university professors. They made outlines, drew pictures, and scribbled notes on the questionnaires. Some of the surveys showed evidence that they had been worked on over time—done with different colored pens or pencils. A few called in to add to their answers. They argued with the questions, made suggestions, and told stories about their careers and their education.

All in all, they did a supreme job of following instructions.

MODEL INSTRUCTORS

Of the almost 100 people who responded, less than half chose a school teacher. Others listed their husbands, their wives, their parents, former bosses, former coaches, present business partners, and friends. Two respondents named people who worked for them, one listed his best friend's father, and another cited a Zen master in the art of the tea ceremony.

Men chose other men as favorite instructors 91 percent of the time. Women weren't so gender conscious. They were divided 50/50 between the sexes in their choices.

All of the respondents were changed in some way by their favorite instructor. They took the lessons into their own lives—professionally and personally. The lessons taught were diverse—from the general to the specific, from serious to silly, from practical to playful.

One of the most specific replies was offered by Jane McLaughlin, the founder and owner of John Riley Associates, an interactive multi-media production company in Olympia, Washington. I had to fight the urge to find her favorite instructor and ask him to teach me the same things. She claimed that her former boss, the late Fred Waldron, who was a manager at Hewlett-Packard, had taught her:

- "How to make people feel good about helping me."

- "How to manage people that don't report to me."

- "How to keep people from giving me a definitive no."

- "How to set people up for success."

- "How to write a good business letter."

What else would you need to know?

Greg Shaw, a partner in the Plant Recording Studio in San Francisco bestowed favorite instructor status on his ninth-grade English teacher, who exhibited an intrepid sense of equanimity in the face of trying circumstances. The teacher came into class one day and announced, "I'm turning the class over to you students to do whatever you want."

"We immediately locked him into a closet in the back of the room and didn't let him out until the class ended," claimed Shaw. "He was patient and appreciative, and he applauded our initiative."

Conversely, graphic designer Massimo Vignelli applauded his teacher, Mies van der Rohe, for his less pliant attitude toward divergent approaches. Vignelli quoted van der Rohe's following response to a question as an example:

Q: "What if somebody wants to open a window in your building?"

A: "Tough luck, baby."

Chicago—1959

For Bill McCaffery, creative director and president of McCaffery & Ratner advertising agency, the ability to give constructive criticism was an essential quality in a model instructor. His most memorable instructor was Professor Albert Gold, who once critiqued his drawing by saying, "McCaffery, that's beautiful. In fact, that's possibly the best drawing of a big toe I've ever seen. Now, if you can just bring the rest of the figure up to that big toe…"

For some, a model instructor is one who can draw from different media to fire all your senses with a picture of an idea. Donald Hamilton, an education development specialist for Rockwell International, cited his friend and former music teacher, Jeff Reynolds, for such mystical abilities. Hamilton, who got into instruction design through his career as a musician and music teacher, applauded Reynolds for his ability to "talk, demonstrate, and relate a concept to art, history, current TV shows. He gave such a complete verbal, aural, and visual image of abstract musical principles that you could almost touch the music, as though a ball was floating in space before you."

Others also turned toward their music teachers for role models. Betsy Davis, a manager of the Inter-active Media Entry Business Unit of Microsoft, Inc., remembered her high-school piano teacher, Mrs. Barton, who would mimic the way Davis played a passage, then play it as it should be so that Davis could hear the difference.

A few were lucky enough to have more than one model instructor in their lives. Miho, the chairman of graphic design at the Art Center College of Design in Pasadena, California, listed Lorser Feitelson, a painting teacher; Rikyu, a Zen master; and architect Louis Kahn. From them he learned how "artists solved very difficult problems, how to put art into historical context, how to see the ordinary in an unordinary way."

James Kramer, chief executive officer of the American Institute of Architects, awarded favorite instructor status to his high-school baseball coach and his grandmother, both respositories of practical advice. His coach taught him how to "tolerate a lot of losses while keeping a vision of success and to expand your skills by applying expertise in one area to another." His grandmother was wise in the ways of working with people and had a firm belief in "honesty, fairness, and high moral conviction."

Shad Northshield, senior executive producer of CBS News, recognized the power of these traits over divergent political viewpoints and personalities in his relationship with a film editor who worked with him covering the Vietnam War.

"He was a supervising film editor; I was his boss. During 1965, we routinely looked at film together; we never disagreed on anything. We had a very intimate professional relationship. After a year and a half, we discovered that he was a totally unreconstructed hawk and I was one of the early doves. Yet during that time, we had never disagreed. It was a stunner. It was a revelation of the total respect that we had for each other that enabled us to work together. From 1965 to 1969, he and I were deciding what Americans saw of the Vietnam War. We learned how unimportant politics were on a personal basis."

Northshield couldn't resist adding a postscript: "Eventually I converted him."

The influence that a quality instructor can have knows no bounds. Charlie Beier, an associate director of the New York Zoological Society, learned from a teacher of European history "to listen, to make bridges between people and events, to view situations in other than logical frameworks, and to focus on a subject. We were taught history through the methodology of a *soap opera*; we learned about the interrelationships of people, not faceless events," he said.

That a good teacher can interest a student in any subject was borne out by Tom Lincoln, a professor of medical information and research pathology who credited a former teacher and boss for his reason for becoming a pathologist. What he learned from the man, who became a friend, was of the broadest application: (1) To do it yourself. (2) To laugh at failure. (3) To be modest in success.

Another person who learned a universal lesson was J. Michael Birch, the director of technology for GTE Imagitrek. His father taught him that

one couldn't really understand something "unless one could explain it simply and clearly to someone else"—one of the best and most effective tests of how well you have learned anything.

From the global to the specific, Doug Wolfe, president of Hawthorne/Wolfe, a corporate communications consulting firm, remembered a former employer, graphic designer Jesse Califano, for teaching him that "no detail is small. Photo-mechanical art always had to be prepared with meticulous detail, even the cover flaps and labels were created in a uniform style—not just to impress the client, who may have reviewed only the art inside, but the printer. I learned why when I accompanied Jesse on a press check at the printers. The press foreman introduced us to the pressman responsible for our job. 'This is Jesse Califano. He's the guy with super accurate mechanicals; he's a tough guy to please, so make sure he's happy with the job.' I quickly grasped the importance of accurately prepared, neat, clean art. It sends the right signal to *all* who come into contact with it. It's as much a psychological tool to achieving perfection as a graphic requirement."

Jim Butler, an associate creative director, also cited a former boss, Mike Tripoli, who headed the graphic design department of an architectural firm. Jim learned that "it's okay to be impassioned about an idea, but you don't have to devote your life to work. It's what you do outside of work that brings depth to your thinking."

Some valued more offbeat lessons. Paul Sparks, who works in educational program development at Rockwell, remembered this scene in a high school history class: "In the middle of a test, the teacher laughed loudly after grading the paper of a troublemaker who defined Chiang Kai-shek as 'the sound metal makes when it hits a cement floor.' The teacher told us this, laughed again, and said, 'Bonus 10 points for creativity.'" The most important thing this teacher taught is that "what matters most is not what is true but what people think is true."

Not everyone looked up to find a model—at least on the conventional status hierarchy. A few people named their own employees as model instructors.

Robert H. Waterman, Jr., co-author of *In Search of Excellence* and author of *The Renewal Factor,* said that Watson Bowes was his favorite instructor. He was a real estate consultant. "When I started work as a consultant in Denver fresh out of business school, I got involved with a client who wanted to locate a new plant site," said Waterman, who is CEO and president of The Waterman Group consulting company. "I knew how to go about the process, but I needed an expert in real estate appraisal. I hired him to work for me, but in a lot of ways, he was really running the project. Because I was so new and inexperienced, he could have taken over the project. What he actually did was act as my consultant and whenever I got stuck, he'd say, 'What do you think?'

"He forced me to put my thinking cap on in a subtle and not so obvious way. In making presentations to a client, again, it might have been much more impressive if he had done it himself, yet he encouraged me to do it. There was an interesting result from the client's point of view. I became their primary consultant. And at one point, the client asked, 'Who is this guy Bowes? Why are we paying him in addition?' He was so willing to be in the background that they didn't even see he was adding value, while he was making a tremendous contribution. He was continually pushing me to do things, in helping develop my self-esteem.

"Interplay between mentor and person being coached depends on the individual personalities. Some people respond well to coaches who are very demanding. I don't. I think that I know myself well enough to recognize that I have relatively high-control needs. In observing coaching relationships, a great coach for one person will not be a great one for someone else. I worked with a lot of bosses who were very demanding at McKinsey. At a conference there, we got into the subject of coaching. Junior and senior partners from all over were asked to name their favorite coach within the company. The guy whose name came up most frequently was a very gentle, quiet man, Gil Klee. He had very high expectations, but they were not unrealistic. Having high expectations could come across to a lot of people as demanding, but I think there is an important difference."

> **"Experience is a thing that enables you to recognize a mistake whenever you make it again."**
> —Franklin P. Jones

Jeremy P. Tarcher, president of a Los Angeles–based publishing company of the same name, listed experience as his model instructor—a conviction that has made him reluctant to instruct others.

> **"Experience is not what happens to a man. It is what a man does with what happens to him."**
> —Aldous Huxley

"Learning ultimately happens from experience and not from a teacher. I cannot instruct experience. I cannot help my employees think the problem through. I can give them pieces, but they have to carry the examples over to the other pieces [on which] I am not instructing them. I hated my schooling until I went to college. I did not like my teachers. Therefore, I do not like being put in the position of one.

"Experience has taught me the limits of individual consciousness. The way I see or experience things and react to them is a reflection of who I am and what I believe, not of the things themselves. Knowledge comes not from someone, but to someone. I have never had someone who taught me in the sense that *doing* has taught me. When experience teaches, the lesson is learned in an unmistakable manner. There is an obviousness, an unavoidability to it. When you do something wrong, you quickly see it.

The moral for instruction-givers here is to build in ways that enable the -takers to learn from their own experience.

"Once I was having an argument with my wife about something that was very important to both of us. I said, 'One moment. Let me try to see it from your point of view.' Somehow I was able to flip out of my perspective. It wasn't that I saw it from her point of view, it was just that I saw her point of view was right. The fact that I deeply held a point of view that I was sure I was right helped me see that, in the end, she was more right than I was. By experiencing the other point of view, I couldn't avoid understanding that this applies with others as well, with the people in my office, with the writers I deal with, with the Ayatollah Khomeini....They hold their ideas with the same sense of rightness that I do. They are right from their point of view. We all go around thinking that the way we see things is the right way."

The intense Tarcher, whose book list could best be described as visionary, did admit that he didn't learn by experience alone and that his wife, Shari Lewis, had taught him many other important lessons. "Her example of efficiency and courage has, I think, been extremely important to me although, because it is part of my life everyday, difficult at some times to recognize for its significance."

Although the respondents chose instructors from a wide variety of backgrounds, a profile of the model instructor began to emerge. The common characteristics are as follows:

"Donald Schon, a professor at MIT and author of *The Reflective Practitioner,* eloquently describes the relationship between knowing by doing and knowledge by learning. His notion of reflection in action is a powerful premise. He states that professionals are called upon to perform tasks for which they were not educated, and where the rules no longer fit the education or the education no longer fits the rule. Professions such as graphic design suffer from shifting ambiguous ends and unstable institutional contexts and are, therefore, unable to develop a stable body of knowledge. The lack of, or limited, exchange between schools of design and practitioners of design separates research from practice and application from education."—Adam Kalish, "Computer Literacy Without a Shared Context," *Statements* (Fall 1989), published by the American Center for Design

- Someone who is able to explain the big picture, the context in which the instructions are set.

- Someone who can teach you to see patterns so that you can transfer knowledge in one area to another.

- Someone who can instill confidence in you.

- Someone who can teach you to ask the right questions.

- Someone who can describe an idea in a variety of ways and thus create a 3-dimensional picture of an idea.

- Someone who is passionate about his or her subject.

- Someone who allows you to make mistakes and encourages you to take risks.

- Someone who sometimes goes in the opposite direction from accepted custom to give instructions.

We asked respondents to check individual characteristics that described their favorite instructors and note the ones they felt were most important. Their choices were patience, intelligence, humor, energy, inspiration, compassion, articulateness, commitment, loving, disciplinarian, toughness, or other. Eighty-seven percent of the respondents described their favorite instructor as intelligent. Over 70 percent described their favorite instructors as having a sense of humor, energy, ability to inspire, and commitment to their work. The attribute most likely to be rated as "most important" was humor, followed by intelligence and commitment.

Toughness, discipline, and *loving* were the three characteristics least used to describe instructors. They were checked in only about a third of the surveys.

Although toughness and discipline weren't rated as important qualities, respondents often described their model instructors as demanding when asked to place their model instructor on a continuum between demanding and docile.

LOOK WHO'S TALKING

We wondered how much the respondents had been influenced by their models and how they rated their own prowess as instructors. So we included a section on their own instruction habits.

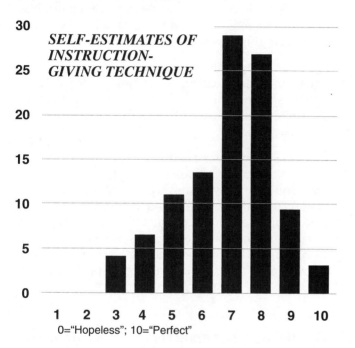

SELF-ESTIMATES OF INSTRUCTION-GIVING TECHNIQUE

0="Hopeless"; 10="Perfect"

On a scale of 1 to 10, 73 percent rated themselves between 6 and 8 as instruction-givers. Then we divided respondents into top management (presidents and CEOs), upper management (vice presidents and directors), middle management (managers and group heads), and academia. Going down the corporate hierarchy tended to raise the respondents' estimate of their instruction-giving skills. The average rating of the top management group was about 7. The average for upper management was 7.5; and for middle management, 8. Apparently, presidents are harder on themselves than managers or they have the luxury of being able to admit their shortcomings. Maybe they just don't get as much practice.

There was some discrepancy when we asked respondents if employees ever complained about being able to understand them. They were asked to check a box marked "Yes" or "No." The next question asked them to specify frequency, if they had answered "Yes" to the previous question. About 40 percent of the people who checked "No" went on to check "Rarely," "Sometimes," or "Often" in the next question, despite their claim that no one ever complained. Apparently, no one ever complains, but they do it sometimes. We think there might be some self-denial going on here.

The most complaints are fielded by upper management and academics; 43 and 40 percent of them, respectively, checked "Yes." Only 17 percent of middle managers and 28 percent of top executives heard complaints.

The most popular explanation for why someone didn't understand a respondent's instructions was that "You didn't give enough information." Next came "The follower was afraid to admit that your instructions were not clear" and "You didn't take into account the ability of the person you were instructing." The least popular explanation was "The follower didn't like the task assigned" or "Didn't understand the reason for the instruction."

DO YOUR EMPLOYEES EVER COMPLAIN ABOUT NOT BEING ABLE TO UNDERSTAND YOU?

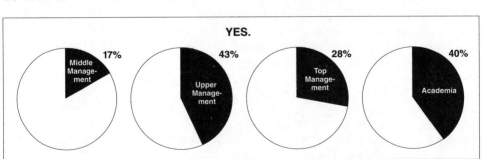

TIME SPENT

Respondents were asked to estimate the amount of time they spent giving as well as receiving instructions.

If instructions are the driving force of communications, then I would expect that giving or receiving them would account for the majority of time spent in the workplace. This was not the case among the respondents.

Only 7 of the 100 people who responded accounted for 100 percent of their work either giving or receiving instructions: Nigel Holmes, graphics director of *Time* magazine (90 percent giving/10 percent receiving); Ian Brackenbury, a systems technology manager for IBM in England (99/1); Jeff Osborne, a design and marketing consultant (95/5); Paul Stafford, director of communication services for McDermott, Inc. (80/20); Jasper T. von Meerheimb, a set designer with Walt Disney Imagineering (50/50); John Greer, a Canadian composer and music professor (75/25); David Kaufman, assistant manager of office services for the Health Insurance Plan of New York (40/60); and Lee Ann Weber, a graphic designer (20/80).

Only one person seemed acutely aware of the universal importance of instructions.

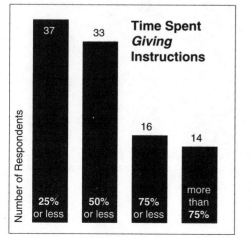

Graphic designer Massimo Vignelli wrote "All" under both categories. Richard N. Carter, who owns a production company, and James Kramer also didn't see giving and receiving instructions as mutually exclusive activities; their combined totals were 130 percent and 160 percent, respectively.

Seventy percent spent less than half of their time giving instructions, and over a third spent less than 25 percent of their time engaged in this activity.

The figures were even smaller for time spent following instructions. Eighty-two percent of those queried estimated that they spent less than 25 percent of their time in this activity.

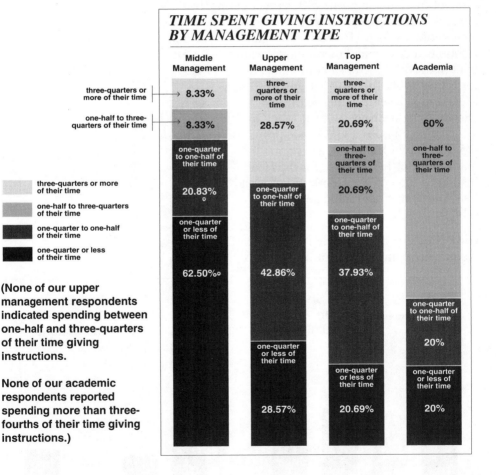

TIME SPENT GIVING INSTRUCTIONS BY MANAGEMENT TYPE

Legend:
- three-quarters or more of their time
- one-half to three-quarters of their time
- one-quarter to one-half of their time
- one-quarter or less of their time

(None of our upper management respondents indicated spending between one-half and three-quarters of their time giving instructions.

None of our academic respondents reported spending more than three-fourths of their time giving instructions.)

	Middle Management	Upper Management	Top Management	Academia
three-quarters or more of their time	8.33%	three-quarters or more of their time	three-quarters or more of their time	
one-half to three-quarters of their time	8.33%	28.57%	20.69%	60%
one-quarter to one-half of their time	20.83%	one-quarter to one-half of their time 20.69%	one-half to three-quarters of their time 20.69%	one-half to three-quarters of their time
one-quarter or less of their time	62.50%	one-quarter to one-half of their time 42.86%	one-quarter to one-half of their time 37.93%	one-quarter to one-half of their time 20%
		one-quarter or less of their time 28.57%	one-quarter or less of their time 20.69%	one-quarter or less of their time 20%

Greg Shaw, a partner of the Plant Recording Studio, must be an easygoing boss, claiming to spend only 2 percent of his time giving instructions and 40 percent following them.

Bill McCaffery spent less time following directions than anyone else—none at all. He was closely followed by Harold Striepe, a marketing manager at Apple Computer, Inc., who spent between 1 and 5 percent.

Eight people accounted for less than 26 percent of their time—for both giving and following instructions. Among them were John Sculley of Apple Computer (25 percent); Robert Ingle, the executive editor of the *San Jose Mercury News* (12 percent); and Cliff Lindsey, chairman of Myriad Research, Inc. (15 percent).

We expected that the higher people were in the corporate hierarchy, the more time they would spend giving instructions, but the survey showed otherwise. About 29 percent of upper management respondents estimated that they spent more than 75 percent of their time giving instructions; only 14 percent of top management did the same.

True to form, the people who were aware of spending the most time giving instructions were also the most conscious of complaints.

FORMULAS FOR GOOD INSTRUCTIONS

The complaints, as well as the wisdom bestowed by favorite instructors, helped the respondents to formulate their own set of requirements for good instructions.

Greg Shaw gave the following requirements of good instructions:

- The audience must be interested in learning the thing at hand.

- The instruction is designed to be conceptually clear and obvious when only minimally described.

- It is funny, sexy, relevant, and clear.

- It is shorter than the attention span of the audience.

Ken Fromm, a software engineer, felt that good instructions must account for the exceptions. There must be information on "how to handle any deviation or exceptions should they occur." And they inevitably do.

For the editor and publisher of the *Electric Word* magazine, Louis Rossetto, "The best instruction is demonstration, *showing* somebody how to do something while explaining enough of the *why* for it to make sense."

Horace Deets, executive director of the American Association of Retired Persons, tersely defined the qualities of good instructions as "clarity, brevity, and logic."

Others also had simple but potent formulas. For Michael Rogers, a senior writer for *Newsweek,* the difference between a good and a bad instruction was a good or a bad listener.

Barry James Linnett, a courseware designer and developer for Microsoft, Inc., was so inspired by the question on good instructions that he developed a full outline on the subject. It included the following ingredients:

- Anticipation. Get them to notice. Hook them.

- Benefit. Show them how *they* will benefit. Motivate them. Focus on the *audience.*

- Coatrack. Give a very concise mental model for the task that they can hang the details on.

- Flow. Make it a story.

- Compare and Contrast. Show examples and nonexamples.

- Practice. Allow feedback.

- Build Upon Skills. Make sure they continue to use skills learned so they don't forget and to build links to new skills.

- Keep Interest. Use humor, suspense, challenges, and dazzle.

- Control. Control the pace, the order, and whether to skip a section or not.

- Recap.

FROM THE PROFESSIONAL STANDPOINT

The people who responded culled their thoughts from personal experiences and individual opinions. Most of them weren't professionally trained as instructors, nor did they necessarily have experience in the field. We wanted some input from someone with vaster experience as an instructor, so we contacted the company that trains more people every year than the U.S. Army. It's also a company with which almost everyone has had some experience.

There's a reason why McDonald's can now be found in 53 countries and everywhere you turn at home, and it isn't only that eight-year-olds have been known to threaten suicide if they can't have a Big Mac in short order. The restaurants work. They serve a phenomenal amount of people in a short amount of time. Whether or not you like the food, you have to admit that McDonald's restaurants are models of efficiency—partly because the company believes in training its employees before they turn them loose on the public.

The McDonald's operations manual is 600 pages long and weighs four pounds. It specifies the exact cooking times for all products and the standard portions for each food item, including the 4 ounces of onions on each hamburger and the thickness of the french fries (9/32 of an inch).

Fred Turner, now the chairman of McDonald's, founded Hamburger University in 1961 in the basement of a company restaurant in Elk Grove, Illinois. Today the 130,000-square-foot facility sprawls over an 88-acre campus in Oak Brook, Illinois, the Chicago suburb where the company headquarters are located. Courses are taught in 9 languages and more than 36,000 people have graduated from the program. And training doesn't

The company employs more than 650,000 people and is the first employer of one out of every fifteen American workers. In its first 30 years of business, it employed about 8 million Americans, who now work in other jobs, or about 7 percent of the country's entire work force. McDonald's has built a kingdom on the concept that you can't be overinstructed or overtrained for a job, whether it be making milkshakes or managing restaurants. Many others have copied their program, but few have managed to enforce it with the rigor and resources of McDonald's.

stop with the bachelor of hamburgerology degree. All employees, even the chairman, spend time training at HU at least once every 5 years. By the time someone becomes a restaurant manager, he or she will have undergone about 2,000 hours of training and management development, about the same amount of classroom time as the graduate of a 4-year college. The company also maintains 30 regional training centers in the U.S. and 10 international training centers, in such places as England, Japan, and Germany.

Other corporations have started colleges that teach skills that can be used on the job. Although they vary widely in the degrees offered, most operated as accredited, nonprofit institutions. For example, the Dana Corporation in Ohio offers managers the chance to earn a master's of business administration while on the job; the National Technological University in Colorado awards master's degrees in engineering; and Thunderbird Management Center in Arizona offers executives international business instruction.

According to Randy Vest, dean of HU, one of the challenges of their training program is "learning how to deal with cultural diversity and how to reach people as individuals by figuring out their differences. What do they need in the way of training and how do they prefer to learn? We try to be observant and gather facts from watching people at work. In this way we learn to separate fact from assumptions."

The training program uses an on-the-job approach based on orientation and observation. Crew trainers go into the restaurants and work alongside the trainees. Operations of the restaurants have been broken down into 25 work stations, and the trainers go through each function until it is mastered. The company also mandates that the trainers give the reasons why each operation is necessary. On-the-job sessions are followed by a classroom session. Each McDonald's restaurant has videotape equipment and a set of regularly updated training tapes on each work station and the procedures involved. Employees are also trained in communication skills, managing people, finished and raw product quality, sanitation, security, and service.

The objective is always to maintain a high and uniform standard without stifling individual initiative. According to John F. Love in his book, *McDonald's: Behind the Arches*, "One of the least understood characteristics of the system is that its fascination with uniformity exists side by side with its less known—but equally strong—respect for the creativity and judgment of its franchisees. 'True, we have procedures that do not allow for a lot of tolerance,' Turner concedes. 'But anyone who concludes that we march around regimenting operators and managers in ninety-three hundred restaurants contributes to the most superficial notion of McDonald's. Anyone who meets our operators knows there is no way those guys could be regimented.'

"....McDonald's is something of an American response to Japan's management by consensus. Without the freedom of franchisees and suppliers to exercise their entrepreneurial instincts, to test their own ideas on new products and procedures, and even to challenge the corporation head-on, McDonald's might still have attained its celebrated uniformity, but at a terrible price. It would lose the grass-roots creativity that diverse franchisees and suppliers provide. It would, in short, lose touch with the marketplace."

THE COMMON DENOMINATOR

I began to notice that McDonald's shared many of the same characteristics of the model instructors described by the survey respondents. The company is passionate about its subject matter and willing to entertain divergent opinions, allows trainees to make mistakes, encourages asking questions, explains the reasons behind the instructions, and instills confidence in its trainees.

Perhaps the real common denominator is the underlying ability behind these characteristics—an ability that seemed to be at the heart of most of the model instructors. They were people who could teach us something that could be applied and expanded to other subjects and endeavors, people who gave us knowledge and information in such a way that we were empowered to act on our own.

In 1990, there were 11,000 McDonald's in 50 countries. The average restaurant does $1.6 million in business.

"I was surprised at how easy it was to get right to the information I needed within the company. I called Simone Skretvedt at Golin/Harris Communications in Chicago, which handles public relations for McDonald's. She sent me a package of information and put me in touch with the training development manager, whose name is actually Gary MacKelfresh. I told him I thought that sounded like a great name for a new McDonald's sandwich, but Gary didn't seem to see the humor in it. I guess I wasn't the first person to point this out. Despite my silly pun, he immediately called Randy Vest, dean of the Hamburger University, who promptly called me, eager to answer any of my questions and send more specific information my way. Consumer electronics manufacturers could learn a few things from McDonald's."

EMPOWERMENT AND THE SPHERE OF VISION

"That man is great who can use the brains of others to carry on his work."

Don Piatt, *Memories of Men Who Saved the Union*: W.H. Seward

The archetypal corporate interpretation of original sin is that all employees are lazy, sloppy, error-ridden potential felons who need to have the fear of God bred into them before they will perform at even the most cursory of levels. Without constant supervision and threats from above, they will lapse into slothful/sinful behavior.

This kind of attitude prompts an approach to management that revolves around crime and punishment. Management watches and waits for their inevitably errant employees to stray from the righteous path, then jumps in for the retribution. Surveillance and repression are the *modus operandi*.

Under the police system, the constant surveillance and repression begin to wear on the employees. They begin to look guilty and start to think of themselves as criminals, who have been imprisoned for crimes they have not yet committed or are unaware of committing.

This kind of regime may insure that rules or instructions are followed, but not in the way that they could and should be followed. Remember that there are several ways that takers can follow an instruction. They can ignore it, deliberately follow it incorrectly, perform the barest minimum to keep the instruction-giver at bay, try to please the taker, or regard the instruction as a means to reach new understandings and acquire new skills. Thus, can they do a better job than the instruction-giver, the sub-rosa hope of most instruction-givers.

Traditional business ideology stifles this last most desirable response. It sends employees looking upward for permission, authority, and direction. While employees thus cast off some of the responsibility for their actions, they are burdened down with a sense of oppression from above. They may find they are absolved from responsibility, but they also forfeit the pride of possessing their work.

Instructions can be the ticket for maintaining the status quo or they can be the means for employees to go beyond the capacity of the instruction-giver. Companies flourish with employees who carry out directives with spirit and enthusiasm.

EMPOWERMENT IS THE WORD OF THE NINETIES

Empowerment is what enables employees to go beyond the instructions given. Empowerment means to give rights and responsibilities to employees, to allow them a say in their work as well as in company business in general. It means to recognize and reward their input. It is a movement designed to nurture human resources and replace the manager-as-warden mentality with the manager-as-aide-to-action approach.

> "We cannot work for others without working for ourselves."—J. J. Rousseau, *The Social Contract*

The difference between an adequate instruction and an inspired instruction is that the latter *empowers* the takers so that they feel possession of the results of their efforts.

Empowerment is about feelings; it isn't an issue of dollars and sense. Feelings have not historically been the stuff of business. In fact, you were supposed to respond to them in the same way you would a drop in earnings: chagrin, embarrassment, and a promise that it won't happen again. Empowerment has assumed cause status. It is a word that was developed to express feelings that may have existed for a long time, enabling the concept to take root and people to focus on the idea.

> "Our mentality has been going through an astonishing transformation. Early human beings were locked into a nonconscious absoluteness, told what to do by hallucinated voices called gods. We possessed a mind without choice, doubt, wonder or ambition. We lacked even a sense of selves. That mind, over the years, has slowly been replaced by introspective consciousness."—Psychologist Julian Jaynes in *Life* (12/88)

"Empowerment is a concept that has gained the sanctity of motherhood and apple pie in corporate America. Indeed, in the years to come your career may well fade or flourish on the basis of how well you master the art of empowering every single individual who works for you," said Peter Block in his book, *The Empowered Manager.*

"We take other men's knowledge and opinions upon trust; which is an idle and superficial learning. We must make it our own."
—Michael Eyquem de Montaigne, *Essays*

Empowerment depends on the will and determination of both management and employees. Empowerment must be both granted and encouraged by the *empowerers,* or instruction-givers, and assumed by the *empowerees,* or instruction-takers, who must recognize that their mission isn't just to realize the dreams of others, blindly following orders like sheep, but to derive their own satisfactions from the instruction-taking process.

THE AGREEMENT

When I was a high school student, I realized that I was only listening to the teacher by my agreement. The teachers couldn't get me to do anything unless I agreed to do it. What could they do if I said I wouldn't go to school? Could they shoot me, put me in jail? We are all educated with the fear that we must do things because we have to. When we walk down a crowded street, we walk to the right and avoid bumping into oncoming people. When we miscalculate, most of us say, "Excuse me." There are no punishments for violations of this rule.

Unless society can inflict pain or punishment for violating the rules, people follow them only because they agree to follow them. **This agreement is the glue of civilization.**

Most people make agreements with society. They promise to make certain compromises—to whisper in the library, wait patiently in line, let a car into a line of traffic—to enjoy the company and good will of others. I've always wondered how those agreements come about. It seems to me that many of the breakthroughs in the arts and sciences have come about because someone broke the agreement. John Cage broke the agreement as to what constitutes music. Radical alternatives are produced by not going along with the rules.

Recognizing that you are the one who agrees to the rules means that you are the one who can chose to disagree as well. Recognizing that you are the one who decides what rules to follow gives you a sense of power. You are the one who makes the choice. I believe that we all have that right.

Great Moments in the
HISTORY OF INSTRUCTIONS

THE FIRST RECIPE:

BOIL WATER!

B-BUT HOW?

You don't *have* to go to work every day. You go because you want something that work gives you—whether it is monetary, emotional, or social satisfaction. I believe that people do what they want to do; they don't always recognize this though. You might dread going to a party and complain about *having* to go, but maybe you want the chance to meet new people or establish business connections, so you go. If you find yourself starting a lot of sentences with "I have to...," keep in mind that you probably don't. There is probably some reason why you "want to." "Want to" is more liberating than "have to."

Isaac Bashevis Singer surmised that when a fatalist crosses the street and starts to run as a car approaches, he probably believes in free will at least for that moment.

This right to follow or to break the rules also gives us the right to ask for what we want. To get what we want, though, means being able to instruct others in our wishes. You can't be upset about the table you get in a restaurant, the benefits you get at work, or even the gifts you get from a spouse unless you have made it clear through instructions about what you wanted in the first place.

I am on planes a lot and I try to make the experience as comfortable as possible. When I fly at night, I like a window seat so I am not disturbed by other passengers getting in and out of their seats. During the day, I like an aisle seat because there is more room and you can get up without disturbing others. I was taking the red eye from San Francisco to New York, so I asked for a window seat as far forward as possible. The airlines complied with my request and gave me a seat in the third row. It turns out that there were only three rows in first class, so I got the seat in front of the bulkhead, which doesn't recline as much. I didn't get what I wanted, which was to go to sleep, because I didn't communicate the right instructions.

All of us could have our way more often if we knew how to communicate it. Each of us has the right. What we need to develop is the ability to ask for it.

If you don't ask, you don't get.

In a restaurant you have the power to get what you want. You are the boss. Most restaurants, especially the better ones, are willing to entertain your specific instructions for food and liquor or substitutions of ingredients. One of the drinks I like is similar to a vodka Gibson—but not exactly the same. I like Absolut vodka with only 2 rocks and a wedge—not a peel—of lime and extra onions. To get what I want, I have to give these instructions. A lot of people don't get what they want. Most people would just order the vodka Gibson. Many restaurants, especially Japanese and Italian, allow you to tailor meals. You can order half portions or full portions, a few pieces of sushi or a platter.

My wife, Gloria, likes chili with a lot of beans. Before she orders it, she will ask the waiter or waitress, "Does it have a lot of beans?" Thinking that she doesn't like beans, sometimes the person will respond, "No it doesn't have too many beans." So she doesn't order the chili, which she would have liked, because she didn't give the order in a way that enabled the server to give her what she wanted. All she would have to say is "I like a lot of beans. Does your chili have them?"

TO OBEY OR NOT TO OBEY?

Along with the freedom and right to get what you want, empowerment brings responsibilities. Employees have the freedom to act or not to act, and they must bear the consequences of the choice. Choice carries responsibilities. An article in *Time* (7/30/90) about how East Germans are adjusting to West German ways of business reported that they were overwhelmed by the number of choices and reluctant to make decisions about what to buy.

The article, "Speeding over the Bumps," by James O. Jackson, stated that "One reason for Eastern docility in the face of aggressive Western sales forces is 40 years of communism. 'It's hard to imagine what the central command system did to people,' says Stahmer [Ingrid Stahmer, West Berlin's deputy mayor in charge of housing and social services]. 'Too many of them just sit and wait for instructions. They lack initiative and judgment. It's a crash course, but they are learning fast.' "

Throughout history, subordinates have attempted to exonerate themselves from guilt by claiming that "I was just following orders."

The Nazi holocaust, the massacre of civilians at My Lai during the Vietnam War, the Iran–Contra affair, the misappropriation of millions in the Department of Housing and Urban Development, and the Exxon Valdez oil spill are only a few episodes that were colored by the "following-orders" defense. Throughout history, some variation of this has been used as a defense for wrong actions in almost every field of endeavor, and time and time again, it has come up short as a justifiable excuse. It drives home the message that at some time in your life, it might be better to not follow orders. Making this decision

"When you think of the long and gloomy history of man, you will find more hideous crimes have been committed in the name of obedience than have ever been committed in the name of rebellion."—C. P. Snow opens a Pandora's box of conflicting emotions and ethics. Do we follow our conscience or our desire to please? The line where a responsibility to obey transgresses into the territory of unethical behavior must be moved toward individual accountability. No instruction should be followed blindly. Just because you are working under the authority of someone else doesn't mean that ill-conceived actions can be absolved by claiming that you were just following orders.

SPHERE OF VISION

Empowerment doesn't mean granting absolute freedom. The boundaries of empowerment are set by the sphere of vision of the instruction-givers. What are the limits of your own vision? Make sure that the people to whom you give instructions understand how far they can go. Then give them the freedom to work within these boundaries.

You have to be clear what the sphere of your own vision is. The trick is to define your sphere so that it is meaningful to employees, large enough not to inhibit your employees' creativity, and small enough so as not to overwhelm them with options.

All of my work has my mark, yet I do hardly any hands-on work at all. The people who work for me have changed over the years, but the imprint of my work has not. This is possible because I empower people to do their work, and then I give the instructions for it to be done. I'll put my work on the line to prove it. It may sound silly and arrogant and it's probably not something you're supposed to say—that I don't do any work—but it's true. Lee Iacocca doesn't build cars, but his vision gave birth to a renewed Chrysler Corporation.

I make a living by doing the opposite of the way other people do things. I look for the patterns in what doesn't work. I find the pattern in failures. Why can't I use the dictionary properly, the telephone book, the *TV Guide*, the *Official Airline Guide*. I'm not self-conscious about saying things that sound simple. This frees me. I have stripped

---

" 'Vision animates, inspirits, transforms purpose into action,' Lincoln Kirstein, founder of the New York City Ballet and School, said. 'My whole life has been trying to learn how things are done. What I love about the ballet is not that it looks pretty. It's the method in it. Ballet is about how to behave.' " —Warren Bennis and Burt Nanus, *Leaders*

"No man is great enough or wise enough for any of us to surrender our destiny to. The only way in which any one can lead us is to restore to us the belief in our own guidance."—Henry Miller, "The Alcoholic Veteran with the Washboard Cranium," *The Wisdom of the Heart*

myself of the pressure of having to sound smart. I can be the professor of ignorance.

As to the creative work that gets done—the phone books, the *USAtlas*, the ACCESS city guides—I've done well, because I have less and less to do with producing things that have more and more of my mark on them. Because I've allowed people the freedom to be creative, they have an identity with the projects. I try to give "happy limitations" so that the projects fall within an acceptable range of the ideas I have for it.

I allow people to be proud of what they have done, to feel that they have ownership or possession of the task. This enlists their energies to produce a better product. I may not sit in front of the computer and do illustrations, yet they are all my inspiration. There is no doubt that my employees create work better than I could.

I empower people by giving them a creativity allowance. I find people who can do better than I can do, but I make sure their work does not pierce the sphere of my vision.

WHAT GOOD IS EMPOWERMENT?

The possibilities of empowerment outweigh the responsibilities for instruction-givers and takers. An empowered work force benefits individual employees as well as groups and organizations.

Empowered employees are more likely to be motivated. Motivation is a higher form of instruction. Motivation can move mountains. Motivated people do exceedingly complex work, which they enable themselves to do by interest. People follow complex pattern instructions because they want to make a dress, but will claim they are baffled by electronic equipment. We learn to do those things we want to do. If I'm on a private plane and the pilot has a heart attack and dies, I'm going to be quite interested in how to fly a plane. As long as the pilot is doing his or her job, I really don't care.

"In a recent national survey asking those at the top what those at the top should do, 53 percent of the respondents rated employee motivation and leadership as the number-one priority.

"The survey, developed by Robert Half International, was based on interviews with vice presidents and personnel directors of 100 of the nation's 1000 largest corporations. Says Max Messmer, chairman of Robert Half International: 'The results of this survey are clearly a sign of the times. American business is experiencing a period of rapid change, and people are asking for leadership and direction to help them set the right goals and objectives.' "—"The Boss's Job," *USAIR* (3/90)

"Leadership is the ability to get other people to do what they don't want to do, and like it."—Harry S. Truman

Empowerment can reduce the reliance on instructions and thus minimize the possibility of misunderstanding them. Giving freedom to employees encourages them to act on their own. By acting on their own, they liberate their superiors (instruction-givers) from having to spell out every detail of tasks.

Empowerment encourages the generation of creative ideas. And the most desirable response to instructions depends on creative ideas. As we moved toward an information- rather than a product-based economy, the business community awakened to the importance of ideas in the marketplace. Ideas aren't as predictable as materials; they cannot be produced with formulas and they require a more flexible atmosphere.

CREATIVITY COMES OUT OF THE CLOSET

Creativity was once viewed as a rather suspicious attribute in business vernacular, married as it was in middle-class minds to words like *wacky, outrageous,* and *bohemian.* Like the offbeat haircuts the creative were known to sport, they were thought to be unmanageable, unruly. But the business world has come to see creativity for what it really is—the ability to generate ideas and solutions.

So companies are searching for new ways to encourage and cultivate creative-thinking among their employees. "In an era of global competition, fresh ideas have become the most precious raw materials. That means companies suddenly want their employees to think on their own, which calls for enormous change at firms where imagination was once considered a subversive trait," said Jay Cocks in an article in *Time,* "Let's Get Crazy!" (6/11/90).

> "Executives from Chevron and Amoco have found themselves in two-day creativity seminars, working on problems like how to raise two candles to eye level in a dark room using only string and paper clips.

> " 'You can't just order up a good idea or spend money to find one,' points out Hallmark's Jon Henderson, director of the company's Creative Resources Center. 'You have to build a climate and give people the freedom to create things.' "

American businesses are beginning to recognize the idea of alternatives—especially when trying to generate creative solutions to workplace problems. Although sometimes just specifying that you want employees to "be creative" can have beneficial effects, companies are looking for more far-reaching and offbeat approaches to establish a work climate conducive to creativity. Companies are reorganizing to facilitate the implementation of new ideas, offering consciousness-raising seminars and creativity counseling, and encouraging their employees to go to attitude-building retreats. Companies send their staff to pitch tents, climb rocks, and row boats to clean out the cerebral cobwebs that have been woven by the drudgery of repetitive duties and stifling office atmosphere. The outdoor-challenge programs relieve stress, build confidence, and motivate employees to elevate their job performance as well as their athletic ability.

One such program is the Maryville College Mountain Challenge in Maryville, Tennessee, located in the foothills of the Great Smoky Mountains. Groups can take on-the-ropes courses and go camping, hiking, rock climbing, rappeling, bicycle touring, or flat-water canoeing and white-water kayaking. All of these activities are designed to promote teamwork, communication, and self-confidence.

Faced with increasing competition and diminishing productivity, American companies, inspired perhaps by New Age culture, have shown a new and uncharacteristic openmindedness when it comes to hiring and inspiring employees.

According to an article, "Software Offers Solid Future," by John Markoff in *The New York*

Times (5/20/90), "when William Gates, co-founder and chairman of the Microsoft Corporation, recruits young programmers, he looks for the sharpest college graduates who excel in mathematics or physics....But when Charles Wang, founder and chairman of Computer Associates in Garden City, Long Island, the nation's largest software vendor, searches for programmers, he takes a less obvious approach. Mr. Wang believes that other talents are often the best indicator of programming skill. 'Producing great software isn't engineering, it's an art form,' he said. 'I find that musicians and philosophy students often make the best programmers.' "

LOOKING FOR INSPIRATION IN ALL THE WRONG PLACES

"Trying to pin down creativity is like trying to nail Jell-O to the wall," said a speaker at a Hallmark card company creativity seminar.

Looking for creative solutions to problems in the office might require looking outside of traditional solutions. You could take a course in creativity or hire a creativity consultant, but there are noncorporate channels that can be tapped.

Sometimes the solutions to problems appear when you are outside of the setting in which they occur. Everyone has found themselves in one place and been struck with an idea that can be applied elsewhere—whether you were scaling Mount Everest or sitting in a sauna. In fact, often just getting outside of the arena of concern will promote a new and refreshing vantage point. Being able to apply metaphors from one area to another permits you to see connections and to broaden your understanding of information. To be able to apply the lessons of gardening to the field of finance is an asset that should, and can, be cultivated.

"Metaphor may indeed be the perfect antidote to the modern mania for high-tech answers. 'It's not that we've become incapable of seeing things [in the workplace],' says Cate Coppotelli, Ph.D., a Jacksonville, Florida, psychologist. 'But we've put too high a premium on being advanced and sophisticated, technical and specialized.' Experiences from fields outside your expertise may be powerful in the same way a fairy tale or myth can say more about pride or greed than the most articulate of preachers," stated Jolie Solomon, in an article, "Management Secrets They'll Never Teach You at Business School," in *Working Woman* (6/90).

CASE HISTORIES: GOING OUTSIDE THE OFFICE TO FIND INSPIRATION WITHIN

Brook Knapp, owner of a private-investment company, flies an aerobatic biplane, after overcoming a fear of flying. "Lesson number one, according to Knapp: 'Change is a constant. When you fly, location, weather, altitude, temperature, alter minute by minute. Even the jet itself feels different with gear up, gear down, flaps up, flaps down; and it grows lighter as it burns fuel.' Knapp used to greet change in the workplace with the same dread she had of airplanes. Now, she says, 'I embrace chaos.' That's a useful lesson for any business person, when you never know from day to day what you'll face in interest rates, junk bonds, or foreign markets.

"....Bill Hunter, a Cherry Hill, New Jersey, consultant, took a small group of clients and friends to Steamboat Springs, Colorado, last winter to see whether the ski slopes could help him teach a few fine points of management. In après-ski chats, Hunter talked about one of the hardest lessons for the new skier: leaning into danger....'It seems unnatural,' says Hunter, who learned to ski at 40. 'Your instinct is to hug the hill.' But by leaning into danger, you actually gain control.

"In business, too, you often can 'get control by giving it up,' says Hunter.

"....Tanya Berezin, artistic director of the Circle Repertory Theatre in New York, finds that some of her exercises from 20 years of acting linger on in her new career as manager. In one method-acting exercise, says Berezin, she uses 'emotional memory,' focusing, for example, on memories of her feelings for her father to pinpoint the essence of her relationship to a character she plays against. She'll think back to a particular moment, concentrating on the texture of the air, the tones of voice, even the feel of a tablecloth, to stay in touch with her instincts. 'The memory comes back, and it enlivens the character,' says Berezin.

"Now, when making a business decision at the theater, Berezin goes through something similar to summon up her gut instincts. Relaxing, concentrating and letting a decision emerge works better, she says, than listing the pros and cons. 'I trust what I know.'

"....Kathy Lang Albright, marketing director at a Cincinnati investment firm, Bartlett & Co, considers herself a recovering workaholic. She was delighted to discover that one of her new passions, gardening, yields dividends at the office, too.

"Lang Albright's first garden was a near disaster. She'd leapt into action, going mostly by color, not planning much. Some things sprouted, of course. But she also ended up with 'sun plants in the shade, shade plants in the sun,' and plants that needed drainage put where they were soaked with every rain.

"The key to gardening—and to management— says Lang Albright, is respect for your environment. 'You can't make a shade plant grow in the sun' she says.

"....Sometimes, says Lang Albright, who has tempered impulse in both places, the garden speaks louder to her than the office. 'Plants only grow so fast. The sun is out only so many hours. There is something crazy about being an overachieving gardener.' "—Jolie Solomon, "Management Secrets They'll Never Teach You at Business School," *Working Woman* (6/90)

The search for relationships between one endeavor and another applies to the giving and taking of instructions as well. As an instruction-giver, instead of stopping at the obvious, look for metaphors and illusions from different arenas to convey your message. Perhaps they will make connections in the mind of the taker that will inspire more creative performance. As a taker, try to relate the message to different situations until you feel comfortable with it. Know the interests and passions of your employees and try to draw metaphors and allusions from them.

Let's say someone on your market research staff is a bit obsessed with his health; you are too diplomatic to say hypochondriacal. You are trying to convince him to continue gathering information when he is sure that you have enough. Perhaps you could instruct him by drawing parallels to antibiotic therapy, which is only effective if continued to a designated point, despite the fact that all of the symptoms have disappeared.

Perhaps you have a trout fisherman in your employ. Allude to *maribou jig* in a conversation and you may enable him or her to make creative connections.

Perhaps you think that sending your employees into the woods, learning to sky-dive, or taking up gardening is too extreme for your taste.

JUST SAY YES

Empowering employees can be done without risking life and limb, without any sporting equipment at all. After all, empowerment is an attitude. At the 1990 International Design Conference in Aspen, Ken Brecher, director of the Children's Museum in Boston, talked about former first lady Nancy Reagan's "Just Say No" campaign against drugs as the antithesis of empowerment. Telling people to "Just Say No" to drugs is authoritarian; it doesn't empower people to make decisions for themselves. Empowerment means telling people that "You could say yes or you could say no. The choice is yours."

Volvo has a team that builds a car. The workmanship, the productivity is high, if you feel you own your work. The antithesis is the assembly line, where each worker repeats some small task that becomes a tiny part of the whole. This hypnotic repetition makes a sense of ownership or authorship of your work virtually impossible. That's what Henry Ford did for this country.

The problem is how can executives give instructions that will enable their employees to go beyond the status quo, to follow instructions to their own satisfaction and growth, yet still realize the ideas and dreams of their bosses? Employees are empowered by:

● Having the option of making decisions about their work and about the company as a whole.

● Being informed about company business—the bad as well as the good.

● Feeling that they own their work. They receive the credit—the criticism and the praise.

● Having the comfort of knowing that they can make mistakes, that mistakes are inevitable on the road to success.

● Understanding corporate goals and the ways those goals can be applied to their work.

● Understanding the sphere of vision of their superiors.

> "At the top, life seeks expression through particular individuals."
> —Simone de Beauvoir

Empowerment depends on the practice of participatory leadership, which recognizes the power of employees and promotes a climate of cooperation.

The applications of empowerment are almost universal. It can be employed to improve office morale, personal relationships, and even political and economic conditions. Jack Kemp, secretary of the Department of Housing and Urban Development under President Bush, suggests that empowerment is the way to solve the homeless problem in this country by allowing tenants to run their own housing projects.

"Empowerment, says Mr. Kemp, is the way to fill the gaps in the Great Society. Mr. Kemp has no time for the negative approach of the libertarians—that government efforts to wage ware on poverty are wrong in principle and bound to fail in practice. Instead he attacks the design of the programs in the 1960s: the way they perpetuated poverty by subsidizing failure rather than rewarding success. He does not want to cut the government out, but to use it to empower the poor with choices.

"Giving them somewhere to live is a pretty good start. In the past, assistance with public housing has meant either providing homes in public estates or providing subsidies to the developers of cheap housing. Mr. Kemp wants to empower the tenants with the management of their own public-housing estates, with subsidies for home ownership and with rental vouchers. He calls his program HOPE (home-ownership and opportunity for people everywhere)."—"A Sword Called Empowerment," *The Economist* (6/2/90)

I predict that leaders will look toward empowerment to solve some of the problems facing the business and political communities today. They will abandon hiring policies that look for yes men and instead forge ones that find people who are allowed to do a better job than their leaders. More leaders will recognize that those who can encourage self-esteem in their employees will get higher quality work than those who are driven by a desire to keep their employees under their thumbs.

I predict that, inevitably, the empowerment movement will redefine the role of leaders in many organizations.

THE NEW LEADERSHIP: CONDUCTORS VERSUS CONTROLLERS

"If the primary aim of a captain were to preserve his ship, he would keep it in port forever."

Thomas Aquinas

*T*he loss of corporate supremacy in the United States has caused the business world to reflect on its historic leadership model based on the image of the autocratic CEO. All power is centralized and all decisions and subsequent instructions must come from one absolute source. No one else can be trusted to make decisions or understand the scope in which they must be made.

What worked so well in the first half of the 20th century doesn't appear to be working as well in the second. An industrial economy based on buying and selling of tangible resources needs a different leadership than one dominated by the gathering, processing, and selling of intangible information. Yet many cling to the old leadership model.

"To know what is possible tomorrow you must be willing to step outside of what is possible today.

"The long view is all."
—Toshiba ad in *The New York Times*

Perhaps people adhere to this idea not only because it has been foisted on them from above but because some part of them wants to escape responsibility for their actions by abandoning them to a higher power. The need to follow leaders might signify a desire to return to childhood, wanting a father figure to "take care of everything," "make it all better." There is little room or tolerance for diversity or originality, but followers can escape blame for the consequences of their actions as well. Moral responsibility is instead borne by the exalted one, which perhaps explains our longing for leaders.

This leadership model is similar to most monotheistic religions. We should follow an all-powerful, all-knowing god who will lead us to a state of grace.

"The weaknesses of the many make the leader possible."—Elbert Hubbard, *The Note Book*

The longing for patriarchs hasn't become extinct. It has only been replaced by the longing for omnipotent CEOs.

This seems to be a peculiarly American outlook toward the chief executive. The word *executive*—with its violent connotations—has no direct counterpart in many other languages. In German, the closest word is *leitende männer,* which translates as "leading men." In Spanish, the counterpart to *executive* is *directores de empreses* or "directors of enterprises." Both of these imply a more egalitarian, less militaristic approach.

ANTILEADER MOVEMENT

We need a more enlightened, less patronizing leadership model, a delegator not a despot. The Japanese espouse a more participatory leadership, in which members of the company share responsibility for its success. The waning of the United States in the world marketplace testifies that it's time for some corporate philosophy transplants here. We need to make a new mold to replace the CEO as a father figure leading a flock of work-force sheep. A more appropriate image might be that of a symphony conductor directing a pool of talented musicians, keeping the tempo, assigning tasks, making sure that tasks harmonize with abilities. Each performer has his or her own expertise and thus his or her own responsibility for the sound of the orchestra.

> "Authoritarian management, which told people what to do and how to do it, worked well in the industrial era, when workers performed manual labor. Today half of the work force attended or graduated from college. Mental tasks have replaced mechanical ones. Information work—of attorneys, salespeople, executives, secretaries—cannot be managed in the authoritarian style. The CEO of the 1990s must win commitment to company objectives by helping people achieve their own goals. When people invest their human resources in a company, they expect a return: personal and career growth. Leaders who bring out the best in people deliver that dividend and attract more good investments."—Patricia Aburdene, "How to Think Like a CEO of the 90's," *Working Woman* (9/90)

P. J. O'Rourke, social gad-fly and author of *Modern Manners: An Etiquette Book for Rude People*, has been baffled with the concept of leadership ever since his Boy Scouts days. In an article, "How to Succeed in Business? Here's the Secret," in *The New York Times Book Review*, (10/29/89), he said, "As I remember, leadership consisted of jumping in an ice-cold lake before anyone else did, and being first to climb out on a high, rotten tree limb. Boys who possessed 'leadership qualities' often died in car wrecks before the age of 20."

"For the most part our leaders are merely following out in front; they do but marshal us the way that we are going."—Bergen Evans, *The Spoor of Spooks and Other Nonsense*

"The information-based organization does not actually require advanced information technology. All it requires is willingness to ask: Who requires what information, when, and where?

"The conventional organization of business was originally modeled after the military. The information-based system much more closely resembles the symphony orchestra. All instruments play the same score. But each plays a different part. They play together, but they rarely play in unison....In the orchestra, however, the score is given to both players and conductor. In business the score is being written as it is being played....If every player has to know the score, there has to be a common language, a common core of unity."

—Peter Drucker, "Playing in the Information-Based Orchestra," *The Wall Street Journal* (6/4/85)

MANAGING WITHOUT MANAGERS

Ricardo Semler, president of Semco S/A, Brazil's largest manufacturer of marine and food-processing machinery, runs a company based on an unorthodox, creative, and *successful* egalitarianism. According to an article he wrote in the *Harvard Business Review* (9-10/89), "I am president of a manufacturing company that treats its 800 employees like responsible adults. Most of them—including factory workers—set their own working hours. All have access to the company books. The vast majority vote on many important corporate decisions. Everyone gets paid by the month, regardless of job description, and more than 150 of our management people set their own salaries and bonuses.

"....The organizational pyramid is the cause of much corporate evil, because the tip is too far from the base. Pyramids emphasize power, promote insecurity, distort communications, hobble interaction, and make it very difficult for the people who plan and the people who execute to move in the same direction. So Semco designed an organizational circle. Its greatest advantage is to reduce management levels to three—one corporate level and two operating levels at the manufacturing units.

"Managers and the status and money they enjoy—in a word, hierarchy—are the single biggest obstacle to participatory management....We don't hire or promote people until they've been interviewed and accepted by all their future subordinates. Twice a year, subordinates evaluate managers....We insist on making important decisions collegially, and certain decision are made by a company-wide vote.

"We have other ways of combating hierarchy too. Most of our programs are based on the notion of giving employees control over their own lives. In a word, we hire adults, and then we treat them like adults. Think about that. Outside the factory, workers are men and women who elect governments, serve in the army, lead community projects, raise and educate families, and make decisions every day about the future. But the moment they walk into the factory, the company transforms them into adolescents. They have to wear badges and name tags, arrive at a certain time, stand in line to punch the clock or eat their lunch, get permission to go to the bathroom, give lengthy explanations every time they're five minutes late, and follow instructions without asking a lot of questions.

"One of my first moves when I took control of Semco was to abolish norms, manuals, rules, and regulations. Everyone knows that you can't run a large organization without regulations, but everyone knows that most regulations are poppycock.

"When we introduced flexible hours, we decided to hold regular follow-up meetings to track problems and decide how to deal with abuses and production interruptions. That was years ago, and we haven't yet held the first meeting."

Sam Walton, the founder of Wal-Mart and one of (if not *the*) the richest men in America has built his fortune around opening the lines of communication with every member of his empire. He is not an all-powerful autocrat who claims to know everything; he is a master at surrounding himself with smart people, then paying attention to their advice. "Ego, in my opinion, is one of the worst things that can happen to a company," says Walton, who drives a 1978 Ford pickup and lives in a modest home in Bentonville, Arkansas. He also shuns personal publicity and plays down his own part in Wal-Mart's success.

"Walton's eccentricities, however, are also his strength. He seems to run Wal-Mart like a larger version of his original dime store. He doesn't bother with pricey industry consultants and marketing gurus. Instead, he relies on the seat-of-the-pants judgments of his employees

and his own ability to keep a close eye on other
regional retail chains....Traveling at least three
days a week, he visits all of his stores at least
once each year. And he drops in on hundreds of
his competitors for good measure....The gospel
according to Sam is paying off. As other retailers
struggle, Wal-Mart regularly posts nearly 35
percent annual sales gains. Profits have soared
an average of 37 percent a year since 1975." —
Tod Mason with Marc Frons, "Sam Walton of
Wal-Mart: Just Your Basic Homespun
Billionaire," *Business Week* (10/14/85)

The company maintains a policy that allows any
employee to discuss his or her ideas with
management and a structure that enables the company
to put new ideas quickly into practice. Store managers
are required to ask every sales clerk what he or she
thinks might improve the operation of the store. To
further interaction between management and
employees, all Wal-Mart executives are required to
spend a week each year working an hourly job in a
Wal-Mart store, so they are informed of the problems
in day-to-day retail operations. The company places a
premium on LTC, Wal-Mart lingo for "low threshold
for change."

Another example of new leadership is the Pritzker
family, who owns Hyatt Hotels. According to an
article on the family by Ford S. Worthy in *Time*
(4/25/88), the family, which is known for its
cohesiveness, has a management philosophy that
allows for great autonomy for the professional
managers who run the diverse companies owned by
the family. "It's like owning my own company but
having the Pritzkers' bankroll a phone call away,"
said Merlin Wille, general manager of a company that
produces ready-mix concrete.

In 1989, the company closed its Chicago headquarters
for a day and sent the 375 corporate employees
around the country to 98 hotels, where they made
beds, carried luggage, and registered guests. The 39-
year-old president, Thomas Pritzker, spent the day at
the Grand Hyatt in Washington, DC, where he
worked 90-minute shifts as a bellhop, cafeteria server,
and deli counterman.

Herman Miller, which was ranked 9th in *Fortune* magazine's survey of American's most admired corporations, is also known for its pioneering management. In the category of management excellence, it moved up to 6th place. Part of its success can be attributed to its former chairman of the board, Max DePree, author of the book *Leadership Is an Art.*

"Leadership is the art of liberating people to what is required of them in the most effective and human way possible....The condition of our hearts, the openness of our attitudes, the quality of competence, the fidelity of our experience—these give vitality to the work experience and meaning to life," said DePree in his book.

The company's chief executive officer, Richard H. Ruch, translates the philosophy into the day-to-day operation of the company, which pioneered participatory management in 1950.

> "An important way of communicating a corporate culture is through tribal storytelling. Those who know the culture pass on real-life stories of the past that symbolize our values. That way, people will know our culture isn't just an abstract idea but is reflected in our day-to-day activities.

> "Herman Miller's culture is based on equity and participation. Every employee is expected to discuss the company's activities and provide input into management decisions. For example, our Monthly Business Review gives employees an opportunity to see senior managers on video discussing the state of the business and corporate direction. Work-team leaders (managers) then open up a discussion with their team.

> "Our work team leaders must have leadership and interpersonal skills. A manager must be willing to accept diversity—including contrary opinions. We evaluate our managers not just on results but also on participative skills, business literacy, innovations, relationships with others,

FOLLOW THE YELLOW BRICK ROAD

spirit, and attitude."—Peter Block, "How to Be the New Kind of Manager," *Working Woman* (7/90)

Robert Waterman, CEO and president of The Waterman Group, Inc., also forecasts a movement toward a more respectful leadership that is not above learning from subordinates. "My view of the world of management—our ability to learn or pass off information—is that America is a *telling* society. We tend to view the teaching/instructing proposition as the big brain telling the little people who don't know so much. I think the basic job of an instructor is to bring out something the learner already knows/can learn himself.

"If you look at the Japanese culture, it's a *listening* society, not a telling society. A lot of what they learned about quality control they learned from looking at American standards. Our model of the boss is very top down. Flip on the television set and watch the way bosses are portrayed. Some guy shouting at someone else. This image of the person on top as giving instructions—as the wise, all-knowing, here's-how-you-do-it kind of guy—is much over done in our society and creates a lot of the difficulty in really learning.

"I think the attitude toward management in America is changing. It's the force of world competition. As we get further and further from the Great Depression and post-war era of 'Gee, I'm lucky to have a job,' people down the line simply refuse to be pushed around, shouted at, and told what to do. Everything we know about quality assurance says that people down the line already know a lot and they seldom get asked about it. Real communication is a two-way street. Too often we treat it as one way. Effective learning is really a dialogue.

"Moving more information, faster, with better manipulation, to more people, by itself will have no positive effect on office productivity."

"I'm much more interested in asking the right questions. If people discover something for themselves, they will really understand how to do it, rather than if someone had told them what to do, 'because I'm smarter than you.' "

Waterman has been putting his ideas into his own practice by trying to devote less of his time to giving instructions and more toward asking the right questions that will enable him to tap into the information possessed by those around him.

THE SEVEN KEYS TO BUSINESS LEADERSHIP

❶ **"Trust your subordinates.** You can't expect them to go all out for you if they think you don't believe in them.

❷ **"Develop a vision.** Some executives' suspicions to the contrary, planning for the long term pays off. And people want to follow someone who knows where he or she is going.

❸ **"Keep your cool.** The best leaders show their mettle under fire.

❹ **"Encourage risk.** Nothing demoralizes the troops like knowing that the slightest failure could jeopardize their entire career.

❺ **"Be an expert.** From boardroom to mail room, everyone had better understand that you know what you're talking about.

❻ **"Invite dissent.** Your people aren't giving you their best or learning how to lead if they are afraid to speak up.

❼ **"Simplify.** You need to see the big picture in order to set a course, communicate it, and maintain it. Keep the details at bay."— Kenneth Labich, *Fortune* (10/24/88)

FROM THE SILLY TO THE SUBLIME

Lately, evidence is mounting that executives are trying to bridge the gap between the leaders and the flock— from increased attention to in-house communication between management and staff, to more resources devoted to communicating company news and a plethora of new open-door policies. There comes other more entertaining evidence in the form of wacky stunts performed by presidents to prove what down-to-earth, approachable guys they really are.

Whereas the stiff upper lip was once de rigueur, executives now are not only getting away with silly, outrageous gestures, they are winning praise for them. Examples both abound and amuse.

"When David A. Sabey, a Seattle entrepreneur, bought the Frederick & Nelson department stores last year, he spoke to 3,300 new employees via video teleconference—dressed as a store doorman. He said it emphasized his bottom-up management style and the importance of customer contact," claimed an article, "When the Boss Wears a Hula Skirt," by Andrew Feinberg in *The New York Times* (5/25/90). "True believers in grand gestures say that even when they bomb, good things may result. 'When you bring the authority figure down to earth an important bonding takes place with employees,' said Warren Bennis, professor at the University of Southern California School of Business. And that may make chief executives feel a bit more human.

"Some, like Herbert D. Kelleher of Southwest Airlines, have a whole array of costumes, ranging from wings to kilts. And an intriguingly large number of top male executives, including Sam Walton of Wal-Mart, Mr. Kelleher and Robert Goodale, president of Finevest Foods, have appeared in women's clothing.

"....'I have two photos on my office walls,' said Mr. Goodale. 'In one, I'm shaking President Reagan's hand. In the other, I'm wearing a hula skirt. The real me is the one in the hula skirt.' "

CHARISMA: COMPLAINT OR CURE

A charismatic leader is made as much from circumstances as from personality. Someone who assumes the top position at a company that is doing well is not likely to introduce radical changes. Tampering with success is not the way heroes are made. A company that is about to go down the tubes, on the other hand, will be ready to try anything, turn the system upside down, act on outrageous suggestions. Anyone who takes over during hard times and manages to pull the company together will be revered. But this is not necessarily the most effective leader over the long haul.

In the 1980s, many companies were known by the personalities of their presidents, and the search for charismatic leaders produced some outstanding examples of why this is not a productive way to define a company. Sometimes these leaders were able to redirect and inject energy to repair faults and forge into new markets that saved ailing enterprises. But the age bore out the fact that the skills needed to turn a company around wouldn't necessarily help the running of one.

Charm and likeability are hardly liabilities, but charisma without a foundation of adaptability and open-mindedness can be. Charming one's peers and the public isn't synonymous with charming the company portfolio and the 1980s bore witness to several charismatic leaders who turned out to be toxic to their companies.

An article, "The Dark Side of Charisma," by Daniel Goleman in *The New York Times* (4/1/90), explained that "the difference between good and bad leaders often comes down to the distinction between healthy and unhealthy narcissism. 'A healthy narcissist knows what he's good at and knows to take advice about what he's not so good at,' says Harry Levinson, a psychologist who directs the Levinson Institute, a consulting firm in Belmont, MA. 'Their self-confidence is the basis of their charisma.' By contrast, unhealthy narcissists combine an almost-grandiose sense of certainty with a disdain for subordinates.

> "Modern armies are large corporate ventures, exceedingly mixed in psychological make-up and labyrinthine in complexity. Some, like Caesar's, Napoleon's, Hitler's, or even McClellan's, are in a sense personal; but because of the sheer numbers involved, the Great Leader can never be real to his troops in quite the way that Charles [XII] was to his. Far from being a disadvantage, this remoteness permits a modern-style leader to create an 'image' of himself often more attractive than the reality might be, the only problem then being to maintain it."—Charles Fair, *From the Jaws of Victory*

"....Pride also prevents some managers from taking advice. 'While any leader needs an inspiring vision, there's trouble if he starts ignoring data about the limits of his ideas,' said Dr. Larry Hirschhorn, a psychologist at the Wharton Center for Applied Research. 'Such a manager only wants to hear what confirms his own ideas; he turns against anyone who challenges him.'

"....Ineffective, narcissistic leaders bring out several forms of behavior in their subordinates."

Hirschhorn cites the following examples:

- **Groupthink.** Workers feel they must censor what they say in meetings because it's too dangerous to challenge the boss.

- **Distortions of the truth.** Subordinates feel an unusually strong impulse to twist facts around to please the boss or agree with whatever the boss says.

- **Tension.** Employees don't feel like themselves in the boss's company.

- **Humorlessness.** The tone is grim; there's no joking around with the boss.

- **Blind loyalty.** The executive makes excessive demands on workers to show loyalty, such as insisting that they not share information with other departments, putting loyalty above doing what is best for the organization.

DIVINE DELEGATOR

The antithesis of the charismatic leader is the divine delegator, who has a secure enough self-image to trust those around him or her to carry out tasks. Divine delegators are willing to allow work that may not be done *exactly* the way they had in mind and to admit that someone else might even be able to the job *better.* Divine delegators do not regard their subordinates as human carbon paper, there to offer ersatz versions of themselves.

This approach requires self-confidence, as well as self-knowledge and strong communication skills. Delegators have to understand and be able to define what they want to get accomplished, and they must be able to communicate their desires through instructions to those around them. They must be willing to rely on and not compete with their staff.

DOWNWARD MOBILITY

In the end, leaders can only be as good as the companies behind them. Their decisions and actions depend on the information generated by their employees.

> "....We must recognize that most of our organizations—public and private, military and economic—have too many chiefs and not enough Indians....Committees proliferate, but the job does not get done....More than half of the modern American corporation consists of workers uninvolved in operations or production work, an astounding fact. At the General Motors Corporation, 77.5 percent of the work force is white collar and salaried, while only 22.5 percent are hourly blue-collar workers. At Mobil Oil, 61.5 percent of the staff is white collar; at General Electric, 60 percent.

> "If the United States is to arrest its decline, two developments need to occur in the near future: first, American business will need to increase the ratio of operators to managerial staff, giving management a much wider purview; second, workers will increasingly come to fulfill a management function. In the more distant future the distinction between white and blue collars may disappear."—Richard Rosencrance, author of *America's Economic Resurgence: A Bold New Strategy, The New York Times* (7/15/90)

Despite some formal models to the contrary, information isn't just something that enters at the top and then filters neatly down through the rank and file of a company. Some information enters in the downward fashion, but there are other means of communicating information—upward and laterally. And decisions are made based on information from each of these three directions.

The traditional order is the boss calling out orders that are carried out by a caste of workers that ripple out in ever widening arcs from the command post. Each tier of management is responsible for overseeing the tier below. The thrust of formal management practice is downward. A wise manager recognizes that the formal chain of command is only one of the communication systems that determines what gets done in the office. Informal systems, lateral communication, the office grapevine, chats around the coffee machine, will influence the nature of work, the interpretation of instructions.

> "The old smokestack division of a firm into heads and hands no longer works. Just as owners once became dependent on managers for knowledge, today's managers are becoming dependent on their employees for knowledge. The knowledge load, and more important, the decision load are being redistributed....As a result 'submissive rule observers, who merely follow instructions to the letter are not good workers,' says a study of employee relations and productivity in the giant Sony Corp. in Japan. In today's fast-change environment, it points out, rules, too, need to be changed more frequently than in the past. And workers need to be encouraged to propose such changes, because the worker who helps frame new rules will also understand why they are necessary and how they fit into the larger picture—which means they can apply them more intelligently."
> —Alvin Toffler, *Powershift*

Downward communication dominates because those above have the clout to initiate communications and can authorize the funds to produce them. No shortage here.

Upward communication needs nurturing. It is a rich and, for the most part, untapped resource in many businesses. Because of the wariness of employees to propose systems or procedures that depart from the accepted rule, upward communications are a delicate affair.

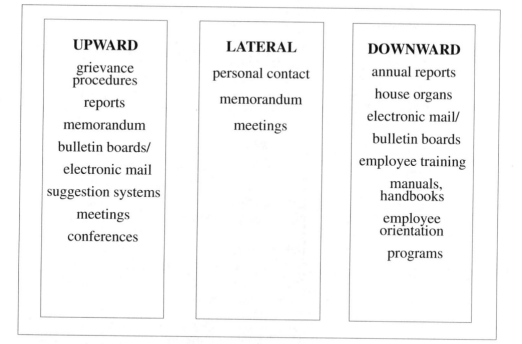

UPWARD	LATERAL	DOWNWARD
grievance procedures	personal contact	annual reports
reports	memorandum	house organs
memorandum	meetings	electronic mail/ bulletin boards
bulletin boards/ electronic mail		employee training
suggestion systems		manuals, handbooks
meetings		employee orientation
conferences		programs

Some companies are beginning to recognize that front-line employees are a rich source of information and are exploring ways of tapping it. Companies can use formal and informal meetings, suggestion boxes, increased contact between different levels of workers, and employee surveys designed to determine their needs, problems, and thoughts on company business.

The popularity of these surveys is on the upswing. As times get tougher and corporations look for ways to pare expenses, ensuring that employees are satisfied becomes not just benevolent concern but sound business sense. Disgruntled employees aren't going to perform well; they tend to take more sick days, lack concentration, make more mistakes, and, in the extreme cases, can sabotage a company.

Ninety-three percent of CEOs believe that employees possess information that can help them make better decisions, but only 14 percent communicate "frequently" with their employees, according to a study conducted by Johnson & Higgins, a New York City benefit consulting firm.

"Slimmed-down companies can ill afford to have disgruntled—and thus, unproductive—employees around. Nor can they keep pouring money into benefits, the most common survey subject. Thus many now hope that surveys will pinpoint ways to keep employees happy without bankrupting the company.

"Johnson Wax, for example, has made career data available to employees via computer, has assigned managers to counsel them about careers, and has otherwise strengthened its career development program—all in response to an employee survey. 'Surveys are the best way to stay in touch with what your employees think and need,' said Gayle P. Kosterman, a vice-president of human resources.

"Nearly half of the 200 companies surveyed last summer by A. Foster Higgens & Company, a human resources consulting firm in Princeton, N.J., said they use employee surveys. And 97 percent of chief executives polled by the firm thought surveys would yield useful information."—Claudia H. Deutsch, "Asking Workers What They Think," *The New York Times* (4/22/90)

Some far-thinking companies are nurturing the future work force by offering mentor programs that allow high-school students to serve work apprenticeships—programs that have been as enlightening to the mentors as to the students. A mentor program at the Federal National Home Mortgage Association with a high school in Washington, D.C., has benefited both sides. The company now uses computer programs written by the students and stays in touch with the customers of the future. And the students get financial support, learn practical skills, and get work experience. Both sides develop enriching social relationships that go beyond the bounds of the office.

"The $1 million program, which Fannie Mae, the nation's largest home mortgage investor, introduced in 1988, brings personal and financial support to students at Woodson [High School], an inner-city school with many low-income students. It is one of many programs nationwide that industry has initiated in recent years to help improve public schools and their students. Companies say that if they want to draw on a well-educated, highly skilled pool of workers, they will have to create it.

"....The program focuses on the most promising of Woodson's 1,200 students. Anyone who earns all A's and B's in a single semester is enrolled in the Futures 500 Club, a membership that brings a mentor, $500 each semester— deposited in an account earmarked for education—and the possibility of getting one of the 20 summer jobs that Fannie Mae opens for Woodson students.

"The mentors' involvement ranges from playing basketball with students on Saturday mornings to helping students apply to college, and they typically do it on their own time. For some students, the most surprising thing about the program is the relationship they develop with their mentors.

"Doresa McCombs, an 18-year-old senior, said her circle of friends now includes Carolyn Fitzgerald, who manages Fannie Mae's mortgaged-backed securities back office....Ms. Fitzgerald and Doresa have conversations by telephone two or three times a week and do things together. Until last year Doresa had never seen a play or been farther from Washington than neighboring Maryland. But since she entered the program, she has seen the Dance Theater of Harlem and has gone to Boston to visit the campus of Northeastern University, where she will enroll this fall to study engineering."—Sandra Salmans, "Nurturing the Next Work Force," *The New York Times* (5/27/90)

HANDS-OFF MANAGEMENT

Another approach to encouraging the input of employees is to de-emphasize authority and rigid chains of command that promulgate the them-and-us mentality between management and employees. This can be accomplished by formal policies letting employees have more say in company decisions, by informal attitudes, and even by the architecture of the workplace.

"I decided that my office wouldn't be my business card; it wouldn't be an icon of my position in the organization. Second of all, Apple is constantly in a state of change—in fact, change is really the fuel of Apple. So, as people have to move around so frequently, I wanted to negate the idea that there was any status attached to having a certain kind of an office. Therefore, I decided that my office would be smaller and less prestigious than that of anybody who worked for me.

"The next thing was that I decided that, basically, for me, an office did not have to connote power, but it ought to connote what I do, and so this is really form follows function; I meet in conversation with people, so a round table works for me; there really is no sense of importance for any one individual over another."—John Sculley, chairman of Apple Computer.

Other companies have resorted to more global measures. Drastic changes in company policy can sometimes be the saving grace for to an ailing business. "Desperation is a good motive," says David Luther, senior vice president and corporate director of quality at Corning. "Customers came to us and said if we didn't change, they'd go somewhere else." According to Jay Cocks in an article, "Let's Get Crazy!" in *Time* (6/11/90), "Corning gave its employees unusual freedom to think of solutions, backing off from hands-on management and organizing the staff into some 3,000 teams of up to 15 members each. One result: profits have risen 250 percent since 1982. 'By the mid-1990s,' says Luther, 'we'll define good management as the ability to get out of the way.' Managers at Eastman Kodak decided to let the folks on the factory floor run the professional-film manufacturing unit. In 1989 the unit, which had run $1 million over budget, came in $2.5 million under."

The motto at W. L. Gore & Associates, the 32-year-old outfit that introduced Teflon products and manufactures everything from electronics to dental products, is "If you're not making mistakes, you're doing something wrong," said Jeanne Ambruster-Sherry, a biologist who works in the company's sales-and-marketing division. The company has gone from a mom-and-pop operation to one with 37 plants worldwide and 5,000 employees, and its success has been credited to the absence of direct control over the workers (or associates in company parlance) and the encouragement to take the long chance.

Many companies are devoting increasing attention to promoting cooperation and esprit de corps. This will require some revising of the corporate totem pole. For example, knowledge workers, i.e., information processors, are regarded as very low on the office totem pole. Yet what they do often determines how a company runs or doesn't run. These people have tremendous power, yet relatively low status. The business community needs to recognize this situation.

By allowing everyone access to information, rewarding the sharing of it, and being lavish in crediting effort, companies support the idea that they operate as a team.

Steve Jobs of Next, Inc., allows everyone access to company information, including salaries. At the Greenwood, South Carolina, fibers plant of Monsanto, employees eliminated the foremen who oversaw the mechanics' work. The mechanics now divide the work among themselves, making their own decisions.

THE MASTER AND THE SLAVE

Too many American companies, though, still practice a master-and-slave approach to the politics of the workplace. The leader as guru to be followed blindly is not a healthy response. It makes a scapegoat of the CEO for the problems or the success of the entire corporation. It lays responsibility for a company on a single person, when in reality the effect that any one individual can have on what happens in a business is minimal.

The CEO of a company is viewed as the company itself, but a corporation can't be represented by one person. Just how much effect one person actually has in the affairs of a corporation pales in light of the imagined impact. A corporation isn't one person—it's countless employees, stock holders, consultants, and even markets.

The American business vocabulary must be adapted to recognize the real power employees have in the day-to-day running of a company. Superiors can make the rules and give orders until they are blue in the face, but they are still dependent on the employees to follow them and get the job done. Thus subordinates have a measure of power in that it is up to them to realize the dreams of their superiors. Who really has the power? The leaders can give the orders, but the employees are the ones who decide how they get followed. It's time for the corporate world to acknowledge this fact in its management practices.

Change occurs only with the perception of catastrophe or in extreme situations. In the environmental arena, for a hundred years we've been pumping toxic wastes into rivers and polluting the air with noxious gases. Yet only in the wake of catastrophes like Chernobyl and the Exxon *Valdez* oil spill has public opinion cried out for action. We only notice the extremes. You wouldn't pay attention to one bump on your arm, but when there's a rash on your whole arm, you call the doctor.

There is a perception in the workplace now of monumental problems. We have been surpassed by the Japanese, by the Germans, by the Koreans. The problems can't be solved with money. They are problems of frustration, of mismanagement, of faulty communications among the lines of command, of failure to adapt to a changing world.

It is one the darkest ironies of history to think that the United States may have handed the economic baton to Japan by dropping the atom bomb on it. After World War II, Japan, like war-ravaged Germany, had no choice but to start from scratch. Factories were rebuilt with state-of-the art

"The search for excellence is giving way to the search for meaning. Whereas career and hustle books were once big business, the new passion is for the courage to let go....Will these ideas inspire a radically new type of business executive? Ideas do have the ability to redirect the attention of our leaders and if these new books are any signal of what is to come, people in business are ready to hone their ability to appreciate more deeply the context, meaning, and subtlety of the world in which they operate and live."—Harriet Rubin, executive editor at Doubleday, "Business Books for New-Age Bosses," *The New York Times* (6/24/90)

"Once you have given up the ghost everything follows with dead certainty, even in the midst of chaos."—Henry Miller, *The Tropic of Capricorn*

equipment, while the United States chugged along patching and repairing machinery that was fast becoming obsolete and lost its manufacturing edge.

It's time to stop pouring millions of dollars into capital improvements and start pouring effort into the development of human capital. It's time to stop patching antiquated management philosophies and replace them with new leadership models based on the leader as a skilled instruction-giver who understands the challenges of communication. This change has nothing to do with money; it has to do with attitude and policy.

America has always excelled in the communication arts—computers, publishing, the news media. Since the communication business is one we do better in than anyone else in the world, this is an obvious industry that we can build upon. This is our long suit.

If we can apply mass-media communication abilities to the infinite interactions—the instruction-giving and taking—that occur every day in the workplace, we can ensure a richer, more productive environment for individuals and for the economy as well.

"The climate which influences one nation to take pleasure in being communicative, makes it also delight in change."
—Charles de Secondat, Baron de Montesquieu, *Spirit of Laws*

AN INSTRUCTION CRIB SHEET

Improving your technique as either a giver or taker of instructions will allow you to function with less frustration in a complex world.

*I*n school, students often resort to crib sheets, writing phrases or words onto a small piece of paper (or the palm of a hand), to summarize information for a test. These sheets help bring up other knowledge. This chapter is the crib sheet. Go ahead, tear it out.

Throughout the book, I've discussed the different issues that affect the giving and taking of instructions, as well as the components of an instruction system. Here you'll find the advice distilled. The first half of this chapter is devoted to the long-term devices for improving the quality of your instructions, such as reworking your general communication patterns and improving work relationships. The rest covers the instruction system and the more specific improvements you can make in your instruction technique. It's divided into the following sections:

- Sharpening your communication skills.

- The instruction system.

- Creating a positive instruction environment.

- Instructions in the workplace.

- The structure of instructions.

- Lamaze for instruction-givers.

- Suggestions for instruction-takers.

- The good, the bad, and the ugly: operating and assembly instructions.

SHARPENING YOUR COMMUNICATION SKILLS

Remember all communication involves translating from one person's understanding to another's. Thus every communication must be filtered through the perceptions and experiences of one person to another. All messages must be translated; people must learn to think, speak, and listen in what might be viewed as a foreign language—the language of the person with whom they are communicating. Both sides will have to make judgments, interpret meanings, and make a leap from one person's biases to another's.

Learn to use context, i.e., the immediate environment and the broader applications, of your messages to surmount some of the difficulties in communication. As an instruction-giver spells out the scope of the instruction, differ-ences in interpretation should appear. Thus, paying attention to the context can be one way of insuring fewer mistakes in translation. You can begin to tell where the definition you use for a word diverges from another's definition of the same word when you can see it in an environment.

Focus on the content and not the form of messages. Try to look beyond a person's idiosyncrasies and styles of communication. If someone uses too many interjections, instead of counting the "Uh, huhs" and "you knows," keep in mind the point of the conversation. If you have some relationship with the communicator, use historic precedent to circumvent potential confusion. Focus on what the person says and does, searching for consistent themes in his or her words and behavior.

Replace abstract concepts with concrete descrip-tions. All language is an abstraction to some degree. Words only represent things or ideas; they are not the things themselves. The more abstract a word is, the greater the margin for misinterpretation. The same concept can almost always be communicated in more concrete terms. By substituting words with a higher concrete value, you will reduce some of the ambiguity of communications.

Make sure your messages are getting through intact to the appropriate target. Build in ways for the listener to respond to you, and pay close attention to the reaction. If the listener starts to look dazed, pained, or dumbfounded, don't proceed blindly on. Stop and rephrase your message; try a new tack.

Hone your question-asking skills to correct misunderstandings and uncover information. Remember the purpose of asking questions is to elicit information and clarify messages, not to show what a brilliant question-asker you are. Let curiosity inspire your questions. Refuse to play God, even unconsciously, Don't guess at another's motivation.

Improve your listening skills. Don't mistake talking with listening. They are 2 different pursuits. Try to encourage a positive listening climate by eliminating distractions, focusing on what the speaker is saying instead of on your own response. Don't be afraid to ask for clarification of confusing messages. The mind has a tendency to meander in a listening mode. Try to be more diligent in returning to the subject at hand. Hone your attention span by looking at the speaker. Don't fidget. Resist the temptation to lead the speaker off the track. Don't claim that you've understood anything that you haven't.

Delay reacting emotionally to a message until you have understood it. Try to the let messages settle before flying off the handle. Most people operate in just the opposite fashion, and wind up in needlessly counterproductive exchanges.

THE INSTRUCTION SYSTEM

Instructions are more than just a message to do something. Like communications, they are part of a system that can be broken down into 5 components—**giver, taker, content, channel,** and **context**. As either a giver or a taker, you should begin to look at instructions from a more global standpoint.

GIVERS originate instructions. They want something done, either consciously or subconsciously. They must then choose who to ask (the taker), formulate a message (content), decide how the instruction should be formed (channel), and take into account the environment in which the instruction is to be delivered (context). Each choice that they make in the process should influence the next step.

TAKERS. In a successful system, those who act on instructions are more than just passive followers.

Instruction-takers should be active; they must interpret a message and perform on it, making decisions along the way. They have a responsibility to communicate their understanding of an instruction to the giver, to let the giver know if they don't understand an instruction.

CONTENT. This is the message itself—independent from the way it is presented. There are essentially 3 kinds of instructions: those that are past-oriented, concerned with transferring knowledge; those that are oriented to present action, such as building something (be it an idea or a tool shed) or operating something; and those that will require some action in the future, such as directions from bosses or even the casual, implied instructions received in social interactions. The content of each should be composed of the same 5 elements: mission, destination, procedure, time, anticipation, and failure (defined later in this chapter).

CHANNEL. This is the form and dressing of the message. Instructions can be expressed by different means—words or pictures—and in different media, or in a combination of these. They can be oral, told as a story or sung in a song, or written in the form of a note or a formal document. They can be illustrated graphically, imaged on videotape, expressed directly or indirectly. The channel is the medium by which the content is communicated.

CONTEXT. The context is the setting in which the instruction is delivered. It is the largest and most complex component in the instruction system. Context has 3 different levels of meaning: the immediate environment in which the instruction is given; the broader applications of a particular instruction, such as what will be affected by performance of it; and the economic or social state of affairs surrounding all parties concerned.

CREATING A POSITIVE INSTRUCTION ENVIRONMENT

Instructions require common sense, perception, intuition, and extraordinary patience, both to give and to receive. Improving your technique as either a giver or taker of instructions will allow you to function with less frustration in a complex world. Start to note all the parts of your commmunications that involve instruction.

The first step toward improving your instruction technique is to recognize your instruction style—as a giver and a taker. Then you can begin to understand problems in your technique. Do you watch over the taker's shoulder? Do people complain about not being able to understand you? Are you reluctant to make decisions on your own? Ask some people who have to follow your instructions to describe your technique. What are your long suits and short-comings as an instruction-giver or -taker?

The following questionnaire will help you assess the role of instructions in your life.

Instruction Questionnaire

Your Name:

Your Title:

I MODEL INSTRUCTORS

1. Most people have someone in their lives that they looked up to as a good instructor, someone who made a difference in their life. It could be a teacher, a parent, a boss, a friend. Who was that person for you?

2. What was his or her job?

3. Put a check in the box beside the characteristics that he or she possessed and put a star by the ones you think are most important.

☐ Patience	☐ Inspiration	☐ Loving
☐ Intelligence	☐ Compassion	☐ Disciplinarian
☐ Humor	☐ Articulateness	☐ Toughness
☐ Energy	☐ Commitment	☐ Other

4. Where would you place this person on the following continua?

	5 4 3 2 1 0 1 2 3 4 5	
Abstract	☐—☐—☐—☐—☐—☐—☐—☐—☐—☐—☐	Concrete
Demanding	☐—☐—☐—☐—☐—☐—☐—☐—☐—☐—☐	Docile
Taciturn	☐—☐—☐—☐—☐—☐—☐—☐—☐—☐—☐	Talkative
Creative	☐—☐—☐—☐—☐—☐—☐—☐—☐—☐—☐	Logical
Humorous	☐—☐—☐—☐—☐—☐—☐—☐—☐—☐—☐	Serious

5. What were the most important things he or she taught you?

6. Give an anecdote or story that illustrates why he or she was such a good instructor.

II INSTRUCTION MANUALS

1. Do you own equipment that you feel you don't use to its fullest? ☐ Yes ☐ No

2. How well can you use the following equipment?

	Can't Operate	Basic Operation	Moderate Proficiency	Use Fully
office phones	☐	☐	☐	☐
computers	☐	☐	☐	☐
fax machines	☐	☐	☐	☐
VCR's	☐	☐	☐	☐
answering machines	☐	☐	☐	☐
microwaves	☐	☐	☐	☐
televisions	☐	☐	☐	☐
bank automated teller machines	☐	☐	☐	☐

3. How many instruction manuals do you have?

4. Which one is the easiest to follow?

5. Which is the hardest?

6. How would you rate the following factors in influencing your decision to buy a piece of equipment?

	Not Important	Somewhat Important	Very Important	Most Important
Product features	☐	☐	☐	☐
Easy-to-follow instructions	☐	☐	☐	☐
Price	☐	☐	☐	☐
Aesthetics	☐	☐	☐	☐

III INSTRUCTIONS IN THE WORKPLACE

1. What percentage of your work involves giving instructions?

2. What percentage of your work involves receiving instructions?

3. How would you rate yourself as an instruction giver?

Hopeless   ☐—☐—☐—☐—☐—☐—☐—☐—☐   Perfect

4. Do your employees ever complain about not being able to understand you?

☐ Yes ☐ No

5. If so, do they complain about it? ☐ Rarely   ☐ Sometimes   ☐ Often

6. What specifically do they complain about?

7. When someone doesn't follow your instructions, do you think it is because: (Check as many as you think apply.)

☐ You didn't consider the abilities of the person you were instructing.
☐ You gave too much information.
☐ You didn't give enough information.
☐ The follower wasn't paying attention.
☐ The follower was afraid to admit that your instructions were not clear.
☐ The follower didn't like the task assigned.
☐ The follower didn't understand the reason for the instruction.
☐ Other

IV OPTIONAL

1. What do you think makes a good instruction?

2. What do you think makes a bad instruction?

3. Why do you think people have such a hard time following instructions?

After you "know thyself" as a giver and taker, you can begin to analyze your instruction relationships with others. Learn to decode the instructions you get from others. People rarely tell you exactly what they are thinking, but often come in the back door to convey what they really mean. Based on close observation and past patterns, you can usually figure out what words or phrases may mean something else. Learn the key words and phrases of the people with whom you interact.

IN THE WORKPLACE

Instructions in the workplace must be understood within the larger context of current affairs and the economy. Create a more fertile atmosphere for giving and taking instructions by:

- Reducing executive isolation by letting employees know that you are always willing to listen—to the bad news as well as the good. Remember information travels in all directions, but upwards is its most fragile direction. It needs to be encouraged.

- Keep employees informed about company business.

- Be lavish with praise and judicious with criticism. Let everyone know that they can make mistakes. And that mistakes are inevitable when you are trying new ideas.

- Define corporate goals. Make sure management policies are as consistent as possible.

- Make sure that individual goals are consistent with company goals, whenever this is possible.

- Reduce interpersonal competition within the company. Encourage the sharing of information.

- Keep in mind that future action is the objective of business, not the storage and handling of records of past actions.

- Build in ways that employees will feel the pride of ownership in their work.

- Look closely at the nature of your work relationships and analyze whom you are dependent on for what and likewise who depends on you for what. This will help in deciding what deserves your attention and what does not.

- Be positive. People want to know what they should do, not just what they shouldn't do. Besides, studies have shown that comprehension of positive instructions is higher than with negative instructions. For example, "Remove hats in the office" is more likely to be obeyed than "Do not keep hats on in the office."

Homer Sarasohn was sent to Japan after World War II to teach the Japanese how to produce electronic equipment and to manage their companies. He (along with engineer Charles Protzman) did such a good job that the United States is now learning from them. According to Robert Chapman Wood in "A Lesson Learned and a Lesson Forgotten" in *Forbes* (2/6/89), their most important lessons were as follows:

- Every company needs a concise, complete statement of the purpose of the company's existence, one that provides a well-defined target for the idealistic efforts of the employees.

- Companies must put quality ahead of profit, pursuing it rigorously with techniques such as statistical quality control.

- Every employee deserves the same kind of respect fellow managers receive, and good management is "democratic management." Lower-level employees need to be listened to by their bosses.

Problem situations. In dealing with an impatient, angry, overly critical instruction-giver or taker, keep in mind that while the anger and ill-will may be directed at you, you are not the cause. People are responsible for their own emotions and reactions. Perhaps the irate one is under pressure from someone else, perhaps he or she had a fight with a spouse or a parent.

- Don't reinforce negative behavior. When someone is impatient with you, the tendency is to defend yourself, but this rarely solves the problem. Try a more unexpected reaction, perhaps a bland stare, a raised eyebrow, a curious gaze. Let the person vent their anger without inciting your own. When it blows over, go after the information you want.

- Try agreeing with the person. Nothing is more unbalancing than to be ranting and raving at someone and have them agree with you. You are absolutely right; boy, did I screw up royally. What can I do about it?

- Try humor. In certain cases, a light remark will enable the steam-blower to see himself or herself in a new light. A friend of mine who always used to enjoy her work told me a story about working in an retail store where everyone lived in terror of a manager who was famous for his tirades. My friend had only been on the job a few days when she was introduced to him. He started laying down edicts about all the things employees couldn't have or do. "I will not tolerate employees sitting down in the store; I will not tolerate sloppy dressers; You may not make more than two trips downstairs while working on the floor. I forbid you to...," he continued. My friend politely let him finish, then asked in her most innocent voice, "Does this mean a putting green in the employee lounge is out of the question?" He was so startled by her reply that he laughed and they became friends. He understood that she wasn't afraid of him, so he could treat her like a person.

- Try looking at the person in a benevolent light. Giving someone the benefit of the

"The best remedy for a cranky boss might be a locked office door and an unplugged phone. The average manager is interrupted every 8 minutes, making what once was one of life's minor annoyances the leading cause of on-the-job stress. Managers in high-tech fields who supervise a lot of workers have it worst. They get interrupted at least once every 5 minutes."—Jo Ann Tooley with Marinna Knight and Joannie Schrof, "8 Minutes Worth of Work," *U.S. News & World Report* (5/22/89)

doubt sometimes allows a difficult person to behave like an agreeable one.

THE STRUCTURE OF INSTRUCTIONS

Both givers and takers need to understand the components of every instruction. This becomes the guide against which you can measure your own instructions as a giver and begin to rehabilitate instructions as a taker. You can determine what is missing, what is incorrect.

Despite the myriad different versions of instructions, there are roughly only three different types.

- Those that involve the *past* as in transfer of knowledge that occurs in school where students learn history, geography, biology, mathematics. Aside from memorization and regurgitation for tests, past-oriented instructions are usually passive; they don't require any immediate action. When you learn about the Battle of Waterloo, you won't have to fight it.

- Those that involve the *present,* such as operating and assembly instructions. "Push this button if you want to send a message." "Turn left at Route 66." Present-based instructions include those for all equipment instructions, as well as directions from one place to another, recipes, assembly manuals. These instructions demand immediate action.

- Those that are *future-oriented.* This is the realm of interest in the workplace and in social relationships. When a boss instructs you to reduce spending in the marketing department, he or she is asking you to do something at some future point. It may be next week, next month, or next year. When a company president talks about corporate goals, he or she may be giving implicit instructions that will dictate future actions. The explicit and implicit instructions that we give to our friends and relatives also fall into this category, whether it be "Pick up a quart of ice-cream on your way home" or "I hate to dance," which carries the implicit instructions to "Stop suggesting that we go dancing."

Each of these can be oriented in a goal-based or a task-based manner, but all are created from the same components.

The basic building blocks of all instructions are:

**❶
MISSION
❷
DESTINATION
❸
PROCEDURE
❹
TIME
❺
ANTICIPATION
❻
FAILURE**

- **Mission.** The mission explains why an instruction is being given. The mission should inspire how the instruction-taker performs. It diminishes the tendency of people to confuse the channel or form with the content, to become distracted by the forms and neglect the spirit of the instruction. Learn to decipher the spirit of a message from the actual words used.

- **Destination.** All instructions should have a destination that is made clear when the instruction is given. The destination defines the scope of the instruction.

- **Procedure.** This is the heart of the instructions, the actual directions toward which all the other components are oriented.

- **Time.** The estimated time it will take to carry out an instruction gives the follower an indication of possible errors and will lessen the investment in fruitless or misguided attempts.

- **Anticipation.** Anticipation is the reassuring element of instructions. This is what the taker can expect to encounter along the way of carrying out the instruction. Anticipation helps correct misperceptions in time and ill-defined goals.

- **Failure.** All instructions should contain indications of when the follower may be in error. This is what is often missing from directions, yet is probably the most effective way of reducing frustration on the part of the follower.

LAMAZE FOR INSTRUCTION-GIVERS

The instruction-givers have 4 factors to consider: the **content** (the message itself), the **channel** (the form the message will take), the **context** (the setting in which the message is delivered), and the **taker** (the person to whom the message is directed.

The instruction process begins when you see a need for an instruction. Before you deliver an instruction, make sure that you are clear on what you want to get done and why you want to do it. Then ask yourself:

- Who is the person who would be most able to accomplish it? Why am I asking this person to do it?

- Can you explain the purpose or the need to that person? Can you explain how the request might benefit the individual and/or the organization?

- What consideration can I give to this person's particular personality and aptitude?

- How can I translate my message to someone else's way of understanding?

- How can I incite this person's creativity and inspire him or her to do a better job than I could do?

The Content. Now that you have a taker in mind, you can formulate the content of the instruction.

- Does it encompass the following components: mission, destination, procedure, time, anticipation, and failure? Do the takers understand the different classes of information?

- Is it delivered in the same order in which it is to be followed? Pay attention to sequence, so each instruction adds to the understanding of the next. First, give the mission, then the destination, procedure, time, anticipation, and failure. Instructions should be like surrogate fingers, pointing you on your way.

● Is the content adequate (i.e., sufficient for the taker) and factually true?

The Channel. Don't confuse the form of the instruction with the content. Don't get trapped into thinking there is a best way or right way to give or carry out instructions. Instructions can be delivered in either words or pictures. Let the instruction determine the choice. Pictures seem to be comprehended easier, but words are important in communicating complex ideas. Don't confuse the dressings with the channel itself. Once you have choosen words or pictures, then you can worry about the form the words and/or pictures should take. The instructions should be presented in a variety of forms to allow for individual learning preferences.

The Context. Look at the instruction in light of the big picture. Where does it fit? What is the desired scope of it? What else might it affect? Have I communicated all of this to the taker?

"The instruction-giver needs to get that the instructions have been gotten before moving on."—Paul Frehe, CEO of Sunstar

Post-Delivery. After you deliver the instruction, ask the taker to repeat it. This is the simplest, most effective way to determine whether or not the taker has understood the request. Still, you should build in ways that you can monitor the compliance as the taker proceeds.

● Follow the stages of action.

● Ask for progress reports at specified intervals. Don't just say, "Keep me posted." To you, this might mean daily reports complete with footnotes. To the person you instructed it might mean an "Everything's just fine, Bud," once a month.

● Remind the taker of your instruction.

● Ask the taker how he or she is doing.

● Bring it up again.

MODEL INSTRUCTORS

Learn from the masters. Everyone has a favorite instructor. What do you like about his or her style? If you can analyze their technique, perhaps you can incorporate it yourself. According to our instruction survey, an ideal instructor is:

- Someone who is able to explain the big picture, the context in which the instructions are set.

- Someone who can teach you to see patterns so that you can transfer knowledge in one area to another.

- Someone who can instill confidence in you.

- Someone who can teach you to ask the right questions.

- Someone who can describe an idea in a variety of ways and thus create a three-dimensional picture of an idea.

- Someone who is passionate about his or her subject.

- Someone who allows you to make mistakes and encourages you to take risks.

- Someone who sometimes goes in the opposite direction from accepted custom to give instructions.

SUGGESTIONS FOR INSTRUCTION-TAKERS

Instruction-takers have different concerns and different responsibilites. Although the shape of the instruction is molded by the giver, the takers can and should be participants in the instruction system. They must be responsible for understanding the instructions and should be free to make suggestions and modify instructions by their responses.

You can't count on everyone around you to pay more attention to their instructions. That means that the instruction burden falls on you. But this isn't as bad as it sounds. There are a multitude of things you can do to improve your own techniques as an instruction-taker.

After receiving an instruction, respond with your interpretation of it. If the instruction is delivered face-to-face, repeat it in your own words. This will give you a chance to correct errors in translating the message from one person's understanding to another's. If it is delivered in writing, you could always send an "As I See It" memo.

If you don't understand the instruction, ask for clarification. Never be afraid to admit you don't understand. The embarrassment of admitting this is bound to be less than getting caught not-knowing down the line after you have invested your time and effort in going in the wrong direction.

Learn how to recognize faulty instructions. The following are the most common causes of instruction breakdown:

- Failure to translate the instruction to the perspective of the taker.

- Failure to take into account the understanding level or the needs of the taker.

- Messages phrased in abstract terms that defy mutual interpretation.

- An excess of information that obscures the intent of the instruction.

- Hiding the clear intent of the instruction under allusions and veiled references.

- Omitting essential pieces.

- Unnecessarily threatening enforcement of compliance with the instruction.

- Lack of context.

- Choice of an inappropriate channel to convey the content of the instruction, so the taker confuses the message.

- Departure from accepted custom without adequate warning.

- False claims or promises.

- Lack of attention paid to human behavior.

- Evoking the parent-child rebellion response.

● Self-destructive instructions.

● Time lapse problems.

● Inadequate incentive to follow.

Before you attempt to follow an instruction, you should ask yourself:

● Do I understand the instruction?

● What is it supposed to accomplish or what is the goal?

● What are the main roads toward this goal?

● What are the offbeat paths?

● What are my own interests and aptitudes?

Be aware that you have the power to choose how you will respond. You could: ignore the instruction; deliberately follow it incorrectly; do only what you think will keep the instruction-giver at bay; do what you think will please the instruction-giver; try to satisfy yourself by looking upon the instruction as a means to reach new understandings and acquire new skills. Obviously, the first 3 responses do not produce desirable outcomes, at least not from the giver's perspective. The 4th approach of trying to make someone else happy may have beneficial effects in the short run. However, only the 5th response will produce the most creative instruction performances. For one reason or another, you may not want to make such an effort, but make sure that your mode of response is a conscious one.

THE GOOD, THE BAD, AND THE UGLY

Operating manuals and assembly instructions are the most universal example of a failure to communicate. Too many of them break every rule in the book when it comes to delivering information.

But we can't resist buying the products. What's a person to do?

How well a product sells is more important to the manufacturer than how well a customer learns to use it. Business is, after all, business. The responsibility lies with the consumer to tie product usability to product purchase. Ask to look at the instructional manual of a product before you purchase it. Ask yourself:

- Is it written in a language that resembles English? Can you understand it?

- Are the basic operations separated from the fancy features?

- Does the diagram in the instruction manual correspond to the actual product? (You would be surprised how many times it does not.)

- Are the sections of the manual organized in an easy-to-find manner?

- Is there a section on what to do if something goes wrong? Trouble-shooting or problem-solving sections are useful, because these tend to be the situations that send you to your manuals in the first place.

- Are the illustrations clear and can you see how they correspond with the actual product?

- Are the parts clearly labeled?

- Is there a phone number to call if the manual doesn't answer all your questions? Any manufacturer who doesn't list a phone number or address up front for more information isn't really committed to customer service.

- Can you talk to a live person?

- Do the instructions tell you what is possible to accomplish by following them, what you can expect along the way, how long they should take to perform, and how can you tell when you've done something incorrectly?

What if it is too late and you have purchased a product, for which you can't understand the instructions, and are too embarrassed to ask for help?

Photographer Herbert Keppler gives some practical suggestions in an article he wrote in *Popular Photographer* (9/88). They were developed for camera equipment, but can easily be applied to equipment of any kind.

- If [the manual] plows right into the main body of instructions, try to locate the parts that explain how to work with the equipment in its simplest mode. Mark these prominently with a colored pen.

- Once you've become familar with the [equipment], you'll find that the complete instructions will be easier to assimilate.

- If you find that your instructions are linguistically tangled, take the time to cross out all those in foreign languages.

- Look for the warnings in the instructions and take them seriously. Never fool around without first reading electrical or electronic equipment instructions.

- Are they up to date? Did you know that manufacturers periodically update instruction manuals, taking out erroneous information, rewriting unclear material, and adding information that has been learned since you bought your item?

Be patient. More manufacturers are bound to realize that good instructions can sell products. Besides, now that you understand instructions so well, you might find that following product instructions is as easy as following the yellow brick road.

APPENDIX: A LOOK AT PRINTED INSTRUCTIONS

CRIB

1. GETTING ACQUAINTED WITH YOUR CRIB :
   It has many convenient uses. CRIB Converts to Mini Youth Bed and seat.
   It is easy to assemble.

2. AS A MINI YOUTH BED:
   When your Child reaches a height of 35 inches (or before), convert to Mini Youth Bed.
   Providing your Child is ready to sleep with out side rail protection.

3. MINI SEAT:
   A comfortable Seat for your Child to play with Toys and Freinds, making it comfy for Child
   to rest and play. To use as SEAT , It is recommended for comfort of child to buy a
   bolster the length of 51 inches or 2 pcs of 25 inches each. (Bolster not included with CRIB
   see below.

When instructions have obviously been translated from another language without the benefit of being editing by a native speaker (left), not only does the manufacturer lose credibility, but things can become can be downright confusing.

Some instruction-givers have attempted to circumvent potential language problems by presenting information by picture or pictogram only.

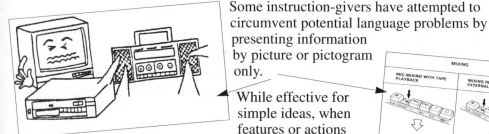

While effective for simple ideas, when features or actions become complex, the specificity and accuracy of words becomes a necessary complement to pictures.

Other manufacturers have taken a different approach—relying on words entirely and losing the potential directness and understandability of a drawing or photo.

Top: Portion of instructions for assembling a crib. Actually bringing up the baby is a breeze compared with putting this crib together.

Middle: Excerpt from instructions for a compact disc player. I guess this is supposed to mean that the CD unit can cause interference with other electonic audio mechanisms.

Below: Excerpt from instructions for the TIME Machine, a digital clock.

Your Desk Clock is capable of display-ing hours, minutes, seconds, month, and date. It can give you a display of either hours and minutes, or month and date. You can set the display to contin-uously switch from the hours and minutes to the month and date and back again. You also have a calendar which will last you a lifetime.

3) Push Button S2 once again and the display will shift to the hours along with an AM-PM indicator. Press Button S1 until the correct hour is showing in the display.
4) Push Button S2 once again and the display will change to the minutes. Press Button S1 until the correct minutes are showing in the display.
5) When finished setting the minutes, push Button S2 once again and the display will show the time. Press Button S1 once to activate the clock.
Note: The clock is not activated unless the colon (:) is flashing.

HOW TO OPERATE THE CLOCK
1) To see the date at a glance, press Button S1 once. The clock will return to the time display mode after a couple of seconds.
2) To see the seconds, press Button S1 twice. To return to the time display mode, press Button S1 once again.
3) To have the display continuously switch back and forth between time and date, press Button S2 once.
4) To stop the flashing back and forth between time and date, go through the entire set cycle. Continue pushing Button S2 until the time appears.

HOW TO SET THE TIME & DATE
1) Push Button S2 two times. This will bring the display to the set mode of the month. Press Button S1 until the correct month is showing in the display.

HOW TO CHANGE PERPETUAL CALENDAR
On the first day of every month, you will need to change

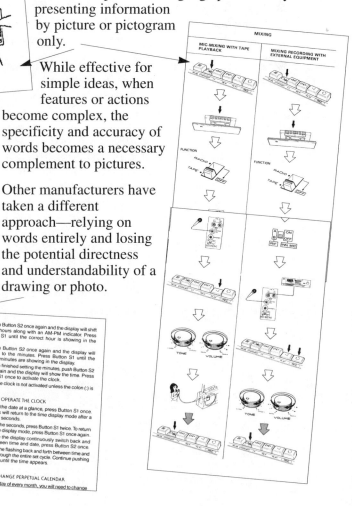

MIXING

MIC-MIXING WITH TAPE PLAYBACK | MIXING RECORDING WITH EXTERNAL EQUIPMENT

375

Big chunks of dense, unrelieved text can discourage even the most determined instruction-taker.

But perhaps as frustrating are instructions which contain a seeming balance of words and pictures, but show the pictures so small or so poorly done that the objective of the communication is just muddled.

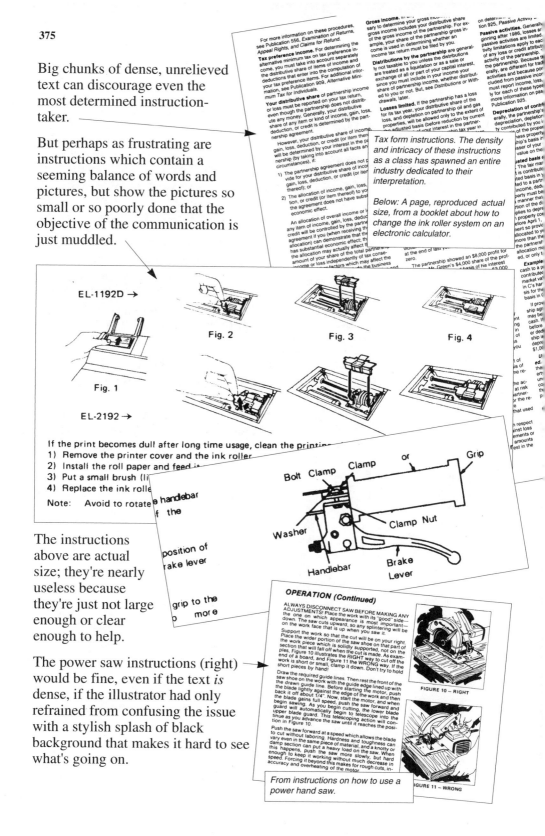

Tax form instructions. The density and intricacy of these instructions as a class has spawned an entire industry dedicated to their interpretation.

Below: A page, reproduced actual size, from a booklet about how to change the ink roller system on an electronic calculator.

The instructions above are actual size; they're nearly useless because they're just not large enough or clear enough to help.

The power saw instructions (right) would be fine, even if the text *is* dense, if the illustrator had only refrained from confusing the issue with a stylish splash of black background that makes it hard to see what's going on.

From instructions on how to use a power hand saw.

#1.DRAWER FACE
#2.BACK DRAWER SIDE
#3.LEFT DRAWER SIDE
#4.RIGHT DRAWER SIDE
#5.MIDDLE BOTTOM BOARD SUPPORT
#6.BOTTOM DRAWER BOARDS (2 PCS.)
#7.LEFT DRAWER SLIDE
#8.RIGHT DRAWER SLIDE
#9.DRAWER COVER SUPPORT (2 PCS.)
#10.DRAWER COVER
#11.MACHINE SCREW(ALLEN WRENCH HEAD)
#12.SCREW(PHILIP'S HEAD 4 PCS.)
#13.DRAWER HANDLE (2 PCS.)
#14.LOCK SCREW (4 PCS.)
#15.ASSEMBLY LOCK (4PCS.)
#16.ALLEN WRENCH

Another excerpt from the instructions for assembling a crib.

These crib instructions have too many details, crowded into a poorly drawn and cheaply reproduced diagram.

Clearly defined sections, such as those in the the the refrigerator instruction manual (below left) or those found throughout the Sony electronic product instruction manuals (below right) really help a person navigate through unfamiliar territory.

But the Sony video camera manual has a problem—it's not until page 36 that we find out how to actually shoot some video! In most cases, consumer instruction manuals would be more effective if the user didn't have to wade through tons of preparatory set-up details just to use the device in a basic way.

Parts and Features

From a well-organized refrigerator care and use instruction manual.

Please read this Owner's Manual before using your refrigerator. This manual explains how to start your refrigerator, clean it, move shelves and adjust controls. It also tells you what new sounds to expect from your refrigerator.

Treat your new refrigerator with care. Use it only to do what home refrigerators are designed to do. Remove the sales labels and tape before using the refrigerator.

To remove any remaining glue:
• Rub briskly with thumb to make a ball then remove.

OR

• Soak area with liquid hand dishwashing detergent before removing glue as described above. Do not use rubbing alcohol or flammable or toxic solvents, such as acetone, gasoline, carbon tetrachloride, etc. These can damage the material. See "Important Safety Instructions" on page 2.

NOTE: Do not remove any permanent instruction labels inside your refrigerator. Do not remove the Tech sheet fastened under the refrigerator at the front.

(Sony would not give us permission to reproduce the cover to their video cameras instruction manual.)

Instruction on using a video camera.

These coffee-maker instructions have a lot of good things going for it. It's organized into well-defined sections. The sequence of actions are described concisely and articulately; there is an accurate and close relationship between text and drawings; the drawings themselves are large enough, clear and in order. Only one important piece is missing—an indication of the time it takes to make yourself a cup of espresso.

Addressing potential failure by including a troubleshooting section does not reflect poorly on a product. On the contrary, the presence of a good guide makes users feel like manufacturers appreciate their position. Manufacturers gain credibility and reduce both frustrations and costs associated with responding to unnecessary questions and complaints.

The best troubleshooting sections are organized by "symptom" in a modified matrix arrangement like this chart for a color TV

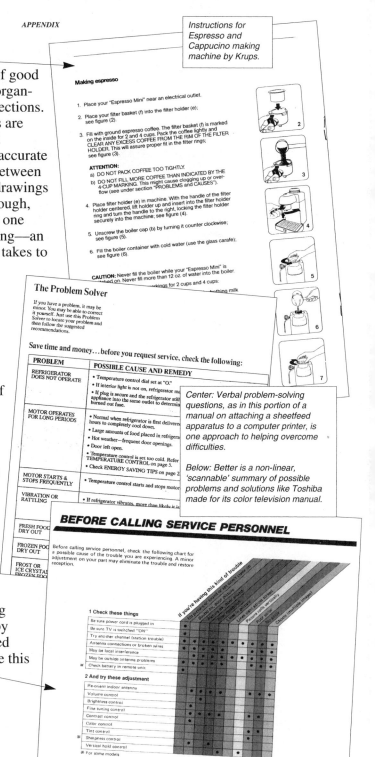

Instructions for Espresso and Cappucino making machine by Krups.

Center: Verbal problem-solving questions, as in this portion of a manual on attaching a sheetfeed apparatus to a computer printer, is one approach to helping overcome difficulties.

Below: Better is a non-linear, 'scannable' summary of possible problems and solutions like Toshiba made for its color television manual.

BIBLIOGRAPHY

Abelow, Daniel, with Edwin J. Hilpert, *Communications in the Modern Corporate Environment* (Englewood Cliffs, NJ: Prentice-Hall, 1986).

Anderson, John Robert, *Language, Memory, and Thought* (Hillsdale, NJ: L. Erlbaum Associates, 1976).

Bennis, Warren, *On Becoming A Leader* (Reading, MA: Addison-Wesley Publishing Co., 1989).

Bennis, Warren, and Burt Nanus, *Leaders: The Strategies for Taking Charge* (New York: Harper & Row Publishers, 1985).

Bentley, Trevor J., *Information, Communication, and the Paperwork Explosion* (New York: McGraw-Hill, 1976).

Berkman, Robert I., *Find It Fast* (New York: Harper & Row, 1987).

Berry, Leonard L., David R. Bennett, and Carter W. Brown, *Service Quality: A Profit Strategy for Financial Institutions* (Homewood, IL: Dow Jones-Irwin, 1989).

Bowbrick, Peter, *Effective Communication for Professionals and Executives* (London: Graham & Trotman, 1988).

Broadwell, Martin M., *The Supervisor as Instructor* (Reading, MA: Addison-Wesley Publishing, 1984).

Bruner, Jermore S., *Beyond the Information Given: Studies in the Psychology of Knowing* (New York: W. W. Norton & Co., 1973).

Burkett, David, *Very Good Management: A Guide to Managing by Communicating* (Englewood Cliffs, NJ: Prentice-Hall, 1983).

Burns, James MacGregor, *Leadership* (New York: Harper & Row, 1978).

Cherry, Colin, *On Human Communication: A Review, a Survey, and a Criticism* (Cambridge: M.I.T Press, 1957).

Crick, Frances, *What Mad Pursuit: A Personal View of Scientific Discovery* (New York: Basic Books, 1988).

Cunningham, Donald H., *Creating Technical Manuals: A Step-by-Step Approach to Writing User-Friendly Instructions* (New York: McGraw-Hill, 1984).

Davies, Ivor K., *Instructional Technique* (New York: McGraw-Hill, 1981).

Diebold, John, *Business in the Age of Information* (New York: American Management Association, 1985).

Dishy, Victor, *Inner Fitness* (New York: Doubleday, 1990).

Drucker, Peter, *The New Realities* (Oxford: Heinemann Professional Publishing, 1989).

Fair, Charles, *From the Jaws of Victory* (New York: Simon & Schuster, 1971).

Ferguson, Henry, *Tomorrow's Global Executive* (Homewood, IL: Dow Jones-Irwin, 1988).

Flesch, Rudolf, *The Art of Clear Thinking* (New York: Harper & Row, 1951).

Gibson, Cyrus F., and Barbara Bund Jackson, *The Information Imperative: Managing the Impact of Information Technology on Businesses and People* (Lexington, MA: Lexington Books, 1987).

Forbes, Mark, *Writing Technical Articles, Speeches, and Manuals* (New York: John Wiley & Sons, 1988).

Graber, Doris Appel, *Processing the News: How People Tame the Information Tide* (New York: Longman, 1984).

Grimm, Susan J., *How to Write Computer Manuals for Users* (Belmont, CA: Lifetime Learning Publications, 1982).

Gropper, George L., *Instructional Strategies* (Englewood, NJ: Educational Technical Publications, 1974).

Halliday, Michael Alexander Kirkwood, *Learning How to Mean: Explorations in the Development of Language* (London: Edward Arnold, 1975).

Hamlin, Sonya, *How to Talk So People Listen: The Real Key to Job Success* (New York: Harper & Row, 1988).

Harrell, Allen T., *The Bottom Line: Communicating in Organizations* (Chicago: Nelson-Hall, 1979).

Hartley, James, Designing Instructional Text, 2nd edition (New York: Nichols, 1985).

Horn, Robert, *Mapping Hypertext: Analysis, Linkage, and Display of Knowledge for the Next Generation of On-Line Text and Graphics* (Lexington, MA: The Lexington Institute, 1989).

How Plain English Works for Business: 12 Case Studies, by the Office of Consumer Affairs, U.S. Dept. of Commerce, editorial services provided by the Document Design Center/American Institutes for Research (Washington, DC: U.S. Government Printing Office, 1984).

Human Service Information Systems: How to Design and Implement Them, Barry Trute, Bruce Tefft, and David Scuse, editors (Lewiston, NY: E. Mellen Press, 1985).

Jackson, Gerald, *The Inner Executive* (New York: Simon & Schuster, 1989).

Johnson, Kerry A., and Lin J. Foa, *Instructional Design: New Alternatives for Effective Education and Training* (New York: Macmillan Publishing Co., 1989).

Jordan, Stello, *Handbook of Technical Writing Practices* (New York: Wiley-Interscience, 1971).

Judgement under Uncertainty, Daniel Kahneman, Paul Slovic, and Amos Tversky, editors (Cambridge: Cambridge University Press, 1982).

Kyle, James, *Sign Language: The Study of Deaf People and Their Language* (Cambridge: Cambridge University Press, 1985).

Language and Communication, Jack C. Richards and Richard W. Schmidt, editors (London: Longman, 1983).

Larson, Charles U., *Persuasion: Reception and Responsibility,* 3rd edition (Belmont, CA: Wadsworth Pub. Co., 1983).

Levin, Tamar, with Ruth Long, *Effective Instruction* (Alexandria, VA: Association for Supervision & Curriculum Development, 1981).

Loftus, Geoffrey R, and Elizabeth Loftus, *Human Memory: The Processing of Information* (Hillsdale, NJ: L. Erlbaum Associates, 1975).

Longuet-Higgins, H.C., *Mental Processes: Studies in Cognitive Science* (Cambridge, MA: MIT Press, 1987).

McKinnon, William T., *Style and Structure in Modern Business Communication* (Irvington-on-Hudson, NY: Columbia University Press, 1980).

Milgram, Stanley, *Obedience to Authority: An Experimental View* (New York: Harper & Row, 1974).

Mindell, Arnold, *River's Way: The Process Science of the Dreambody: Information and Channels in Dream and Bodywork, Psychology and Physics* (London: Routledge & Kegan Paul, 1985).

Murphy, Kevin J., *Effective Listening: Hearing What People Say and Making It Work for You* (New York: Bantam Books, 1987).

Neway, Julie M., *Information Specialist as Team Player in the Research Process* (Westport, CN: Greenwood Press, 1985).

Ornstein, Robert Evans, *On the Experience of Time* (Baltimore, MD: Penguin Books, 1969).

Norman, Donald A., *Psychology of Everyday Things* (New York: Basic Books, 1988).

Patton, Forrest H., *Force of Persuasion: Dynamic Techniques for Influencing People* (New York: Prentice Hall Press, 1986).

Penzias, Arno, *Ideas and Information: Managing in a High-Tech World* (New York: W.W. Norton & Company, Inc., 1989).

Phillips, Bonnie D., *Business Communication* (Albany, NY: Delmar Publishers, 1983) [JLE 86-411].

Pirsig M. Robert, *Zen and the Art of Motorcycle Maintenance* (New York: William Morrow, 1974).

Poundstone, William, *Labyrinths of Reason: Paradox, Puzzles, and the Frailty of Knowledge* (New York: Doubleday, 1988).

Rand, Ayn, *The Voice of Reason: Essays in Objectivist Thought* (New York: Penguin, 1988).

Rifkin, Jeremy, *Time Wars: The Primary Conflict in Human History* (New York: Simon & Schuster, 1987).

Robbins, Larry M., *The Business of Writing and Speaking: A Managerial Communication Manual* (New York: McGraw-Hill, 1985).

Rubin, Michael Rogers, Mary Taylor Huber with Elizabeth Lloyd Taylor, *The Knowledge Industry in the United States 1960-1980* (Princeton, NJ: Princeton University Press, 1986).

Ruch, William V., *Corporate Communications: A Comparison of Japanese and American Practices* (Westport, CN: Quorum Books, 1984).

Rushdie, Salman, *Grimus* (London: Grafton Books, 1977).

Silverthorn, James Edwin, and Devern J. Perry, *Word Division Manual: The Twenty Thousand Most-Used Words in Business Communication,* 3rd edition (Cincinnati: South-Western Pub. Co., 1984).

Simon, H.A., and J.R. Hayes, "Understanding Complex Task Instructions," *Cognition and Instruction,* edited by D. Klare (Hillsdale, NJ: Lawrence Erlbaum Associates, 1976).

Smith Curtis G., *Ancestral Voices: Language and the Evolution of Human Consciousness* (Englewood Cliffs, NJ: Prentice-Hall, 1985).

Steil, Lyman K., *Effective Listening: Key to Your Success* (Reading, MA: Addison-Wesley, 1983).

Stephan, Peter M., *Writing User-Usable Manuals: A Practical Guide to Preparing User-Friendly Computer Hardware & Software Documentation* (Salt Lake City, UT: Wredco Press, 1984).

Subject Retrieval in the Seventies: New Directions, Hans (Hanan) Wellisch and Thomas D. Wilson, editors (Westport, CN: Greenwood Publishing Co., 1972).

Tannen, Deborah, *You Just Don't Understand: Women and Men in Conversation* (New York: William Morrow, 1990).

The Executive Mind, edited by S. Srivastva (San Francisco: Jossey-Bass, 1983).

The Great Conversation: A Reader's Guide to Great Books of the Western World, Philip W. Goetz, editor (Chicago: Encyclopaedia Britannica, 1990).

The ISTC Handbook of Technical Writing and Publication Techniques: A Practical Guide for Managers, Engineers, Scientists and Technical Publications Staff, Mike Austin and Ralph F. Dodd, editors (London: Heinemann, 1985).

Weiss, Edmond H., *How to Write a Usable User Manual* (Philadelphia: ISI Press, 1985).

Whyte, William H., Jr., *Is Anybody Listening?* (New York: Simon & Schuster, 1952).

Wilensky, R., *Understanding Goal-Based Stories* (New Haven: Yale University, Computer Science Department, Research Report #140, 1978).

Wilensky, R., *Planning and Understanding* (Reading, MA: Addison-Wesley, 1983).

Winograd, *Terry, Understanding Natural Language* (New York: Academic Press, 1972).

Winograd, Terry; and Fernando Flores, *Understanding Computers and Cognition: A New Foundation for Design* (Norwood, NJ: Ablex Publishing, 1986).

Wurman, Richard Saul, *Information Anxiety* (New York: Doubleday, 1989).

ACKNOWLEDGMENTS

From the moment a book begins as a viable idea through the moment it comes off the printing presses, instructions are what move the book along. Instructions fly back and forth between the author, writer, editor, publishers, copyeditor, the sales department, the art department, and the printer. And somehow, it is only because of this instruction field day—however complex, confusing, and confounding as it can be—that an idea can turn into a book. We'd like to applaud the following people for their remarkable abilities as instruction givers and takers.

Michael Everitt, an information designer and founder of the design firm, InForm, has been a pioneer in the field of desktop publishing design. We have worked together for 11 years now and he has helped to bring my ideas into workable realities.

When we first met **Tom Dyja,** he was wearing tortoise shell glasses and a bow tie. We shook our heads. But, almost instantly, we realized that behind the Cambridge attire was a real *mensch*—and an elegant editor. He nurtured the book; he understood the book; he could help us to see what the book wanted to be even when we lost sight of it; and he made us laugh and carry on when we sometimes contemplated giving up.

Ed Victor, my agent with the silver tongue and convincing eyes, made all this possible in selling the book when it was only an idea.

Illustrators **Larry Gonick** and **Ed Koren** added a piquancy to the book with their drawings and cartoons, reminding us through their offbeat imaginations that instructions have a lighter side.

In his insightful introduction, **John Sculley**, chairman of Apple Computer, helped us to see how the instructions that run technology have lessons for human communication as well.

Copy editor **Miriam Berg Varian** had a sharp eye and a gentle touch. She understood the spirit of the book and cared for it as if it were her own.

John Porter, my assistant, and **Rachel Repetto**, his predecessor, performed the laborious and frustrating task of securing permission to reprint material from other sources.

Ellen Reinheimer, director of research at Research on Demand, conducted several on-line information searches for background material. She was able to translate the concept of the book into search terms that yielded a quantity of applicable and amusing information.

Over 100 people responded to our instruction questionnaire, overwhelming us with the thoughtfulness of their responses. They provided invaluable feedback and influenced us in our treatment of subject matter throughout the book.

While the following people enjoyed no formal relationship to the book, they played a vital role in the finished product by reading portions of the book, suggesting new directions for the manuscript, contributing pertinent marginalia, listening to our books troubles (among others), and encouraging us along the Yellow Brick Road: **Paul Temme**, members of the **Washington Heights Writers' Workshop, Chris Fortunato, Debra Parker,** and **Martha Collins.**

RSW & LL

RICHARD SAUL WURMAN

With the publication of his first book in 1962 at the age of 26, Richard Saul Wurman began the singular passion of his life: that of making information understandable. In his best-selling book, *INFORMATION ANXIETY*, in 1990, he developed an overview of the motivating principles found in his previous works. *FOLLOW THE YELLOW BRICK ROAD* is the second book in a trilogy. Each book focuses on some subject or idea that he personally had difficulty understanding. They all stem from his desire to know rather than from already knowing, from his ignorance rather than his intelligence, from his inability rather than his ability.

Along the way, Richard Saul Wurman has received both M. Arch. and B. Arch degrees from the University of Pennsylvania, where in 1959 he was graduated with the highest honors, and where he established a deep personal and professional relationship with the architect Louis I. Kahn. He is a fellow of the American Institute of Architects (FAIA), a member of AGI (Alliance Graphique Internationale) and served as vice-president of the American Institute of Graphic Arts. He has been awarded several grants from the National Endowment for the Arts, a Guggenheim Fellowship, two Graham Fellowships and two Chandler Fellowships.

A parallel channel for his ideas about communication has been the creation and/or chairmanship of a number of conferences such as the International Design Conference in Aspen in 1972, the First Federal Design Assembly in 1973 (co-chairman), the national AIA convention in 1976, and the Technology Entertainment Design (TED) conferences (co-chairman): TED 1 in 1984, TED2 in 1990, and TED3 in 1992 in Monterey, California.

His career has spanned from a 13-year architectural partnership to teaching (Cambridge University in England; City College, New York; University of Southern California, Los Angeles; Washington University, St. Louis; Princeton University; North Carolina State University, Raleigh), to serving as dean at California State Polytechnic University in Pomona, to participating in city government as Deputy Director of Housing and Community Development in Philadelphia and as consultant to the Jerde Partnership and Charles Eames.

He founded ACCESS Press, Ltd., in 1984 and The Understanding Business (TUB) in 1987. A major project of TUB was the restructuring and design of the 40,000,000 Smart Yellow Pages directories distributed in California by Pacific Bell Directory annually. In addition to the ACCESS city travel guides to London, Paris, Rome, Tokyo, San Francisco, Los Angeles, New York, Washington, D.C., Hawaii, Chicago, Boston, San Diego and Barcelona, the latest of his over 50 publications include the *Wall Street Journal Guide to Money and Markets*, *Polaroid Access*, guides to the 1984 & 1988 Summer & Winter Olympics, *Football Access, Baseball Access, Medical Access* (a guide to diagnostic tests and surgical procedures), *What Will Be Has Always Been: The Words of Louis I. Kahn*, and *USATLAS* (a new road atlas of the United States), as well as *ON TIME*, a monthly airline and travel guide.

Richard Saul Wurman has been a regular consultant to major corporations in matters relating to the design and understanding of information. Among these are News Corporation, TV Guide, Encyclopaedia Britannica, Knight-Ridder, LA Times, AARP, The Taubman Group and Lotus.

Richard Saul Wurman is married to novelist Gloria Nagy, has four children and lives in Manhattan and Bridgehampton, New York.

LORING LEIFER

Loring Leifer is a former design editor of *Interiors* magazine and the "translator" of *INFORMATION ANXIETY*. After graduating from the University of Wisconsin-Madison, she worked as a staff writer for a newspaper and then headed the corporate communications department of a health agency. For the last 10 years, she has worked as a freelance writer on a wide variety of projects, including feature articles for newspapers and magazines, a biography of a media hoaxster, and a screenplay. She lives in New York, but grew up near Dorothy in Prairie Village, Kansas.